DIVERSE MILLENNIAL STUDENTS IN COLLEGE

STUDENTS IN COLLEGE

Implications for Faculty and Student Affairs

Edited by

Fred A. Bonner, II, Aretha F. Marbley,

and Mary F. Howard-Hamilton

1996–2011 15TH ANNIVERSARY

Sty us

PUBLISHING, LLC.

STERLING, VIRGINIA

COPYRIGHT © 2011 BY
STYLUS PUBLISHING, LLC.

Published by Stylus Publishing, LLC
22883 Quicksilver Drive
Sterling, VA 20166-2102

Library of Congress Cataloging-in-Publication-Data
Diverse millennial students in college : implications for faculty
and student affairs / edited by Fred A. Bonner II, Aretha F.
Marbley, and Mary F. Howard-Hamilton.—1st ed.
      p. cm.
   Includes bibliographical references and index.
   ISBN 978-1-57922-446-2 (cloth : alk. paper)
   ISBN 978-1-57922-447-9 (pbk. : alk. paper)
   ISBN 978-1-57922-711-1 (library networkable e-edition)
   ISBN 978-1-57922-712-8 (consumer e-edition)
   1. Library users—Effect of technological innovations
on—United States.   2. Libraries and students—United
States.   3. Generation Y—Attitudes—United States.
I. Bonner, Fred A.   II. Marbley, Aretha Faye.
III. Howard-Hamilton, Mary F.
Z665.2.U6D58   2011
378.1'98—dc23   2011015595

13-digit ISBN: 978-1-57922-446-2 (cloth)
13-digit ISBN: 978-1-57922-447-9 (paper)
13-digit ISBN: 978-1-57922-711-1 (library networkable
e-edition)
13-digit ISBN: 978-1-57922-712-8 (consumer e-edition)

Printed in the United States of America

All first editions printed on acid free paper
that meets the American National Standards Institute
Z39-48 Standard.

Bulk Purchases

Quantity discounts are available for use in workshops
and for staff development.
Call 1-800-232-0223

First Edition, 2011

10   9   8   7   6   5   4   3   2   1

I dedicate this book to my friend and mentor Dr. Melvin Cleveland Terrell, Vice President Emeritus at Northeastern Illinois University. Navigating the academic terrain has been profoundly more manageable due to my ability to seek wise counsel from my guide. Thank you for investing your time and energy in my journey.

—FRED A. BONNER, II

I would like to express my thanks to my own Millennial, my son Courtney, and four incredible and awesome women: Ms. McLarty (my 1st grade teacher); Ms. Lyles (my 4th grade teacher); Ms. Jones (my 7th grade teacher); and Ms. Williams (my 10th and 11th grade French teacher), who more than four decades ago, managed to see beyond my shabby exterior and feed my hunger and thirst for knowledge, and to nurture my tender and fragile inner potential three generations before Courtney.

—ARETHA F. MARBLEY

There are scholars who impact our lives vicariously and such is the case with Dr. Manning Marable, a socially conscious activist and great analytical historian of African American people, who passed away April 1, 2011. It is my hope that this book leaves a legacy that is near the magnitude of the amazing works that Dr. Marable penned over the course of his illustrious life. May we all continue to educate and uplift our people.

—DR. MARY HOWARD-HAMILTON

CONTENTS

ACKNOWLEDGMENTS

We wish to acknowledge the administrators, faculty, staff, and students in the Lone Star College System; you have truly made this work on Millennial college students soar. Additionally we would like to recognize the many students in the Student Affairs Administration in Higher Education (SAAHE) program at Texas A&M University who allowed us to vet with them our many assumptions and theories related to this generational cohort. Additional recognitions go out to the students at Indiana State and Texas Tech University for their efforts in helping us "ground" this work. Also, Eric Hoover at the *Chronicle of Higher Education*, Gary Reger at Trinity College in Hartford, Connecticut, and David Cofer at Intern Bridge for providing us with a platform to talk about the importance of diversity when focusing on this population of collegians. Finally, we thank Gifted Child Today (GCT) and the National Association of Student Affairs Professionals (NASAP)—two refereed publication outlets that supported us in getting the message out about diverse Millennial students across the P–16 continuum.

INTRODUCTION

The thieves are at it again, stealing my piece of
mind . . . but, they won't win because my soul
they'll never find.

       —Rhian Benson, Soul and Jazz Singer

Those of us who call academe home have often acted as bandits, thieves if you will, who steal bits and pieces of our students' identities to mold and shape into forms that we deem developmentally palatable. From the age-old process of producing *gentleman scholars* to the more contemporary aim of creating an engaged and learned citizenry, much of our focus in higher education has been to advance a holistic understanding of student learning, growth, and development. Too often the methods used to gain insight about our collegiate cohorts have been deductive and riddled with attendant problems associated with this approach (i.e., a priori assumptions, rigid one-size-fits-all perspectives, reductionist views of collegiate populations).

Promising is the research and the researchers who have dared to enter these discussions through a different door—one that provides entrée into a discourse about inductive processes that seek to provide critical constructivist-based opportunities to listen and discern through perspective, voice, and worldview a more authentic rendering of what identity feels like from where "real" people sit. *Diverse Millennial Students in College* (DMC) provides a front row seat to readers who desire to gain knowledge about the diverse population of students in our nation's postsecondary institutions, what we refer to in this book as Millennials. DMC eschews the tendency to force students into constraining frameworks that require them to jettison parts of their identities.

What the term *Millennial* has tended to convey is a focus on the characteristics that define a generation of people born somewhere between the early

1980s to the late 1990s. Beyond this age and time span, labels serve as cynosures to explain who and how these individuals are supposed to behave. Achieving. Confident. Conventional. Pressured. Sheltered. Special. Team oriented. These labels (introduced by Howe and Strauss in their book *Millennials Rising*) have been used primarily to "story" the existence of this generation. Although provocative and insightful in offering some descriptive details about this group, lost in translation with the use of these monikers have been the renderings of black, brown, red, and yellow perspectives; successes and challenges of bi- and multiracial voices; and the cogitations of gay, lesbian, bisexual, transgender, and queer minds. What has been missing is the engagement of people and positions that problematize the assumption that all in the Millennial cohort are the same.

Contextualized in the postsecondary setting, DMC provides an active treatment of diverse groups and their nuanced sense of agency in creating a Millennial framework of their own. In my capacity as a professor of higher education and student affairs administration and as a university administrator, I come in direct contact with Millennial college students as well as the faculty who instruct them. In addition the graduate-level course I teach, Advanced College Student Development Theory, is populated each semester by Millennials who offer their unbridled opinions concerning their portrayal by the media, parents, and professors who "just do not seem to understand" them. Especially for the diverse Millennials in my class, they advance even deeper levels of concern about these incongruent labels: "Is this also supposed to refer to African American Millennials? Because this doesn't sound like me!" "As a gay male, I have been made to feel anything but special." "Biracial students are never fairly represented in these models—we are expected to choose or just fit in!"

DMC in its seminal stance offers viable solutions to these conundrums that continue to perplex those who seek an understanding of this collegiate cohort. Yes, the thieves in academe may be at it again; however, the scholars commissioned in this volume have provided diverse Millennials with critical insight on how they can not only win but also maintain their peace of mind.

Fred A. Bonner, II, EdD
Professor of Higher Education Administration

PART ONE

DIVERSE MILLENNIALS IN COLLEGE: A NATIONAL PERSPECTIVE

I

A NATIONAL PERSPECTIVE

Testing Our Assumptions About Generational Cohorts

Gwendolyn Jordan Dungy

Introduction

Labeling generations has become a lucrative career line for entrepreneurs, authors, and consultants. Once a generation is labeled, however, there is a tendency for our students to become strangers to us. Rather than testing our own observations and checking our own assumptions, we begin to ask the "experts" to tell us what our students are like. After my review of the material available on contemporary college students, the majority of them labeled Millennials, I can only conclude that the jury is still out on who these students are as a generation. What we do know is that there are some similarities among students who complete secondary school and enter college as a cohort. We also know that these similarities are gleaned, for the most part, from a small survey conducted in an affluent suburb of Washington, D.C., which has "one-third fewer African Americans than the rest of the United States" (Hesel & May, 2007, p. 18).

I became interested in the characteristics of African American Millennials in the spring of 2007, when I spoke to approximately 400 African American students at the Southwest Black Student Leadership Conference at Texas A&M University. To test my assumptions about Millennials and African American students, I engaged the students in discussions about whether the descriptors generally given for Millennials were accurate for them. I was surprised that most of the students had not even heard of the term *Millennials*. And in most instances, they said the descriptors might apply to White students but not to them.

During my observations of students, in general those who had begun college in 2000 and after, I found that while there were similarities across the board, there were also distinctions between what I call the first-wave Millennials, those who had begun college in 2000, and the second-wave Millennials, those who had begun college in 2004–2005 or after. In talking with these first- and second-wave Millennials, it was obvious that some were able to see they have some characteristics of this generation of students (in college since 2000) and some characteristics of the previous generation of students. More than one person I interviewed who fell within the first wave of Millennials said that they were on the "cusp" of the Millennials with many characteristics of the previous generation of students, referred to as the "Transitional Generation" by Levine and Cureton (1998, p. 156). *Transitional Generation* did not take hold as a label, so Millennials may be referring to what we called *Generation X* (or Gen X).

Students who have attended college during the first decade of the 21st century are either undergraduate students now (second-wave Millennials) or they are graduate students, coworkers, employees, or even supervisors. Making the effort to understand characteristics of all our students is a duty and an obligation of every educator. However, it is important to check assumptions and avoid falling into the trap of applying generalizations across the board.

I am convinced it is important that we understand who our students are in order to create a campus climate that supports their learning and success. Knowing who our students are is "more than a notion," as this generation of students' great-great grandparents might have said. We must consider the multifaceted identities that characterize our students—including, but certainly not limited to, race, class, gender, and sexual orientation—and how these different identities intersect. We also want to see how this generational cohort is similar across all groups, and how they may differ depending on demographics and particular identities. Beyond this, we need to explore how students relate to their respective colleges or universities. That is, what do they want out of college, what motivates them, and how do they prefer to learn? To answer these questions, we will need more research and we will need to observe and test many of our commonly held assumptions.

Similarities Among All Millennials

According to Levine and Cureton (1998), it is possible to develop a broad-brush understanding of our college student populations mainly because,

Every college generation is a product of its age. The momentous occur-
rences of its era—from wars and economic shifts to the elections and
inventions of its times—give meaning to the lives of the individuals who
live through them. They also serve to knit those individuals together by
creating a collective memory and a common historic or generational identity. (p. 19)

Through informal conversations with students and new professionals
(those who began college in 2000 or later and are now in the workforce), I
began to test some of the assumptions regarding the Millennial generation.
These conversations took place over a period of 2 years (2007–2009) in my
travels to various campuses and conferences across the country. Following
are some of the responses given when I asked these students and new professionals what they saw as defining moments for their generation:

1. September 11, 2001
2. Reality television
3. Mobile phones and social networks
4. Virginia Tech and Northern Illinois University mass killings
5. YouTube
6. Recession of 2008
7. Wikipedia and mass collaboration
8. Election of President Barack Obama

Although these events have had an impact on how they see and relate to the
world, in the final analysis, as educators we will have to consider each student
as an individual. We will need to know how students make sense of their
world and what their perspectives are.

Technology

The Millennials, as a group, have been labeled the *net generation* and the
digital generation because of their reliance on and facility with technology.
However, all technology is not created equal when it comes to that which is
used for social activities or to access information that contributes to learning
and success in college. In the *NASAP Journal* article "African American Millennial College Students: Owning the Technological Middle Passage" (Marbley, Hull, Polydore, Bonner, & Burley, 2007), the authors noted that
"African American children own cell phones, iPods and MP3 players, CD
and DVD players, and yet . . . are lagging behind when it comes to having

computer tools and Internet access" (p. 12). This is of particular concern for colleges and universities that may make the assumption that all students have access to and facility with online learning. Hawkins and Oblinger (2006), for instance, suggested consideration of the following questions:

1. Do we know whether students have a computer? Do we know their skill level? . . . Is ownership the same for all students, or are there significant differences between groups? . . . Are there different needs based on academic discipline?
2. Do we look beyond who has Internet access to consider online skills? What online skills, support, and freedom of use define an appropriate threshold for digital access and use on campus?
3. Do we limit the definition of digital divide to a haves and have-nots dichotomy? . . . Beyond computer ownership lie issues of Internet access at a reasonable speed, as well as availability of support.
4. How limiting will inadequate online skills be to students? . . . If students are regularly expected to participate in online discussions or use tools such as wikis, campuses should provide reasonable support to ensure that students can participate effectively and autonomously. (p. 13)

Social Justice, Change, and Service

An African American female student who is among the first wave of Millennials said that many of her peers have deep desires to understand the world and what it will take to make it a place where humans are valued and life is affirmed. To this end, she said that her generation is "hell-bent on change." Her cohort and the current cohort of Millennials are action oriented, particularly in regard to social justice and environmental issues. One professional who works with student groups concurred, saying, "These students are about action, and they will fight for social justice as they define it based on where they fall on the conservative–liberal continuum."

The Millennials are particularly known for taking action through service, contributing more hours in this effort than preceding generations (Stone, 2009). An Asian American male, first-wave Millennial commented that second-wave Millennials "don't have money to give to charity, but they are eager to give their time if the activity taps into their passion."

Some professionals, while acknowledging the service students provide, have concerns about the amount of time many students commit. These professionals note that some of the best students are overcommitted in their volunteer and out-of-class activities and have high stress levels. In response to an advisor's caution about the potential negative impact of outside activities on grades, one student responded, "After all, employers don't look at transcripts!" For this student, service took priority over going to class and getting the best grades.

Professionals also comment on group accountability. One attitude seen among students is that people cannot expect them to be held accountable for all that is expected of them in service positions since they are only volunteering. Some supervisors observe that they seem not to have qualms about the impact on others with whom they are working or the reputation of the organization if they do not fulfill their commitment. Because of this attitude among some Millennials, a professional who gave me written comments about Millennials expressed skepticism about whether the amount of service students did correlated with their degree of altruism. It seems that the reasons for service are not always clear.

Although some of the students who are putting innumerable hours into service projects may not be entirely committed, a number of Millennials, whether first wave or second wave, are choosing careers from among nonprofit, service-oriented fields. Although their reasons for participating in service activities as students might be unclear, student affairs professionals note that some are choosing careers in the areas in which they may have provided service, and these are decidedly different choices from those selected during the previous generation, when "enrollment patterns peaked in careers with a vocational orientation such as business" (Levine & Cureton, 1998, p. 120).

Impact of Parenting

Parents became the focus of attention with the initial class of Millennials. Because parental involvement was a new phenomenon, some administrators saw the involvement of parents as a nuisance, and the best way to deal with it was to find humor in the situation and share these incidents with colleagues. When professionals came together for meetings it was almost a "one-upmanship" atmosphere, where each successive horror story of parental involvement was worse than the previous one. The term *helicopter parents* became the generally accepted term to describe these parents. Today college educators are much more prepared to collaborate with parents on helping students become successful. Some educators said, "If you can't beat 'em, join 'em," while others realized that students really wanted their parents' continuing involvement in their day-to-day activities. Given the advances in communications technology, this generation of students agrees that they are always connected, and that connection extends to parents.

Experts on Millennials seem to agree that the parents of Millennials were the ones who made the "Baby on Board" sign in cars ubiquitous. This generation is known as the most-loved and the most-wanted generation in history. Howe and Strauss (2000), in *Millennials Rising*, gave the following examples to describe how the times and parents' attitudes changed for this new generation of children:

> *The era of the wanted child had begun.*
> *The era of the protected child had begun.*
> *The era of the worthy child had begun.* (pp. 32–33)

In *Generation Me*, Jean M. Twenge (2006) wrote that "Parental authority also isn't what it used to be," citing a *Chicago Sun-Times* article in which family studies Professor Robert Billingham notes that "Parents are no longer eager to be parents. They want to love and guide their children as a trusted friend" (p. 30).

It appears that parents really have become their children's best friends, especially when it comes to discipline. Penn's (2007) book *Microtrends* presented the results of a poll in which parents were asked what they would do if their 9-year-old son cursed at them and said he hated them. "Overwhelmingly, the top answers, across age and gender of parents, were 'sit down and ask him why he feels that way' and 'tell him that you're sorry he feels that way, but that you love him anyway' " (pp. 114–115). Although these responses were consistent across age and gender, they were not compared across ethnicities and racial categories, and perhaps more saliently, across class lines. What is more, when it came to consequences, the poll showed that "barely 2 in 10 parents said they would take the child's privileges away for at least a week" (Penn, 2007, pp. 114–115).

Perhaps related to this is the lack of respect for older adults and hierarchy that many first-wave Millennials with whom I spoke pointed out about the Millennials who followed them. The first-wave Millennials also said that, more than their cohorts, the second-wave Millennials seemed to think that "their parents would be a constant source of economic and emotional support."

Work Expectations and Work Ethic

A first-wave Millennial said that she came into the workforce with the expectation of working her way up. By contrast, she sees the second-wave Millennials coming into the workforce wanting to be treated as equals immediately because they have a lot of skills. Noting what she sees as a lack of perspective and interpersonal skills, she said, "They seem to have super high expectations and lack humility."

This observation is confirmed by Bruce Tulgan (as cited in Jayson, 2009), who stated "The classic thing is they show up on Day One and want to tell you how to change your business" (para. 18). Tulgan is founder of Rainmaker Thinking, a research and management training firm in New Haven, Connecticut, and author of multiple books advising employers about Millennials. He describes this generation as upbeat, self-confident, prone to customizing their work and personal life, and expecting to be "thrilled" by their employers while enjoying a comfortable work environment (Tulgan & Martin, 2001).

In looking at similarities across Millennials, there seems to be a consensus or stereotype that expectations are high. Tulgan and Martin (2001) found that Millennials have lofty goals, and they fully expect to meet those goals: It is not a matter of high hopes, but rather of high expectations. According to Eric Chester, president of the consulting firm Generation Why, these different expectations often lead to misunderstandings in the workplace: "[Millennials] may have skills and are techno-savvy and book-smart and streetwise, but they don't understand what the big deal is if they're five minutes late" (quoted in Jayson, 2009, 17).

William Galston of the Brookings Institution in Washington, D.C., stated: "Such attitudes aren't just about work but rather about hierarchy. . . . These young people have grown up in very flat, horizontal relationships. So, the idea of deferring to someone older, simply because that person is there, is not part of their makeup" (Jayson, 2009, para. 20).

Some have said that the work ethic is dead with this generation. Millennials reply that they "work to live"; they do not "live to work." This ethic and the matter of work expectations are both areas that experts note when they label Millennials the "Entitlement Generation." What are the characteristics that earn Millennials this label?

> They are . . . the upstarts at the office who put their feet on their desks, voice their opinions frequently and loudly at meetings, and always volunteer—nay, expect—to take charge of the most interesting projects. They are smart, brash, even arrogant, and endowed with a commanding sense of entitlement. (Halpern, 2007, para. 3)

Despite this kind of description of our new and future workforce, Michael S. Malone (2009) wrote in *The Future Arrived Yesterday* that we, as a nation, "need these young people desperately because they are bright, (infinitely) confident, and entrepreneurial" (p. 12). Although previous generations too often concentrate on what they perceive as the negative qualities of those that follow, it is important that we honor in a positive manner what each successive generation offers and use that constructively to facilitate learning. Each generation is "right" for its time, and the Millennials are right for this time. It falls to educators to meet students where they are and actively engage them in learning.

Materialistic

Another common characteristic that has stuck to today's college students is that they are materialistic. Whether they describe their penchant for material things with hip-hop language such as "the bling-bling generation" (Dilworth & Carter, 2007) or whether they want to buy more things for privacy and to distinguish themselves (Twenge, 2006), they agree that they want to own things that make them stand out as different. Twenge (2006) further stated that they don't want to share rooms, and the iPods and headphones give them their own private world of selected music; they want their own ringtones and special combinations of coffee choices. An advertisement in an upscale catalog appealing to the Millennial generation read, "You are the I in Icon."

By contrast, at least one student affairs professional who works with Millennials daily suggested that "we think about the 'silent majority' of Millennials who do not fit the general consensus about feelings of entitlement and materialism." After all, materialism may be a symptom of age. Each generation of a certain age may appear materialistic from the perspective of the mature generations that came before them. Twenge (2006) allows that "GenMe has always lived in a time when possessions were valued" (p. 99).

Do Cultural Differences Matter?

Economic class and immigration status are two defining variables for first-generation students. While Millennials may cohere because of their age, common contextual experiences, and interests, first-generation college students and their more privileged peers occupy two different worlds as members of the academic community.

Where one comes from is particularly salient for African American male students. Because of the economic class from which they come, many African American males may be the first—not only in their families, but in their neighborhoods or communities—to attend college. To their peers, going to college may be seen as betrayal and going over to the other side. In a discussion with several African American male students who attended a conference with their mentor and faculty member from Morgan State University, these traditional-aged students shared that communities from which first-generation students come in many cases do not value education. For example, one said, "A brother coming home from prison will get a bigger party in the neighborhood than a brother graduating from college."

Data from the 2009 NASPA Assessment and Knowledge Consortium survey on "Ethnicity Differences in Diversity/Multiculturalism" clearly demonstrate the effect of race on students' perspectives on campus climate and the campus's engagement in diversity-related issues:

- Not surprisingly, White students felt more positive about the campus climate and campus's response to diversity issues than Asian/Pacific Islander and Black/African American students. They also felt more positive about the campus climate than students who are multiracial. White students were least likely to have been the target of potential discriminatory or harassing events.
- Black/African American students perceived significantly more racial/ethnic tension on campus when compared to White and multiracial students and students who preferred not to respond to the ethnicity question.
- White students were the least engaged with diversity-related issues on campus (significantly so when compared to Asian/Pacific Islander, Black/African American, Latino/a/Hispanic, and multiracial students). Black/African American students were the most engaged with diversity-related issues (significantly more than all groups other than indigenous/Native American students).
- Multiracial students were the most likely to have learned more about diversity from their families (significant compared to White and Asian/Pacific Islander students and students who prefer not to respond to the ethnicity question).
- Black students were the most likely to report having learned more about diversity in workshops (significant compared to White, Asian/Pacific Islander, and multiracial students and students who prefer not to respond). Black/African American students were the most likely to report learning more about diversity in dialogue groups (significant compared to White, Asian/Pacific Islander, Latino/a/Hispanic, and

multiracial students and students who would prefer not to respond to the ethnicity question).

- White students were least likely to report having learned about diversity from their families (significant compared to Black/African American, Latino/a/Hispanic, and multiracial students). White students were also least likely to report having learned more about diversity in workshops (significant compared to Asian/Pacific Islander, Black/African American, and Latino/a/Hispanic students). White students were the least likely to report learning more about diversity in dialogue groups (significant compared to Asian/Pacific Islander and Black/African American students).

Our assumptions about how students experience the college or university climate should be tested in order to address feelings and perspectives of all students. Dialogue is needed throughout the campus in order to create a campus climate that supports students. The recommendation for dialogue throughout the campus should be taken seriously because White students and students of color experience the campus differently, and these differences could have a powerful impact on their success. According to researchers (Marbley et al., 2002), "Recent literature suggests that the academic success of students of color is due in part to those higher education institutions with knowledge, understanding, and cultural sensitivity, as well as responsive pedagogy and activities that integrate cultural differences" (p. 43). Strayhorn (2007) found that African American Millennials have lower aspirations than White Millennials and lower aspirations than preceding cohorts of African American college students. What might be the cause of lower aspirations among African American students?

When I asked first- and second-wave African American Millennials about their thoughts on achieving "The American Dream," none were familiar with the phrase, yet when Levine and Cureton (1998) described characteristics of students between 1992–1997, they said that they were "optimistic about our collective future and desperately committed to preserving The American Dream" (pp. 156–157). By contrast, one of the students I spoke with said that "if this is some ideal, I've not seen a lot of evidence of this for Black people." She said that she was aware of a lot of hard-working Black people who, despite their efforts, will never achieve what might be called "The American Dream."

Dilworth and Carter (2007) completed focus groups with African American students and found:

These students viewed economic prosperity as something that they were working toward instead of something that they or their parents had already achieved. While financial security and social perceptions were important themes, race was embedded in almost all of the students' responses. . . . Students' responses tended to suggest that the millennial descriptors capture the experiences of their white peers. (pp. 122–124)

Race does matter. However, we must keep in mind that "students of color are not monolithic in nature" (Rendón, 2004, p. 182), a truism that holds for any given demographic or identity group. Rendón speaks of the "complexities inherent in their lives" that make it imperative that educators understand the nuances of "regional differences and diversity within and across groups" (p. 182). Class differences, for instance, may mean that more affluent African Americans find more in common with their White peers with a similar socioeconomic background than with their Black peers who experienced a less privileged upbringing.

At the 2007 Institute on College Males at Morehouse College co-sponsored by ACPA—College Student Educators International and NASPA—Student Affairs Administrators in Higher Education and held in Atlanta, Georgia, I observed a group facilitated by Shaun Harper, assistant professor at the University of Pennsylvania, on the topic "Men of Color." The majority of the participants at this professional development opportunity were African American males. It became clear during the discussion that these students, staff, faculty, and administrators thought that gender made a difference. They did not think the African American female college experience was the same as the experience of African American males at predominantly White institutions. Some of their comments included the following:

1. Men on campus are not taking charge as leaders.
2. Black men of a certain class and low economic status can't go home after attending college. There is no support group.
3. Black males on campus, for the most part, are in subservient roles and are not considered as role models.
4. African American men tend to remain in college for longer periods than expected but their rate of graduation does not seem to increase.
5. Many African American males are athletes first and they are often underprepared for the academic rigor expected. They also are not involved in the college beyond their sport affiliations.

6. There should be more attention to the celebration of the African American males who are being successful and less time focusing on African American males who are failing or at risk.
7. We must help African American males find space to dialogue with one another on questions such as "Am I who society says I am?"
8. Educators need to learn more about identity development in African American males and men and masculinities.

During this discussion, the participants noted that programs should be created for *all* men of color, as many of the same issues named for African American males also apply to indigenous peoples and Latino males in predominantly White colleges and universities.

Gender also makes a difference in how contemporary students relate to technology. In the use of the current most popular social networks among college students, preliminary research at one institution indicates that women report using social networks at higher levels than male students, and students of color use social networks more frequently than their White counterparts (Strayhorn, 2009).

Cooper and Longanecker (2009) found that race matters in college enrollment and college completion; fields of study and graduate education; perceptions of campus climate; and hiring, tenure, and compensation policies. They questioned "Why the difference? Is it because we all see the world from our own worldview, and that worldview is shaped by our race and ethnicity?" (para. 10). They recommend that colleges and universities use today's increasingly bitter racial climate to "begin a dialogue on race in our institutions—and not just in orientation and freshmen seminars, but also in faculty senate meetings, staff retreats, board meetings, and the like" (para. 13). The authors encouraged "faculty and administrators to engage students, inside and outside the classroom, to have deliberative dialogues on topics of race" (para. 13).

Implications for Learning and College Success

Students' motivations for attending college are powerful incentives for them to do what is necessary to be successful in college. Their motivations vary both across and within generations. When the freshman class of fall 2008 was polled on "Objectives considered to be essential or very important," 76.8% of the respondents chose "Being well off financially," 75.5% chose

"Raising a family," and 69.7% chose "Helping others who are in difficulty" (UCLA Higher Education Research Institute, 2009).

The responses to this inquiry confirm some of the characteristics that Millennials share:

- They want material things because they are accustomed to having what money can buy;
- They value family and will strive for balance between work and family; and
- They will most likely continue their habit of service that they have developed during their developmental and college years.

We need to consider what may be the most effective way to reach Millennials in order to encourage their learning. That is—how do they prefer to learn? The context for learning is different from when most educators were students. Educators held the keys to information and knowledge. Although educators still have the keys to knowledge, many students are not aware that there is a difference between that knowledge and the vast amount of information to be found (and even created) by anyone on the Internet.

Teaching will prove more effective if the attention of contemporary students is captured by tailoring instruction to their strengths and interests. Several researchers have explored why computer and video games are so compelling. They have found that the many intrinsic motivations that are built into games are elusive to educators. Millennials are action oriented and they want to try out rather than just read or hear about something. They want to know how it works. They want to conquer the challenge. According to Jenkins (2005), "Games foster a sense of engagement through immersion. . . . [Students] can manipulate variables and see the consequences of their choices. . . . Games create a social context that connects learners to others who share their interests" (p. 50).

James Gee, professor of education at the University of Wisconsin, Madison, is a pioneer in the use of video games in teaching. He believes that this new generation of students will be out best models to demonstrate that learning is both academic and developmental. Gee stated that "Research shows . . . that people learn best when they are entertained, when they can use creativity to work toward complex goals, when lesson plans incorporate both thinking and emotion, and when the consequences of actions can be observed" (quoted in Carlson, 2003, p. A31).

As noted earlier in this chapter, race, class, and gender do matter. They matter in how to reach students. I found that when I met with Black student leaders at their conference in 2007 at Texas A&M, they were eager to speak when I brought up topics related to popular culture. When I attempted to engage them in discussion about then-Senator Barack Obama's book, *The Audacity of Hope*, they were mildly interested. When I tied the idea of hope to songs in the current popular film *Dream Girls*, however, there was much greater interest and participation. There was little response when I asked who had read the two popular books by Senator Obama (*The Audacity of Hope* and *Dreams From My Father*), but when I asked how many had seen the film *Dream Girls*, almost all had seen it. They knew the music and could share their thoughts about audacity and hope as dramatized in the film and through the music.

When we consider the motivations of contemporary students, colleges and universities are demonstrating openness to looking at how the curriculum could change to be more congruent with the current context. Although colleges may not be ready to redesign the system of higher education to become more interdisciplinary rather than segregated by major and minor, student demand and workforce demands are the incentives for some new majors such as service science, management and engineering; health informatics; computational science; and sustainability (Glenn & Fischer, 2009).

Conclusion

Recalling the comment of a student who thought she was on the "cusp" of the previous and current generations, I think there is wisdom in her observation that we tend to give a tremendous amount of weight and credibility to those similarities among generations of students identified by the entrepreneurs, consultants, and authors who have been deemed experts on generations. Some of the information will appear to apply to many students, and some of it won't seem remotely descriptive of the students we encounter. These experiences signal that we must make our own observations. Notwithstanding the need for more research, if we gave equal attention to our own observations and to those of our colleagues, as well as to the thoughts and feelings of students themselves, we might come closer to understanding our successive generations of students.

Our observations must include getting to know students by talking with them about who they are, what they value, and what they want from their educations. If we discover through conversations and observations that African American students do have lower expectations than other groups of students and even lower expectations than cohorts of African American students that came before them, we must help them see their potential beyond the context that might have shaped their limiting aspirations. Acknowledging that environment has influenced them, we have an opportunity to help them understand that they need not limit their vision based on what has come before.

If we find that today's students are, indeed, always connected, we must connect with them in the manner that is most appealing to them, such as texting rather than e-mailing them. If they share that they have high expectations and we think that these expectations might be unrealistic given the way in which they are pursuing their educations, then we must help them see that the pathways to their expectations may be different from the ones they are on.

Rather than assuming that each new generation of students is completely different from the previous generation, we might begin to see students as what famed researcher Zogby (2008) calls "composites" rather than differences. From surveys, he finds that "First Globals" (his term for Millennials) are highly materialistic and self-absorbed, as well as caring, tolerant, and possessed of wisdom well beyond their years. He stated that they are the "clear and direct inheritors of the age cohorts stacked above them" (p. 191).

It is both comforting and scary to think that each generation of students is building on the foundation of the generations that preceded it. One issue that remains for each cohort of students over the decades is how we tolerate and engage with difference. If we want college students to become the citizen leaders of tomorrow, we need to address how we as educators are helping them move forward morally and ethically on the issues of diversity and multiculturalism.

It comes as no surprise that the generation of students born in the 1970s and early 1980s were uncomfortable even engaging in conversations about diversity and multiculturalism. Levine and Cureton (1998) said that students of this generation would rather share intimate details of their sex lives than discuss race relations and multiculturalism. When the authors conducted focus groups with students and interviewed chief student affairs officers between 1992 and 1997, they found that students were confounded and emotional about discussions centering on multiculturalism and that "tension regarding diversity and difference runs high all across college life" (p. 75).

The authors concluded that "Multiculturalism remains the most unresolved issue on campus today" (p. 90).

Although issues surrounding multiculturalism remain unresolved, Zogby (2008) noted that "No group of Americans more appreciates the multiethnic, multiracial world in which we all live than today's teens and young adults, and none is anywhere near as accepting of the full range of the human experience" (p. 92). As we prepare to effectively work with students for their academic and personal success, we will need to keep alert to the common contextual experiences that students share as well as their individual experiences that are influenced by cultural differences and how each uses these experiences to help them make sense of the world. As educators, we believe in the power of learning, and we are eager to share this power with each generation of students.

References

Carlson, S. (2003, August 15). Can grand theft auto inspire professors? *Chronicle of Higher Education*, A31.

Cooper, M. A., & Longanecker, D. A. (2009, September 3). Race still matters. *Inside Higher Education*. Retrieved from http://www.insidehighered.com/views/2009/09/03/cooper

Dilworth, P. P., & Carter, S. M. (2007). Millennial versus hip hop: Exploring black undergraduate students' perspective on socially constructed labels. *NASAP Journal, 10*(1), 70–84.

Glenn, D., & Fischer, K. (2009, August 31). The canon of college majors persists amid calls for change. *Chronicle of Higher Education*. Retrieved from http://chronicle.com/article/Amid-Calls-for-Change-Coll/48206/

Halpern, J. (2007, September 30). The new me generation. *Boston Globe Magazine*, 36–39, 47–49. Retrieved from http://www.boston.com/news/globe/magazine/articles/2007/09/30/the_new_me_generation/

Hawkins, B. L., & Oblinger, D. G. (2006, July–August). The myth about the digital divide. *EDUCAUSE Review, 41*(4), 12–13. Retrieved from http://www.educause.edu/EDUCAUSE + Review/EDUCAUSEReviewMagazineVolume41/TheMyth abouttheDigitalDivide/158073

Hesel, R., & May, S. B. (2007, February). Student recruitment: Dispelling the millennial myth. *CASE Currents, 33*(2), 16–22.

Howe, N., & Strauss, W. (2000). *Millennials rising: The next great generation.* New York: Vintage Books.

Jayson, S. (2009, August 12). Parents, kids today more in harmony than prior generations. *USA Today*. Retrieved from http://www.usatoday.com/news/nation/2009-08-12-generation-gap-pew_N.htm

Jenkins, H. (2005). Getting into the game. *Educational Leadership, 62*(7), 48–51.

Levine, A., & Cureton, J. S. (1998). *When hope and fear collide: A portrait of today's college student.* San Francisco: Jossey-Bass.

Malone, M. S. (2009). *The future arrived yesterday: The rise of the protean corporation and what it means for you.* New York: Random House.

Marbley, A. F., Butner, B. K., Burley, H., Bush, L. V., Causey-Bush, T., & Mc-Kisick, S. (2002). It takes a village: The retention of students of color in predominantly white institutions. *NASAP Journal, 5*(1), 40–49.

Marbley, A. F., Hull, W., Polydore, C. L., Bonner, F. A., & Burley, H. (2007). African American millennial college students: Owning the technological middle passage. *NASAP Journal, 10*(1), 7–19.

Penn, M. (2007). *Microtrends: The small forces behind tomorrow's changes.* New York: Twelve.

NASPA. Assessment and Knowledge Consortium. (2009). *Ethnicity differences in diversity/multiculturalism* [survey data]. Washington, DC: Author.

Rendón, L. I. (2004). Transforming the first-year experience for students of color: Where do we begin? In L. I. Rendón, M. Garcia, & D. Person (Eds.), *Transforming the first year of college for students of color* (pp. 177–184). Columbia, SC: National Center on the First Year Experience and Students in Transition.

Stone, Andrea. (2009, April 13). 'Civic generation' rolls up sleeves in record numbers. *USA Today.* Retrieved from http://www.usatoday.com/news/sharing/2009-04-13-millenial_N.htm

Strayhorn, T. L. (2007). Educational aspirations of black millennials in college. *NASAP Journal, 10*(1), 20–34.

Strayhorn, T. (2009). Sex differences in use of Facebook and MySpace among first-year college students. *Ejournal, 10*(2). Retrieved from http://studentaffairs.com/ejournal/Summer_2009/SexDifferencesinUseofFacebookandMySpace.html

Tulgan, B., & Martin, C. A. (2001). *Managing generation Y: Global citizens born in the late seventies and early eighties.* Amherst, MA: HRD Press.

Twenge, J. M. (2006). *Generation me.* New York: Free Press.

University of California, Los Angeles (UCLA) Higher Education Research Institute. (2009, August 24). Attitudes and Characteristics of Freshmen at 4-Year Colleges, Fall 2008. *Chronicle of Higher Education.* Retrieved from http://chronicle.com/article/AttitudesCharacteristi/48030

Zogby, J. (2008). *The way we'll be: The Zogby report on the transformation of the American dream.* New York: Random House.

PART TWO

AFRICAN AMERICAN MILLENNIALS IN COLLEGE

2

AFRICAN AMERICAN MILLENNIALS IN COLLEGE

Terrell L. Strayhorn

A few years ago, I was invited to present a session on first-year college students' use of social networking sites (SNSs), such as Facebook and MySpace, at the annual meeting of the National Association of Student Personnel Administrators, affectionately known as NASPA. Drawing on survey results from over 700 first-year college students, I provided evidence that today's college students use technology and SNSs frequently and in varied ways, ranging from word processing to electronic mail, from posting images online to sharing news about upcoming events. Results also seemed to suggest that most first-year collegians use SNSs to reestablish old or maintain previously existing relationships with friends and family; very few seem to establish new relationships that depend on SNS contact only. Additionally, survey findings indicated that the frequency of students' use varies by both sex and race or ethnicity (Strayhorn, 2009d; Strayhorn & Blakewood, 2009).

At the end of the session, a member of the audience, who identified himself as an "associate director of undergraduate admissions at a small college in the Midwest region of the United States," raised his hand to ask a question. With twisted, uneven brows, clearly conveying his confusion, he stated: "Wow! These results are fascinating, especially since all the literature suggests that Millennials are very high-tech. So, is this true for Millennials of color? And, if not, are there other differences that we don't know about? [laughing] I mean, we need to know this stuff so we can know how to work best with today's student." And as he took his seat, I realized that additional research was needed to understand whether and how the central tendencies often associated with today's college students related to students of color, specifically African American Millennials, who are the focus of the present chapter.

This chapter is organized into three major sections. First, I briefly review the existing literature and theory about Millennial college students. Next, a study in which national data were analyzed to measure the extent to which today's African American Millennials compared to Black students in previous generations is introduced. After summarizing the results of that study, I discuss their relevance to student affairs practice, policy, and future research.

What Do We Know From Research?

Three major conclusions can be gleaned from the existing literature about Millennial college students. First, they are the largest generational cohort ever (Howe & Strauss, 2000). Census figures suggest that approximately 80 million Americans were born after 1980 (Yax, 2004). Census projections indicate that with the influx of immigrants and increased birthrates among racial or ethnic minorities, the size of this generation could exceed 90 million. That is, Millennials "could be 33% larger than the Baby Boomer generation" (Coomes & DeBard, 2004, p. 13) and thus, by size alone, warrant additional research attention.

Second, Millennials are the most diverse college-going generation ever (Coomes & DeBard, 2004; DeBard, 2004; Howe & Strauss, 2000). Racial and ethnic minorities make up a larger proportion of this cohort than in preceding generations such as Generation X. Indeed, these groups constitute a larger fraction of the college-going population today than even possible in some preceding generations such as the Baby Boomers or the GI generation, which were eras marked by racial segregation and limited educational opportunities for African Americans (Williams, 1988). Increased diversity brings with it both a number of new opportunities and potential challenges. Understanding the challenges faced by today's diverse learner is critical to creating campus environments that are conducive for success; thus, the experiences of racial or ethnic minority Millennials warrant special attention.

Finally, it is assumed that the Millennial generation will achieve greatness (Howe & Strauss, 2000; Martin & Tulgan, 2001; Sax, 2003). This is based on the premise, in part, that generations vacillate between being dominant and recessive (Table 2.1). Following the recessive Generation X, also referred to as the Thirteeners (Strauss & Howe, 1991), Millennials are

TABLE 2.1
Description of Generations

Generation	Years Included	Presidential Administrations Included
Lost	1883–1900	Arthur to McKinley
GI	1901–1924	Roosevelt to Harding
Silent	1925–1942	Coolidge to Roosevelt
Baby Boomers	1943–1960	Truman to Kennedy
Generation X	1961–1981	Johnson to Carter
Millennial	1982–2002	Reagan to Clinton

expected to be a dominant generation whose "members . . . need to respond to crises as they move into rising adulthood and elderhood" (Coomes & DeBard, 2004, p. 9). In contrast, Generation X was considered recessive due to the absence of social movements and the need to respond to national crises.

In light of Millennials' promise, more information is needed about today's college students so that educators can foster conditions and environments that facilitate their growth and development. Indeed, studies show that Millennials hold relatively high educational aspirations, although this may not be true for Black Millennials (Strayhorn, 2007a). For instance, in a previous study, I analyzed data from the National Center for Education Statistics' National Postsecondary Student Aid Study (NPSAS) and found that African American Millennials had lower aspirations than their White counterparts. Perhaps unexpectedly, Black Millennials also reported lower educational aspirations than African American collegians from the preceding generation (i.e., Generation X). These results seem to challenge those reported for Millennials "in the aggregate" by Howe and Strauss (2000) and they also await replication.

Although certainly useful, the existing literature is limited in at least three ways. First, the weight of empirical evidence on Millennial college students describes this generation as a monolithic group, whose experiences are much more similar than different. Subgroups such as African American Millennials are rarely studied exclusively. This has resulted in significant confusion about the applicability of the "Millennial framework" (Howe & Strauss, 2000, 2003) to the study of today's African American college students and the unique attributes of Black Millennials. The study that informs the present chapter addresses this shortcoming by focusing on African American students exclusively.

The Study

Since I was interested in studying whether and how African American Millennial college students compared to Black students in previous generations, I sought out national data that permitted analysis of such trends. Several possibilities existed including a handful of national surveys conducted by the U.S. Department of Education's National Center for Education Statistics (NCES) including the Beginning Postsecondary Student Survey (BPS). A major strength of the BPS is that it includes results from thousands of new and entering college students. Serious weaknesses of the database, given my focus for this study, range from issues of measurement to sampling. For instance, very few measures of student engagement *in* college are included on the survey; therefore, I would be limited to comparing students on mostly personal traits and educational backgrounds. And, until recently, BPS data were only available for students who began their postsecondary careers in 1996—members of Generation X, not Millennials (Wine et al., 2002).

Two other national databases proved useful for my purposes: the Cooperative Institutional Research Program (CIRP) and College Student Experiences Questionnaire (CSEQ). Both of these longstanding national surveys allowed for cross-sectional trend analysis and included a sufficient number of African Americans in the samples upon which statistical analyses were based. Finally, measures of students' opinions, aspirations, and engagement were included that allowed me to examine the extent to which Black collegians from different generations compared on measures that seem to tap the "central tendencies" identified in the existing literature on Millennial college students (Howe & Strauss, 2000).

To make sense of these data, I conducted several analyses using a combination of descriptive statistics and mean difference significance tests. Findings are summarized below and discussed in the context of the existing literature about Millennial college students. Implications for higher education professionals, supervisors, and educational researchers also are presented.

Major Findings and Generational Comparisons

College Enrollment Trends

Scholars argue that today's college students are "more numerous, more affluent, better educated, and more ethnically diverse" than previous generations (Howe & Strauss, 2000, p. 4). Results from the present study generally support these conclusions for African American Millennials. Analysis of data from the U.S. Department of Education (2006) indicates significant growth in college enrollment among African Americans over the past three decades. In 1976 African Americans (approximately 943,000) composed 10% of total undergraduate enrollment in degree-granting institutions and about 8% of college freshmen. By 2006 Black representation (approximately 1.96 million) increased to approximately 13% of total undergraduate enrollment and 10.5% of freshmen enrollment. Taken together, these figures represent a 107% increase in total African American undergraduate enrollment in just 30 years. Indeed, African American Millennials are more numerous than their same-race predecessors.

Although growth in college enrollment among African American Millennials is significant and undeniable, my analysis revealed that stubbornly persistent gender disparities among African American populations exist. Results from the CIRP Freshman Survey analysis suggest that, consistent with national trends showing most entering students are women (55%), women also are a sizable majority among African American Millennials and the "gender gap" (Sax, 2008) has widened over time. Whereas Black women composed 54.5% of Black freshmen undergraduates at 4-year institutions in 1971, this proportion increased to 59.3% by 2004. Furthermore, gender disparities in college enrollment are most pronounced among African Americans, with Black women outnumbering their same-race male counterparts by a margin of two to one (Cuyjet, 2006; Strayhorn, 2008a, 2008c). This points to an important nuance in the story about today's Millennial college students. Although Millennials as a group are "more numerous" when considered in the aggregate (i.e., all races and both sexes combined; Howe & Strauss, 2000), African American male Millennials are not more numerous than in previous generations. As I have noted elsewhere, "there has been little to no progress in increasing the college-going rates among Black men over the past quarter century" (Strayhorn, 2009a, p. 124). We will return to this point later in the chapter. Table 2.2 presents a summary of these trends by sex.

TABLE 2.2
African American First-Year Undergraduates, by Sex, 1971–2004

Sex	1971	1984	1994	2004
Women (%)	54.5	57.7	60.4	59.3
Men (%)	45.5	42.3	39.6	40.7
Total	72,199.6	114,240.8	108,121.5	120,494.0

Family Income

Other interesting demographic trends were identified. Similar to the broader population of Millennials, African American Millennials are generally more affluent than Blacks from preceding generations. Today, students from the lowest income groups make up a smaller proportion of the total Black freshmen population than in 1971. For instance, CIRP data revealed that, in 1971 (i.e., Generation Xers), approximately 94% of African American first-year undergraduates reported a family income of less than $20,000 annually, compared to only 22% of Black Millennials (2004 cohort). Results also suggest that African American Millennials are more likely to hail from higher-income families than their same-race predecessors. The proportion of Black collegians whose family income ranged from $20,000 to $29,999 increased from about 4% in 1971 to approximately 15% by 2004. In some ways, this reflects the growing "middle class" among Blacks in America during this time span (Graham, 1992; Pattillo-McCoy, 1999; West, 1993). Perhaps most striking, however, is the exponential growth among Blacks from even higher income families. In 1971, 0.2% of Black Generation Xers reported family income as above $50,000 per year; a much larger proportion (42.5%) of African American Millennials hail from affluent family backgrounds. Table 2.3 presents a summary of these results.

Demographic Traits and Characteristics

Although most of my findings illustrate how Black Millennials differ from their Black predecessors, several figures challenge the assumption that today's African American college student population is vastly different from those

TABLE 2.3
African American First-Year Undergraduates' Parents Income, 1971–2004 (percent)

Income Range	1971	1984	1994	2004
Less than $6,000	41.0	16.5	9.4	—
$6,000 to $9,999	28.5	11.3	6.4	10.2
$10,000 to $14,999	18.1	16.3	8.7	6.3
$15,000 to $19,999	6.1	11.1	7.8	5.8
$20,000 to $29,999	4.4	18.5	16.1	14.6
$30,000 to $49,999	1.7	18.9	22.0	20.6
$50,000 or more	0.2	8.0	29.6	42.5

of bygone eras. For instance, Black Millennial freshmen are overwhelmingly single (98.6%) versus married (0.6%); predominantly full time (94.8%) versus part time (6.2%); and largely traditional age (i.e., 19 years or younger [91.6%]), much like previous generations of Black collegians. Still, there has been some increase in the number of nontraditionally aged Black freshmen, who represented 4.4% of Black Generation Xers (1985 cohort) yet 6.5% of Black Millennials (2004 cohort). Although almost 50% of Black Generation Xers reported being first-generation (FG) college students—that is, neither parent attended college (Strayhorn, 2006)—FG students composed only 48% of Black Millennials surveyed in 2004.

Academic Preparation and Achievement

Most evidence about today's college students supports the notion that they are among the "best and brightest" ever to enter higher education. And all of us are probably familiar with the long list of accolades that college presidents and other senior-ranking administrators use to introduce the entering class of "four years from now." Consider the following excerpt from Chancellor Robert Holub at the University of Massachusetts, Amherst (formerly Provost at the University of Tennessee, Knoxville where I served as his special assistant):

> Last year we received a record number of applications for admission; over 30,000 young people wanted to come to Amherst to pursue their studies, and we offered admission to the lowest percentage of applicants in our history. . . . As a result of the record number of applications, we had a first-year class that broke the previous high-water marks for both SAT scores and high school grade point average. We also welcomed to campus the most diverse class we have ever had.

So, is this true for African American Millennials? Comparative statistical analysis of African American Generation Xers (1985 cohort) and Black Millennials (2004 cohort) provides supportive evidence. For instance, 15.4% of African American Generation Xers reported earning "mostly As" in high school, whereas 33.1% of African American Millennials did so. And a small proportion of African American Millennials (0.2%) compared to Generation Xers (1.9%) reported low performance in high school.

Howe and Strauss (2000) noted that "a much higher share of today's kids are taking advanced placement [AP] tests" (p. 18). Findings from a secondary analysis of College Board data are inconsistent with this general conclusion for African Americans. That is, although participation in the AP program has grown steadily nationwide, with more than 15% of recent high school graduates passing at least one AP exam in 2008, African American students are still far less likely than White, Latino/a, and Asian students to have taken or passed an AP exam (Lewin, 2009). Representing 14% of high school graduates in 2008, African Americans made up only 8% of students taking AP exams and only 4% of those earning a passing score—that is, a score of 3 or higher.

Values and Attitudes

Not only have previous scholars assumed that Millennials are the most diverse college-going generation ever (Coomes & DeBard, 2004; DeBard, 2004; Howe & Strauss, 2000), but they also tend to assume that Millennials' values and attitudes are favorable toward issues of equity, diversity, and social justice. For example, one might assume that today's college student would be more open to homosexuality and gay marriage, especially since anywhere from 3% to 10% of today's teens believe themselves to be gay, lesbian, bisexual, or questioning (Howe & Strauss, 2000). Additionally, Howe and Strauss pointed out that "sexual preference is far more widely discussed [today] than it was in earlier generations at the same age" (2000, p. 228). They conclude that the mass of Millennials envision a future community that encompasses gays, lesbians, and straight men and women.

Results from my analysis of CIRP data from 1985, 1998, and 2004 suggest that there may be cause for concern with African American college students. For instance, 22% of Black Generation Xers "strongly agreed" that legal marital status should be granted for same-sex couples, while 30% "strongly disagreed" with that perspective. Similarly, only 25% of Black Millennials "strongly agreed" with gay marriage and about 29% "strongly disagreed" with the issue. On the other hand, 21% of Black Generation Xers "strongly agreed" with the statement that "homosexual relations should be prohibited," whereas 17% of Black Millennials did so. Perhaps this reflects a downward trend in Black students' negative attitudes toward same-sex relationships, although change appears slow and gradual.

Use of Technology

Returning to the opening topic in this chapter discussion, most authors argue that today's college student population is highly skilled with using technology, and they use it frequently in varied ways. Interestingly, both the

1985 CIRP and 2004 CSEQ databases included an item that asked students to rate the frequency with which they "use[d] a personal computer." African American Generation Xers reported the following: very often (24%), often (42%), occasionally (32%), and never (2%). African American Millennials, however, reported more frequent use: very often (75%), often (15%), occasionally (8%), and never (2%). Independent samples t-tests affirmed that this difference is statistically significant [t (11,910) = 383.86, p < .001], with the mean of Black Millennials (M = 3.64, standard deviation [SD] = 0.169) far exceeding the mean of Black Generation Xers (M = 2.89, SD = 0.022). Combined with the findings presented earlier in the chapter (Strayhorn, 2009d; Strayhorn & Blakewood, 2009), it seems clear that African American Millennials tend to use computers and other technologies (e.g., SNSs) more often than preceding Black generations.

Discussion

This chapter was designed to provide information that will aid in understanding whether and how the central tendencies often associated with today's college student population relate to African American Millennials. Several major conclusions can be drawn from the evidence presented in the previous section. First, indeed, African American Millennials are more numerous than their same-race predecessors, and this trend seems to hold across racial and ethnic lines (Howe & Strauss, 2000). College student educators should consider these results when working with today's college student and anticipating the demographic complexion of future generations. Increased racial and ethnic diversity brings with it exciting opportunities, as well as a number of challenges. Learning more about students' racial and ethnic backgrounds, creating campus environments that affirm diverse cultural backgrounds, and promoting meaningful engagement among students with individuals whose race or ethnicity differs from one's own are important ways to maximize the educational benefits of increased structural diversity.

Second, results reveal that stubbornly persistent gender disparities exist in terms of African American college student enrollment, with women representing almost 60% of African American collegians nationwide. National statistics of this kind turn much-needed attention to the experiences of African American male collegians who, according to research (Harper, 2003; Harper & Nichols, 2008; Strayhorn, 2008a, 2008b), face a number of unique challenges and barriers to their success in college. The weight of evidence seems to suggest that additional resources are needed to assist African American males in completing high school, preparing for college, and earning their degrees in a timely fashion. So, although the Millennial framework tends to imply that today's college students are more numerous than ever, scholars and researchers should consider the research results in this chapter when noting the limitations of the framework's applicability to Millennials of color and even the within-group heterogeneity that exists among African Americans (Harper & Nichols, 2008).

Third, African American Millennials are generally more affluent than Blacks from preceding generations, similar to conclusions drawn by Howe and Strauss (2000) about the population as a whole. This finding may reflect the once growing "middle class" among Blacks in America (Graham, 1992; Pattillo-McCoy, 1999; West, 1993); recently, scholars have argued that the Black middle class is disappearing due to the economic recession and workforce reductions. Furthermore, my findings show that there has been exponential growth in the number of Black college students from the highest income families. This may be the result of several educational policy shifts over time. First, the price of college has increased remarkably over the past few decades, and regrettably this has restricted access to higher education, in some places, to those who can afford to go (Strayhorn, 2007b). The popular press is full of stories about the rising costs of college, the struggle of middle-class families to finance a college education, and questions about the value of high-priced postsecondary education (St. John, 2003). In 1985, 63% of first-year students had concerns about financing their college educations; a decade later, 70% were concerned, and 18% had major concerns. If these trends continue, we can anticipate that few issues will concern American families as much as the spiraling cost of a college education (Baum, 2001). And African American students of future generations will likely hail from high-income families, while those from middle- to low-income families will have limited options for further education. A second reason for the shift toward enrolling students from higher income families is student financial aid policies have shifted from need-based grants to merit-based scholarships, which tend to provide funds to students and their families without reference to need (Strayhorn, 2007b). Policymakers and campus leaders should consider these results when establishing new or revising existing student aid programs, paying particular attention to reconciling the tensions between affordability and access.

Fourth, despite the aforementioned differences, Black Millennials are similar to previous generations of Black students in several ways. Black Millennials tend to be single not married, enrolled full time, largely traditional age, and about 50% first generation to college, much like previous generations. These issues point to an important caveat in the story. Howe and Strauss's (2000) Millennial framework may be useful for investigating and understanding the perspectives, behaviors, and values of today's college students and even today's African American college students. Yet, it is unlikely to be helpful with *all* students, at *all* times, given the differences presented throughout this volume. Future research might proceed in a number of directions. For example, researchers might draw on studies like those presented in this volume to formulate a theory or framework that applies to today's college students of color. Studies of this kind would provide college student educators with guidance to support today's students in effective ways.

Fifth, African American Millennials, on average, performed much better than their same-race Generation X counterparts in high school, although they continue to lag behind their White, Latino/a, and Asian counterparts in terms of AP exam participation and success rates. This has implications for teaching and learning in higher education. For instance, instructors who rely on the Howe and Strauss (2000) framework might conclude that today's college student is academically superior to previous generations, thereby requiring advanced teaching and learning strategies that capitalize on their intellectual acumen. Results presented here and elsewhere (Adelman, 1999) temper such conclusions and suggest the need to provide additional academic and social supports to some African American students that will likely enable their success in college. Precollege outreach programs, summer bridge programs, AP exam preparation activities, first-year seminars, and compensatory programs in college are likely to yield positive educational outcomes for such students (Strayhorn, 2009b, 2009c).

Although Howe and Strauss (2000) posit that anywhere from 3% to 10% of today's teens believe themselves to be gay, lesbian, or questioning, and although sexual preference is more widely discussed today than in generations past, there is little empirical evidence from my analyses to suggest that African American Millennials are more accepting than Blacks of previous generations of same-sex relationships, gay marriage, or similar liberal political opinions. What seems evident is that African American Millennials' attitudes and beliefs about issues of sexuality are virtually unchanged, compared to Blacks in preceding generations. This may be the result of well-documented homophobia within the Black community (Clarke, 1983; Mitchell, 2006) and fairly conservative political opinions among today's college students (Pryor, Hurtado, Saenz, Santos, & Korn, 2007). Indeed more information is needed and these results warrant additional testing.

Lastly, most evidence seems to suggest that African American Millennials use computers and emerging technologies frequently and perhaps in varied ways, although other research reveals the "digital divide" between Black students and their non-Black counterparts (Marbley, Hull, Polydore, Bonner, & Burley, 2007; Vinson, 2007).

Conclusion

Although prospects for this generation are generally positive, there are potential dangers and obstacles that deserve mention. First, most scholars agree that Millennials have positive self-confidence, boundless optimism, and high aspirations (Strayhorn, 2007a). And while these traits are certainly admirable, the personal and social consequences can be quite serious if their aspirations are thwarted (Howe & Strauss, 2000). College student educators, parents, and mentors would do well to help today's college students acquire skills and strategies for maintaining their aspirations in the face of challenges, as well as managing their emotions when failure occurs. It is also true that, as Howe and Strauss rightly said, the Millennial persona is distinguished by several major traits including a sense of being "special." And special people tend to sport feelings of entitlement while demanding special treatment. College student educators and parents might consider this chapter and others in the volume to provide guidance routinely to students about the importance of balancing positive self-confidence and high aspirations with a reasonable portion of modesty so that students can set realistic expectations and work with college personnel in mutually rewarding ways.

References

Adelman, C. (1999). *Answers in the toolbox: Academic intensity, attendance patterns, and bachelor's degree attainment.* Washington, DC: U.S. Department of Education, Office of Educational Research and Improvement.

Baum, S. (2001). College education: Who can afford it? In M. B. Paulsen & J. C. Smart (Eds.), *The finance of higher education: Theory, research, and practice* (pp. 39–52). New York: Agathon Press.

Clarke, C. (1983). The failure to transform: Homophobia in the Black community. In B. Smith (Ed.), *Home girls: A Black feminist anthology* (pp. 197–208). New York: Kitchen Table Press.

Coomes, M. D., & DeBard, R. (2004). A generational approach to understanding students. In M. D. Coomes & R. DeBard (Eds.), *Serving the Millennial generation* (pp. 5–16). San Francisco: Jossey-Bass.

Cuyjet, M. J. (2006). African American college men: Twenty-first century issues and concerns. In M. J. Cuyjet & Associates (Eds.), *African American men in college* (pp. 3–23). San Francisco: Jossey-Bass.

DeBard, R. (2004). Millennials coming to college. In M. D. Coomes & R. DeBard (Eds.), *Serving the millennial generation* (pp. 33–45). San Francisco: Jossey-Bass.

Graham, S. (1992). Most of the subjects were White and middle class: Trends in published research on African Americans in selected APA journals, 1970–1989. *American Psychologist, 47*, 629–639.

Harper, S. R. (2003). Most likely to succeed: The self-perceived impact of involvement on the experiences of high-achieving African American undergraduate men at predominantly White universities. *Dissertation Abstracts International, A64*(6), 1995.

Harper, S. R., & Nichols, A. H. (2008). Are they not all the same? Racial heterogeneity among Black male undergraduates. *Journal of College Student Development, 49*(3), 199–214.

Howe, N., & Strauss, W. (2000). *Millennials rising: The next great generation.* New York: Vintage.

Howe, N., & Strauss, W. (2003). *Millennials go to college.* Great Falls, VA: American Association of Registrars and Admissions Officers and LifeCourse Associates.

Lewin, T. (2009, February 5). Blacks less likely to take A.P. exam. *New York Times,* p. A19.

Marbley, A. F., Hull, W., Polydore, C. L., Bonner II, F. A., & Burley, H. (2007). African American millennial college students: Owning the technological middle passage. *National Association of Student Affairs Professionals Journal, 10*(1), 7–19.

Martin, C. A., & Tulgan, B. (2001). *Managing Generation Y.* New Haven, CT: HRD Press.

Mitchell, B. C. (2006). *Exploring levels of homophobia in minority college students.* Unpublished doctoral dissertation, The University of Houston, Houston.

Pattillo-McCoy, M. (1999). *Black picket fences: Privilege and peril among the Black middle class.* Chicago: University of Chicago Press.

Pryor, J. H., Hurtado, S., Saenz, V. B., Santos, J. L., & Korn, W. S. (2007). *The American freshman: Forty year trends.* Los Angeles: Higher Education Research Institute, UCLA.

Sax, L. J. (2003). Our incoming students: What are they like? *About Campus, 8*(3), 15–20.

Sax, L. J. (2008). *Gender gap in college: Maximizing the developmental potential of women and men.* San Francisco: Jossey-Bass.

St. John, E. P. (2003). *Refinancing the college dream: Access, equal opportunity, and justice for taxpayers.* Baltimore: Johns Hopkins University Press.

Strauss, W., & Howe, N. (1991). *Generations: The history of America's future, 1584 to 2069.* New York: Morrow.

Strayhorn, T. L. (2006). Factors influencing the academic achievement of first-generation college students. *NASPA Journal, 43*(4), 82–111.

Strayhorn, T. L. (2007a). Educational aspirations of Black Millennials in college. *NASAP Journal, 10*(1), 20–34.

Strayhorn, T. L. (2007b). HOPE for success: State aid, access, and persistence. In B. Longden & K. Harris (Eds.), *Research, theory, and practice in higher education* (pp. 46–61). Amsterdam: European Association of Institutional Research.

Strayhorn, T. L. (2008a). Fittin' in: Do diverse interactions with peers affect sense of belonging for Black men at predominantly White institutions? *NASPA Journal, 45*(4), 501–527.

Strayhorn, T. L. (2008b). The invisible man: Factors affecting the retention of low-income African American males. *National Association of Student Affairs Professionals Journal, 11*(1), 66–87.

Strayhorn, T. L. (2008c). The role of supportive relationships in facilitating African American males' success in college. *NASPA Journal, 45*(1), 26–48.

Strayhorn, T. L. (2009a). African American male graduate students. In M. H. Howard-Hamilton, C. L. Morelon-Quainoo, S. D. Johnson, R. Winkle-Wagner, & L. Santiague (Eds.), *Standing on the outside, looking in: Underrepresented students' experiences in advanced-degree programs* (pp. 124–146). Sterling, VA: Stylus.

Strayhorn, T. L. (2009b). Bridging the gap from high school to college for "at risk" first-year students. *E-Source for College Transitions, 6*(3), 9–11.

Strayhorn, T. L. (2009c). An examination of the impact of first-year seminars on correlates of college student retention. *Journal of The First-Year Experience and Students in Transition, 21*(1), 9–27.

Strayhorn, T. L. (2009d). Sex differences in use of Facebook and MySpace among first-year college students [Electronic Version]. *Student Affairs Online: A Quarterly e-Journal, 10.* Retrieved from http://www.studentaffairs.com/ejournal/Summer_2009/SexDifferenc esinUseofFace bookandMySpace.pdf

Strayhorn, T. L., & Blakewood, A. M. (2009). Racial differences in first-year students' use of MySpace and Facebook [Electronic Version]. *NetResults.* Retrieved from http://www.naspa.org/membership/mem/pubs/nr/default.cfm?id = 1674

U.S. Department of Education, National Center for Education Statistics. (2006). *The condition of education 2006* (NCES 2006-071). Washington, DC: U.S. Government Printing Office.

Vinson, B. M. (2007). African American millennial college students and the impact of the digital divide. *National Association of Student Affairs Professionals Journal, 10*(1), 63–69.

West, C. (1993). *Race matters.* New York: Vintage.

Williams III, J. B. (Ed.). (1988). *Desegregating America's colleges and universities: Title VI regulation of higher education.* New York: Teacher's College Press.

Wine, J. S., Heuer, R. E., Wheeless, S. C., Francis, T. L., Franklin, J. W., & Dudley, K. M. (2002). *Beginning postsecondary students longitudinal study: 1996–2001 (BPS:96/01) methodology report* (No. NCES 2002-171). Washington, DC: U.S. Department of Education, Office of Educational Research and Improvement.

Yax, L. K. (2004). Projected population of the United States, by age and sex: 2000 to 2050 (Vol. 2004). Washington, DC: U.S. Bureau of the Census.

3

THE PERSON, ENVIRONMENT, AND GENERATIONAL INTERACTION

An African American Rural Millennial Story

Corey Guyton and Mary F. Howard-Hamilton

A marginalized and isolated Millennial population of students are from the rural areas of the United States. According to the U.S. Department of Agriculture (2003), a city or town that has a population of fewer than 50,000 residents is considered a rural environment. Within these rural areas are students of color who are surrounded by a confluence of family, peers, teachers, and devoted community residents who have a tremendous impact on their futures. The rural Millennial students may not have the advantage of having an expansive network of individuals who can assist them with transition to a college campus, career decisions, and ultimately the move away from their rural homes. According to Carr and Kefalas (2009), "Residents of rural America are more likely to be poor and uninsured than their counterparts in metropolitan areas, typically earning 80 percent what suburban and urban workers do" (p. B7). This crisis is exacerbated by the fact that many of the rural Millennial students who do leave their small town environments do not return once they have completed their academic work (Carr & Kefalas, 2009).

Based on the overall description of students who are from the rural Millennial generation there is a group of African Americans who are faced with challenges exponentially greater than their counterparts' (Hebert & Beardsley, 2002). The impact of the financial burden of living in a rural environment is magnified for African Americans. There are an overwhelmingly high percentage of rural Blacks, 97%, living in the South (Hebert & Beardsley, 2002). Concomitantly, the lower socioeconomic status combined with limited academic access outside the rural environment could lead to a cycle of poverty over multiple generations (Hebert & Beardsley, 2002). The rural African American Millennial student may be uniquely challenged when matriculating to a predominantly White campus and becoming connected to a nonrural environment. This chapter provides a narrative analysis, or first-person account, of the lived experiences of the first author who is a rural African American Millennial student (Merriam, 2002). The story will be bracketed by an ecological theoretical framework to understand how the person telling the story, his race, as well as his departure from a rural environment to a predominantly White institution intersect to create situations that continue to expand the list of traits describing this unique generation.

Corey's Story

I was born in 1983 and by most standards I would be considered a member of the Millennial generation. As I began to learn more about Millennials and their traits, I realized there were a large number of traits ascribed to the Millennial generation that I did not possess. My initial thought was that since I was born during the first years of the Millennial generation, I did not possess the traits of what others described as being a Millennial.

Although there may have been some validity to this assumption, I realized that most of my peers born during the same time period carried more Millennial traits than I did. As I began to have conversations with peers, colleagues, and mentors, I realized that my rural roots had a large influence on my lack of "traditional" Millennial traits.

The Town

I was born and raised in an unincorporated town located in southern Georgia less than 2 miles from the Florida state line. The nearest city, which I will call the "big city," is approximately 15 miles north. The big city had a population of about 18,000 residents.

Within the confines of my small town, there were no stop lights, no police stations, no medical facilities, no mayor, no schools, a dormant volunteer fire station, two churches, one unnamed country store, and a large sawmill that was considered the main attraction.

The town had a population of less than 200 residents and most of them were from families who have lived in the town for decades. There was little racial diversity, meaning the town was composed of only Black and White residents. Most White residents were self-employed and their primary source of income was agriculture, while most Black residents worked in nearby cities.

Due to the very rural location of the town, cell phones did not pick up signals. Within the past 5 years, cable television made its way to my small town. Prior to cable television, satellite was the only source of television outside the traditional analog channels. During storms, lights could go out for days and families would have to rely on kerosene lamps and gas stoves. In the case of an emergency, assistance from the police, ambulance, or fire department could take a considerably long time because they are dispatched from the big city.

The Community

White residents in the community were direct descendants of slave owners and Confederate soldiers of the Civil War. They were very proud of their Southern heritage and they worshiped the Confederate flag. Normal attire for White residents was a pair of blue jeans and a camouflage Dixie Outfitters shirt. They generally wore the Confederate flag on most apparel and had it visible in their yards and on their vehicles.

Black residents in the community were direct descendants of slaves. Their sense of Southern pride was different from that of White residents. Black residents' Southern pride comprised an appreciation for the obstacles they had overcome through the years. Many Black residents placed value on the land they owned. They put a lot of energy into keeping their land groomed and maintained because they knew their families had fought really hard to obtain it. Most Black families agreed to never sell their land because of its rich history.

Black and White residents in the community have strong conservative values. Most families function in a very traditional Southern way, in which the man is the provider and the woman is the nurturer. The general role of the male is taking care of the outside responsibilities such as mowing the grass, taking out the garbage, gardening, chopping wood, and other outside chores. The general role of the female is cleaning the house, cooking dinner, nurturing the kids, and tending to other inside responsibilities.

Most people in the community identify as being Christian. Due to the strong Christian beliefs and strong conservative values, there is a very strong opposition to homosexuality. Homosexuality is rarely seen in the community and in the rare instance that it is public, there could be various forms of discrimination exhibited toward the individual(s).

Interracial relationships are also frowned upon in the community. Although a few residents have engaged in interracial relationships, the notion of Black and White intimate relationships is foreign. In the community, Black people marry Black people and White people marry White people.

The town has a love–hate relationship among Black and White residents. The love is shown when the community is forced to show unity. This becomes evident when outside entities come into the community and try to create change. In this type of situation, residents come together regardless of race.

Over the years the two races have learned to coexist. Although they have learned to tolerate each other, there is an understanding that each race really feels negatively toward the other. A typical conversation in my family was talking about how the "White man" or "Cracker" thinks he is better than the Black man.

My Education

My parents did not attend college. My father was a part of the first group of Black students to integrate the local high school in the 1960s. He dropped out during his senior year due to large amounts of racial discrimination. My father explained that he dropped out because White teachers allowed White students to call them "Niggers" and hit them with paper without doing anything about it. My mother graduated from high school but did not attend college because she was pregnant with my oldest sister during her senior year.

Although my parents did not attend college, my mother always felt like college was my ticket out of the rural community. She did not push my oldest sister or brother as hard as my youngest sister and me because they were in school during the 1970s and 1980s. During the 1970s and 1980s, high school diplomas were considered valuable enough to obtain a decent job. My youngest sister and I were in school during the time (millennial generation) when college education began to become a necessity.

Elementary School

My family did not travel to the big city much when I was a kid. We specifically traveled to the big city for groceries and other shopping, but outside of that we spent most of our time in my small town. I did not have the luxury of going to the skating rink on the weekends, eating large amounts of fast food, or doing other things that most kids in the city experienced.

My true experience of the big city came when I started elementary school in 1988. My small town did not have an education system so residents of my community attended school in the big city. Elementary school was my opportunity to live the life that I did not get to live in my small town. This was my opportunity to learn about the things that city kids did.

In elementary school, I put a strong emphasis on making good grades. My mother held me to very high standards because she wanted me to succeed in life and have more opportunities than she had. She did not allow me to come home with anything less than the letter grade of "A." In kindergarten she instilled in me the value of college and told me I was going to attend because she knew college was the way to more opportunities and a way out of the small town. I excelled through elementary school with high merit.

Middle School

I moved forward to middle school in the fall of 1994. During middle school, I began to really see how living in a small rural town limited my life experiences. This was when my classmates began to make their weekend outings to the skating rink, theater, bowling alley, dating, and other social activities. I did not get to experience many of these activities because my family would have to travel too far to drop me off and pick me up.

During middle school, I began to play after-school sports. Although I did not get a chance to do a lot of social activities, sports filled the void. I continued to excel in my academic achievement and was an "A" and "B" honor roll student. My mother gave me a small amount of autonomy, but did not let me slack on my studies.

High School

In 1996 my life changed dramatically. I can recall the day a salesman arrived on my family's front doorstep with a new product. The salesman was a representative for DirecTV and he was marketing satellite television to families in rural areas. This was an amazing product because cable television did not reach my rural area and we were stuck with analog stations such as ABC, CBS, and NBC. My sister and I begged my parents to purchase this product. They granted our wishes and this was the day I truly became connected to the world.

After getting DirecTV, I finally had an opportunity to see an actual "music video." My peers would always tell me about MTV and BET, but I had no way to watch those channels. DirecTV made viewing these channels possible and I spent many hours watching various programs. I can honestly say that DirecTV had both positive and negative effects on me.

A lot of the things in the world that I was not exposed to began to pour into my psyche. I began to mimic things I saw on television such as rap artists, movie stars, comedians, and other idols. I also was exposed to nudity and sex during this time, because satellite channels such as HBO and Cinemax broadcast R-rated movies. The closest thing I had seen to nudity and sex prior to DirecTV was a *Sports Illustrated* Swimsuit Edition magazine.

In 1999 I was exposed to college life. I got nominated for the Governor's Honor program, which was a program for students who excelled in technology in the state of Georgia. The interview for the program was in Atlanta, Georgia, at Clayton State University (CSU). I went to the interview and fell in love with the campus.

What really caught my attention while at CSU were students carrying black CSU backpacks. I inquired about the backpacks and found out that every student who attended CSU received the black backpack and a laptop for class. This was amazing to me because I did not have a computer.

In the fall of 2000 during my senior year, I began to really consider college. I knew I needed to take the SAT in order to successfully get admitted into an institution, so I signed up to take the SAT without any guidance or studying. I scored a 930. I knew I was smarter than a 930, but I had major challenges with the verbal section. I studied for the verbal section in hopes of raising my score. A few months later, I took the SAT for a second time and scored 1010.

During the beginning of the spring semester of my senior year, I met with my guidance counselor to ask about possible college opportunities. I expressed interest in the University of Georgia (UGA), but she told me I did not have a chance of getting admitted with my SAT score. My spirits were crushed because most White kids in my graduating class were getting accepted into UGA. My spirits were crushed even more when a White girl in my class with an SAT score lower than mine got accepted into UGA.

Around March of my senior year, I was thinking about possible schools to which I might apply. I recalled the school that gave students laptops that I had visited during my Governor's Honor's interview. I went to the school's website and did research on it and realized that I met the school's admissions requirements. I sent my application packet to Clayton State and a few weeks later I was accepted. At the point of acceptance, I quit searching for other schools and set my sights on Clayton State.

My parents could not help me with the admissions process because they did not know anything about college. I did not feel comfortable going to my admissions counselor because I did not feel she treated me fairly in my quest to attend UGA. I took matters into my own hands and called Clayton State. I asked a lot of questions about starting my college career. I created a to-do list based on the items the admission's representatives told me I needed. I called financial aid frequently and other departments to figure out the process of obtaining housing, paying tuition, and getting enrolled. The financial part was fairly easy, because I received the HOPE scholarship. The HOPE scholarship paid full tuition since I kept a high school GPA of at least 3.0.

Undergraduate

I graduated from high school in May 2001. I moved to Atlanta, Georgia, in August 2001 to live with my uncle for about two weeks prior to the start of school. A week before school started, I went to orientation. Orientation for me was my first "true" experience of being on a college campus. The day I walked into orientation was the first time I was on Clayton State's campus since the Governor's Honor's trip during my junior year. It felt like heaven because I saw a lot of people who came from different backgrounds.

A week after orientation, school began. I walked on campus and really felt a sense of culture shock. I began to see things I hardly ever seen at home. The first thing that caught my eye was a group of guys who identified as being homosexual and showed many feminine qualities. This posed a major problem for me because I was raised in an environment where men were supposed to have masculine qualities and were supposed to only date women.

The second thing that caught my eye was interracial couples. I began to see White men with Black women, Black men with White women, Black men with Asian women, and a large number of other interracial combinations. This was really eye-opening because I thought people would stick to dating within their own race. I admit that I saw a few interracial couples prior to arriving on campus, but it was nothing close to the number I was exposed to on campus.

One final thing that caught my eye when I arrived at college was the caliber of White people. I was used to being around White people who self-identified as being "redneck." Most White people who were in my hometown were Confederate flag–wearing, NASCAR-loving individuals who farmed and mud bogged as a social activity. If I had to compare the type of

White people I was used to seeing to a cartoon, it would be the characters on *King of the Hill.*

At Clayton State, the White people were far from "rednecks" and did not do many of the things I was used to seeing White people do. They also seemed to accept Black people more, which was a conflict, because although I coexisted with White people in my hometown, I did not fully trust them. It took me a while and many good experiences to realize that it was the White people in the world who genuinely cared for Black people.

There were a number of other things outside the college environment that I had to become familiar with. To most people, these things were pretty standard. For example, gaining an understanding of how to use a parking meter was a tricky task for me. I did not know how much money I needed to put into the meter or what happens if I did not put money into it. I had to learn how to parallel park because in my small town we did not have to parallel park. I had to learn what a "city block" was and what it meant when someone told me "it's three blocks up the street." I also did not adjust well to traffic and hated the fact that I had to sit at the same stoplight for several minutes.

Something as little as moving to an apartment was big for me. Prior to moving to Atlanta and getting an apartment, I thought people who lived in apartments were poor. Since most people in my small town owned land and homes, I assumed you were poor if you did not. I looked at apartments in the same manner I viewed housing projects.

After moving into an apartment, there were issues I had with my roommates. The first issue was locking doors. I had to get used to locking my car and apartment doors. The culture in my hometown was that everyone left their doors unlocked and no one touched your possessions. My roommates were from areas that forced them to lock their doors because if they did not, they would lose their possessions.

I had to adjust to eating fast food on a regular basis. My family did not eat fast food much so I was used to eating home-cooked meals. I was extremely excited when I arrived on campus because Kroger (grocery store) and Walmart were 2 minutes away rather than a 25-minute drive.

The final adjustment and most difficult was communicating with others. I think this adjustment had the biggest impact on my life. When I arrived on campus, I thought I talked normal. I began to realize that people talked completely different from me and that my dialect was funny to everyone.

Simple words like "back" and "black" I pronounced completely wrong, more like "bike" and "blike."

I was so embarrassed by the way I pronounced words that I began to practice each night saying words correctly. I would continuously repeat the word "back" hundreds of times so it would become ingrained into my memory. This was the point when I really began to despise my K–12 education because I felt my teachers should have corrected me when I was pronouncing words incorrectly in their classes.

Graduate School

During my senior year of college I was approached by the vice president for student affairs at CSU. He asked me about my plans after graduation and I told him I wanted to progress to graduate school but did not know much about it. I expressed that I did not know many people from my area who possessed a degree higher than a bachelor's. He began to tell me about master's and doctorate degrees and that he believed I was capable of achieving them.

Following that conversation, I began to research graduate programs. While researching programs, I discovered I had to take the GRE. I took the GRE and scored fairly low, considering I made a 320 on the verbal section. I did fairly well on the math portion of the test. My results on the verbal part of the GRE were fairly consistent with the results I had on the verbal section of the SAT. Despite my low score, I applied to a graduate program at the University of Georgia. I was denied admission to UGA. Following the denial, I discussed alternatives with my mentor. He told me about the University of Louisville and I applied. I got accepted into a graduate program at the University of Louisville (U of L).

In 2005 I graduated from Clayton State University with a bachelor's of applied science degree and moved to Louisville, Kentucky, to attend U of L. My experiences at CSU gave me a better understanding of the world and I felt more prepared for my move to Louisville. There were some cultural adjustments I had to make when I moved to Louisville, but for the most part I was well adapted by then to people who were different from me. I spent 2 years in Louisville and completed my master of education degree.

Upon completing my master's degree in 2007, I obtained a job at Indiana State University. While at Indiana State, I decided to further my education and pursue my doctorate degree. I was accepted into a doctoral program and I am currently completing my program.

Summary

The personal narrative of Corey's journey from his home in Georgia to Indiana provides the reader with an overview of the additional challenges rural Millennial students encounter in a society that often assumes that all educational systems and environments are created equal. The human ecology theory acknowledges that individuals must adapt to their environments and alter what they have learned to exist in their new surroundings (Evans, Forney, Guido, Patton, & Renn, 2010).

Recommendations and Conclusion

The use of narratives or life stories to gain a deeper understanding of people's unique environment and how it impacts their psychological and social development can be useful for higher education faculty and administrators (Evans et al., 2010). The ecology theory adds a new lens to the development of the Millennial student, emphasizing the reciprocal relationship of person and environment impact (Evans et al., 2010). The institution that pays attention to the environmental impact of student development could create a campus culture that is supportive of rural millennial students of color. There would be fewer assumptions that all students enter college with a set of skills that are comparable, such as technological prowess and the ability to negotiate an "urban" environment. There are several areas within the institutional organizational structure that may need a review of its policies with regards to effectively communicating with the rural African American Millennial. Specifically, when the admissions office begins recruiting these students they should be aware of the need for these students to spend additional time with the school administrators and the students' families to acclimate them to the differences between the high school rural environment and systems compared to the bureaucratic nature of higher education. The assignment of a specific administrator to monitor the applicant's progress through the system beyond orientation and preferably the end of the first semester may assist in buffering the culture shock a rural Millennial of color may encounter. "Rather than mark these so-called nontraditional students as somehow not fitting into the campus environment, ecology models, with their emphasis on reciprocity and dynamism, call on student affairs educators to adapt the environment to serve these students" (Evans et al., 2010, p. 173). Moreover, listening to the life stories of the rural Millennial of color will add to the breadth and depth of our understanding and adaptation of college campuses to assist in making their college years engaging, successful, and generationally empowering.

References

Carr, P. J., & Kefalas, M. J. (2009, September 25). The rural brain drain. *Chronicle of Higher Education*, B7–B9. Retrieved from http://chronicle.com/article/The-Rural-Brain-Drain/48425/

Evans, N. J., Forney, D. S., Guido, F. M., Patton, L. D., & Renn, K. A. (2010). *Student development in college: Theory, research, and practice* (2nd ed.). San Francisco: Jossey Bass.

Hebert, T. P., & Beardsley, T. M. (2002). Jermaine: A critical case study of a gifted Black child living in rural poverty. In S. B. Merriam (Ed.), *Qualitative research in practice: Examples for discussion and analysis* (pp. 201–232). San Francisco: Jossey Bass.

Merriam, S. B. (2002). *Qualitative research in practice: Examples for discussion and analysis.* San Francisco: Jossey Bass.

U.S. Department of Agriculture. (2003). *Rural education at a glance.* Washington, DC: Author.

PART THREE

ASIAN AMERICAN MILLENNIALS IN COLLEGE

4

ASIAN AMERICAN AND PACIFIC ISLANDER MILLENNIAL STUDENTS AT A TIPPING POINT

Mitchell James Chang

Asian American and Pacific Islanders (AAPIs)[1] are perhaps one of the most misunderstood populations in U.S. higher education. According to Frank Wu (2002), "Asian Americans are at once highly visible in popular culture and virtually invisible in serious discourse, allowing popular culture to define serious discourse" (p. 26). In higher education, one popular cultural characterization that has endured for over 40 years and continues to shape the discourse on AAPI students is the "model minority myth," which stereotypes AAPIs, especially East Asians, as hardworking, problem free, over-achievers. Curiously, Li and Wang (2008) clearly stated in their edited book, *Model Minority Myth Revisited*, that individuals who are most directly affected by the *model minority* label do not necessarily share a common culture, language, heritage, socioeconomic status, political persuasion, immigration experience, religious or philosophical orientation, or worldview.

Despite this population's extraordinary diversity, however, the model minority stereotype continues to capture the imagination of educators and policymakers, sustaining its powerful and lasting grip on AAPIs. Although the U.S. Department of Education reported in 2005 that well over 1 million AAPI students were enrolled in higher education and represented 6.4% of all students, Museus and Kiang (2009) would agree with Wu that the model minority myth continues to create misunderstandings about AAPI students, rendering them invisible in higher education discourse. For example, Museus and Kiang reported that despite the tremendous growth in the enrollment of AAPIs in higher education over the past two decades, virtually no attention has been given to them in five of the most influential academic journals in the field of higher education. Li and Wang (2008) have documented the deleterious impact on students related to this oversight, which renders AAPIs invisible and exacerbates problems associated with mental health and exclusion from educational resources and opportunities.

Given this backdrop, this chapter adds to the knowledge base about AAPI undergraduates by focusing on the characteristics and concerns of AAPI Millennial students. Although much has been written about Millennials, as referenced throughout this book, there are fewer empirical sources to draw from to understand this generation of AAPI students since they have been regularly overlooked in higher education research. In 2007, I coauthored with my colleagues, Julie Park, Monica Lin, Oiyan Poon, and Don Nakanishi, a report titled *Beyond Myths: The Growth and Diversity of Asian American College Freshmen, 1971–2005.* This report was based on a sample of 361,271 Asian or Asian American first-time, full-time college students from 1971 to 2005, representing the largest compilation and analysis of data on Asian American college students ever undertaken. The national data came from the Cooperative Institutional Research Program (CIRP) Freshman Survey administered by the University of California, Los Angeles (UCLA) Higher Education Research Institute, which focuses on 4-year colleges where 55% of all Asian American students were enrolled nationwide. Since the report was essentially a trend analysis of how incoming freshmen characteristics, behaviors, attitudes, and viewpoints have shifted over time, I believe that its findings serve as an ideal starting point to offer an empirically based understanding about AAPI Millennials. Moreover, such a trend analysis comes to understand AAPI Millennials relative to previous generations of AAPI students rather than to a majority group. The latter approach that usually uses White students as a reference group can wrongly portray AAPIs as an immutable group of students and, subsequently, reinforce the model minority mythology.

As such, the following sections highlight five key areas of findings from the report so as to help faculty, administrators, and student affairs personnel adapt and respond better to the needs of current and incoming cohorts of AAPI undergraduates. Unless noted otherwise, the data in those sections are drawn from the findings of the CIRP report. In considering the implications of these findings, readers should keep several shortcomings in mind. First, our report focused only on first-time, full-time college students enrolled in 4-year institutions, so it does not capture the attributes of those enrolled in 2-year institutions. This is critical because approximately 45.3% of AAPI students enrolled in higher education in 2004 attended those institutions, and according to a recent report sponsored by the College Board (National Commission on Asian American and Pacific Islander Research in Education, 2008), AAPI enrollment is increasing at the fastest rate in public 2-year community colleges. Additionally, a disproportionately larger number of Pacific Islanders and Southeast Asian Americans of Vietnamese, Laotian, Cambodian, Thai, and Burmese descent begin their postsecondary studies in those institutions as opposed to 4-year institutions. To offset the report's emphasis on a particular sector of higher education and subsequent biases on certain groups, I will highlight trends that might also be relevant to those in community colleges. Another shortcoming is related to the applicability of the report's findings to the Millennial generation since the last point of data analyzed was collected on freshmen entering college in the fall of 2005. Although many, but not all, of those who responded to the survey that year have since graduated, we noticed from studying trends that span over 30 years that major shifts typically occur gradually over more than a decade rather than dramatically within only a few years. Therefore, the trends observed up to 2005 would certainly apply to current students and would also likely apply to those who will soon be entering college. Still, I will consider key historical or social forces in a separate section of this chapter to further consider the relevance of those trends identified through the report. Those forces may either accelerate or decelerate identified trends, which result in what is often referred to as *period effects*.

Reported Results

More Diverse Demographically

As a group, expect AAPI Millennials to be even more diverse than previous cohorts on campuses. Certainly, they will be even more ethnically diverse and continue to expand toward one that represents the full range of subgroups. Although few colleges will presently need to identify the 43 self-identified subgroups reported in the 2005 American Community Survey, the typical subcategories of Japanese, Chinese, and Koreans often used by enrollment managers will become increasingly less useful for disaggregating data and capturing the diversity of ethnic origins of this group of students.

Also, expect greater diversity in socioeconomic status among AAPI Millennials. Although we found in our *Beyond Myths* report that the average level of parental educational attainment of entering AAPI undergraduates has increased steadily since the 1970s, 30.9% of entering students in 2005 came from families with a household income of less than $40,000 per year. By comparison, 22.7% of the national first-time, full-time college student population had estimated household incomes of less than $40,000. Those AAPI students who are nonnative English speakers are even more likely to come from low-income families. While increasingly more AAPI freshmen are reporting that English is their native language, there is still great diversity here with over 40.0% reporting that English is not their first language. The language diversity evident among this population, however, should not lead to the misconception that AAPI students tend to be foreigners. Nearly all of the entering freshmen in recent years reported to be U.S. citizens (over 82%).

More Financially Dependent

Perhaps unlike other students, expect economic circumstances to play an even more prominent role in the lives of AAPI Millennials. First, they are increasingly more likely than previous generations of AAPI students to report that receiving financial assistance was a key factor for why they chose their particular college, with about one-third reporting this in 2005. Similar to previous generations, however, AAPI students continue to be loan adverse and overly rely on family and personal savings to cover educational expenses. Subsequently, increasingly more entering AAPI freshmen expect to work during college, with over half of the low-income students reporting in 2005 that there was a "very good chance" that they would need to do this to help pay educational expenses. The current poor economic conditions will likely accelerate these trends and put greater pressure on incoming students to make college choices based on affordability and to work more during their college years.

Less Constrained Academically

Put to rest the academic stereotypes and expect AAPI Millennials to explore the full range of academic options. First, they enter college with a much higher sense of self-confidence than previous generations of AAPI students. This elevated level of confidence does not apply only to academic skills, but also to social skills, leadership, public speaking, writing, and artistic abilities.

Despite this higher level of confidence than previous generations of AAPI students, Millennials do not appear to be too proud or overprepared to consider remediation. Nearly 20% of AAPI first-year students in 2005 reported that they believe they will need special tutoring or remedial work in English during college. This proportion is similar to that for incoming Latino/a students (20.9%) and higher than that for all other racial groups (Pryor, Hurtado, Saenz, Santos, & Koon, 2007).

Also, expect them to enter college with a broader range of academic interests beyond the sciences and with intentions of eventually seeking advanced degrees. With respect to undergraduate majors, a concentration in "business" was the most popular major in 2005. Also in the same year, nearly three of every four incoming AAPI students reported that earning advanced degrees was an important reason they were going to college. If enhancing their earning power is the main interest for seeking an advanced degree, than expect this trend to be even stronger for future cohorts of students as economic interests continue to preoccupy popular concerns.

More Civically Engaged

Similar to their peers, AAPI Millennials also seem to be less interested in politics as usual, yet still interested in making a political difference. Since 1990, there has been a steady decline in the percentage of AAPI entering freshmen who indicated that "keeping up to date with political affairs" was a "very important" or "essential" objective for them. Yet, at the same time, there has been an overall increase in the proportion of incoming Asian American undergraduates who consider it "essential" or "very important" to "influence the political structure." Also, a growing percentage of Asian American students over the decades reported having participated in an organized demonstration prior to college, with 46.3% in 2005 reporting to have done this.

They also appear to be increasingly more civically minded. A larger proportion of 2005 AAPI freshmen than in previous years reported to have performed at least 3 hours of volunteer work per week during their senior year in high school and to be interested in participating in volunteer or community service work during college. Also, the proportion of entering AAPI students stating that it was either "very important" or "essential" for them to become a community leader almost tripled over the decades, from 13.0% in 1971 to 32.3% in 2005. There is no reason to expect a downturn regarding this trend, as will be discussed later in this chapter.

Middle of the Road Political and Racial Attitudes

Politically, expect AAPI Millennials to be slightly more liberal oriented than conservative leaning, with the majority reporting to be middle of the road politically. The overwhelming support among college students for President Barack Obama in the 2008 election will likely sustain if not accelerate this trend toward a more liberal political orientation. It is less clear how connected and devoted as a group, Millennials are to their racial identity.

Although over 80% of entering AAPI freshmen in 2005 viewed racial discrimination as a major problem, fewer of them in recent years "consider it important to promote racial understanding." Likewise, AAPI students appear to be divided on whether "affirmative action in college admissions should be abolished," with slightly over 50% of AAPI respondents supporting affirmative action in college admissions. Again, with the election of President Obama, the trend may well lean toward views that the significance of race in U.S. society is declining.

Trends in Context

Although the above characterization of AAPI Millennials is empirically based and drawn almost entirely from findings reported in *Beyond Myths*, one shortcoming noted earlier was that the last year of data analyzed for this report was collected in the fall of 2005. One way to assess whether the above highlighted trends would still apply to the fall 2009 entering freshmen class and also other entering classes in the immediate future would be to consider key social or cultural trends in recent years. According to Coomes and DeBard (2004), "Two powerful forces—history and popular culture—play an important role in shaping the values, beliefs, attitudes and worldviews of individuals and groups" (p. 87). If so, what might be some key events or cultural shifts that could moderate those trends in the four areas identified in this chapter, namely the diversity, financial dependency, academic interests, civic engagement, and attitudes of AAPI Millennials?

Downward Spiral of Economy

Let's first consider perhaps one of the most worrisome national problems at the moment, the economy. Currently, the nation is considered to be facing the worst set of economic circumstances since the Great Depression of the early 1930s. The graduating class of 2009 faced one of the worst employment prospects of any graduating group in recent memory. As alluded to earlier, the current economic crisis will no doubt affect some of the trends based on 2005 student surveys. For example, it might affect the economic diversity of the AAPI population at 4-year institutions, since college choice decisions for this group are closely coupled to financial capacity and less expensive options such as starting in community colleges will likely become more attractive. Given the stark average income differences across AAPI subgroups (U.S. Government Accountability Office, 2007), members of some groups will be more negatively affected than others. The economic crisis might also affect undergraduate major choices, and here we may see a trend toward majoring in areas that offer better chances of obtaining a good paying job after graduation. If so, this will likely turn students away from majoring in fields such as the fine arts and humanities and perhaps have the overall effect of narrowing major choices overtime. Likewise, with the poor economic outlook for entering students, perhaps staying longer in school will become an even more attractive option for some AAPI students who can afford to, and so the desire to pursue a graduate degree may accelerate.

War in Middle East

Another major national concern is U.S. military involvement in the Middle East. More AAPIs are serving under the U.S. flag in this war than ever before. One consequence for higher education related to this war is the increased enrollment of military veterans. In 2009, President Obama presented a new GI Bill that is considered to be the most comprehensive education benefit offered to veterans since President Franklin Roosevelt signed the original one in 1944. The new bill will not only enable eligible veterans, reservists, and National Guard members to pursue an undergraduate or graduate degree, but will also allow for the transfer of tuition benefits to their spouses or children. The *Los Angeles Times* (Silva, 2009) reported that the Department of Veterans Affairs has, as of July 2009, already processed more than 112,000 claims for tuition under the new GI Bill, and it is anticipated that nearly half a million veterans and family members could participate in the first year alone. It is unclear how the increasing numbers of AAPI veterans on college campuses over the course of this decade will affect the trends identified earlier. What is clear, however, is that these students will have unique needs that will require special attention, and educators should not assume that they share the same characteristics, attributes, or interests as their peers.

It should also be noted that the war on terrorism at home struck a sensitive nerve with AAPIs. Japanese Americans are aware that such a "domestic war" heightens the risk of suspecting and detaining innocent victims based on their cultural roots or physical features, as was the case with the internment of Japanese Americans during World War II. If these sentiments resonate with AAPI Millennials, it may have the effect of elevating race consciousness, as will be discussed later in this chapter.

Diversity in Government

Another recent set of events concerns historic changes in the representation of political leaders, beginning with the election of the first African American president in U.S. history. As discussed earlier, this may enhance political interest among AAPI Millennials, but may also affect their perspectives on the significance of race in U.S. society. More certain is that the trend of greater civic engagement will likely persist as the composition of political leaders continues to diversify in ways that inspire Millennials of color. During the summer of 2009, for example, we witnessed other historic changes in the nation's highest positions of leadership. They included the election of the first Chinese American woman to the U.S. Congress, Judy Chu, and the appointment of the first Latina into the U.S. Supreme Court, Sonia Sotomayor. Also within 100 days after President Obama took office, he appointed Nobel Laureate Steven Chu to serve as the secretary of energy, General Eric K. Shinseki to serve as the secretary of veterans affairs, former Washington state Governor Gary Locke to serve as the secretary of commerce, and actor Kal Penn to serves as an associate director in the White House Office of Public Liaison to work in Asian American and Pacific Islander communities. In all likelihood the inclusion of more AAPIs in political office will inspire the civic interests of AAPI Millennials, but it remains to be seen if it will enhance a unique AAPI political consciousness or movement.

Asian American Studies

One trend that will likely enhance Millennials' consciousness as being uniquely "Asian American" is the growth of Asian American studies and its significance in understanding the domestic relevance of the emerging economic and political clout of Asian nations. Although not nearly as ubiquitous on college campuses as African American studies, the fast-growing numbers of Asian American studies programs have paralleled the growth of the population in higher education and have provided students with access to an important knowledge base that is otherwise absent from their regular coursework

(Chang, 1999). The scholarship in that field has also become more important in understanding the domestic perception and treatment of AAPIs as Asia, especially China and India, carve out increasingly more prominent roles on the world stage. A more developed AAPI consciousness shaped in large part by Asian American studies has also influenced federal legislation. For example, folded into the 2007 College Cost Reduction and Access Act was a provision that created a federal designation for Asian American– and Pacific Islander–serving institutions, making available funding to better serve AAPI students. Although the amount of funding was relatively modest, the creation of a federal designation for AAPI-serving institutions is a major step toward greater recognition and understanding of the needs of AAPI students, as well as a sign that AAPI advocacy on Capitol Hill is maturing (Park & Chang, 2010).

Influencing Campus Culture

As the enrollment and presence of AAPIs increase, so too has their influence on campus culture. There are already several campuses including a few University of California institutions and the University of Hawaii, Mānoa, where AAPIs compose the majority of the undergraduate population. On those campuses, Asian culture also is viewed as being more "mainstream" than "foreign," exposing all students to a wider range of cultural opportunities. For example, on campuses where there is a critical mass of AAPI students, there is also a proliferation of AAPI student groups that focus on a wide range of interests, including but not limited to specific careers, politics, religions, and ethnic cultures (Chang, 2002). There are also Asian-interest fraternities and sororities that function in ways more similar to their African American counterparts than to the mainstream Greek letter organizations. Moreover, both on and close to the UCLA campus, students can purchase sushi, Boba (bubble tea), Asian-style frozen yogurt (e.g., Pinkberry and Red Mango), and other Asian items. They bring to campus the music of Korean pop stars and magazines from Japanese anime artists. These and other cultural options are accessible year round and not limited to just a cultural appreciation evening or restricted to May, deemed Asian American History Month. As these options are made widely available to more students on more campuses, they will likely be viewed by AAPI Millennials as being essential to campus life rather than a unique privilege.

Accessibility to Technology

Even if those options are not available for AAPI students, they will not likely feel nearly as racially isolated on campus as did students of previous generations. Improvements in and accessibility to high technology enable students to build communities that extend beyond their physical campus ones. This enables them to establish a sense of racial or ethnic identity and connection even on campuses where the proportion of AAPIs are small and where Asian American studies is not offered. As with previous generations and given AAPI Millennials' willingness to organize, as previously discussed, this can result in more frequent and sophisticated demands on administration to address the needs of AAPI students. The Internet also enables AAPI Millennials to respond to discriminatory and offensive incidents that otherwise would not receive much attention on their respective campuses but can now quickly turn into national incidents. For example, when the retailer Abercrombie and Fitch, a brand that is popular among college students, produced T-shirts in early 2000 that showed stereotypical caricatures of Asian Americans doing laundry, it created outrage among college-age AAPIs. The successful activism that resulted in getting the company to remove those T-shirts from their stores was fueled largely by electronic communication.

Even though there appears to be more and better resources available for AAPI Millennials to actively contribute to distinct AAPI interests, whether a broader sense and identification with AAPI interests will strengthen over time will highly depend on a few key future developments. Curiously, as the AAPI population becomes increasingly more diverse economically, culturally, and politically, their bond as a group will weaken. For AAPI Millennials, they may come to share little collectively besides a distinct vulnerability to certain stereotypes and their ensuing discriminatory effects. If that is the case, being made aware of the risk of being regularly stereotyped as model minorities or perpetual foreigners, for example, and subsequently disqualified or held under suspicion should strengthen a collective AAPI consciousness. The beating of Vincent Chin in 1987, for example, fueled a broader and deeper AAPI awareness because it made many feel more vulnerable to acts of racial violence and, subsequently, inspired more intense AAPI activism. Since Chin's death, there have been many other notable events, such as the Wen Ho Lee case whereby a Chinese American researcher was wrongly accused in 1999 of spying for China, concerns raised about the war on terrorism, as noted earlier, the scores of local incidents involving acts of racial antipathy aimed at AAPIs on campus, and the countless negative portrayals of AAPIs in the media. Such incidents will continue to fuel AAPI activism in ways that enhance their collective consciousness. Since these racist acts have not abated, there will always be the potential for galvanizing AAPI students in a racially focused way that bonds the range of subgroups. How

Millennials address those issues will likely be more sophisticated and perhaps even more influential than the approaches taken by previous generations of students.

Conclusion

Certainly, AAPI Millennials are similar in many ways to their same-age counterparts, but they are distinctively different from previous generations of AAPI students. What makes this population particularly unique is that when they arrive on college campuses, they still run a high risk of being treated in ways that are based on longstanding stereotypes applied across generations of AAPI students. Whatever "truth" there was to the model minority stereotype of the "passive" Asian student or the Asian "science nerd," it applies even less so to this generation of students. Subsequently, educators' willingness to cling to those stereotypes will result in even more severe problems and conflicts with this generation of students. Based on findings from the *Beyond Myths* report and consideration of key historical events, AAPI Millennials will likely exact even greater real costs, financially and politically, on institutions that continue to consider them in stereotypic ways. As a group, they are significantly stronger than previous generations in terms of numbers, leadership potential, confidence, activism, and accessing knowledge and networks of influence.

Without those stereotypes obstructing decision making, faculty, administrators, and student service staff can better deliver what AAPI students really need to succeed and maximize their educational experiences. One important need is to receive better access to and outreach for important services, especially those related to counseling. Not only with regards to mental health counseling, which AAPI students tend to underutilize (Leong & Lau, 2001), but also with financial aid counseling, as noted earlier, so that they can expand their options for funding their college education. AAPI students also benefit when institutions expand their Asian ethnic subcategories for data collection, which establishes a more accurate account of the diversity of backgrounds and potential needs within an AAPI undergraduate student body. This is especially important on those campuses that are experiencing a steady growth in the enrollment of AAPI students. A 2007 U.S. Government Accountability Office report concluded that AAPI "subgroups differ in their levels of academic preparedness, ability to pay for college, and their need to balance academic, employment, and family obligations" (p. 4). Along with this growth and diversity will be greater interest among students to access Asian American studies, establish new student organizations, and have available a wider range of cultural options especially related to dining and entertainment. Those interests should not be confused with a desire to self-segregate, as Asian students have been regularly accused of doing. These are interests that expand students' options, typically made available to majority students but inaccessible to AAPI students. By expanding those options, other students might also benefit from being exposed to a wider range of ideas and cultural practices and, subsequently, develop a stronger willingness and more confidence in associating with a wider range of individuals.

Growth in enrollment, presence, and level of influence of AAPIs, however, has historically faced harsh backlashes and today anti-Asian sentiments can be readily found on the Internet. AAPI Millennials are better equipped than previous generations to confront this sentiment. Given how cohorts of AAPI students have changed over the past three decades, it can be said that with the Millennial generation, AAPI students have reached a critical moment or what sociologists call a tipping point. According to Gladwell (2000), tipping points are the levels at which the momentum for change becomes unstoppable and is the moment of critical mass, the threshold, the boiling point. That on July 17, 2009, the California legislature approved a landmark bill to apologize to the state's Chinese American community for racist laws enacted as far back as the mid-19th century Gold Rush is another example, along with the others noted throughout this chapter, of this tipping point momentum.

AAPI Millennials will certainly continue to benefit from the civil rights–related progress already made, but they will also be expected to contribute to that progress. On September 6, 2006, the *Washington Post* ran an ad sponsored by several benefactors including the 80-20 Educational Foundation, which is devoted to furthering equal opportunity in the workplace and equal justice for Asian Americans. The main points of this ad were that "Asian Americans yearn to make greater contributions to our country. However, today, Asian Americans have the least opportunity to enter management and the slowest rate of progress towards equal employment opportunity, despite having the highest educational attainment" (p. D12). Given my analysis of Millennials, I suspect that if this generation of students reaches their potential, this ad and the problems identified in it will soon be a historical relic rather than a pressing challenge to a generation of college students.

Note

1. Although this umbrella term is insufficient because it refers to a very diverse range of ethnic groups, I still use it here because individuals of those groups share a

vulnerability to unique forms of discrimination and stereotyping widely prevalent in the U.S. educational context.

References

Chang, M. J. (1999). Expansion and its discontents: The formation of Asian American studies programs in the 1990s. *Journal of Asian American Studies, 2*(2), 181–206.

Chang, M. J. (2002). Racial dynamics on campus: What student organizations can tell us. *About Campus, 7*(1), 2–8.

Chang, M. J., Park, J., Lin, M. H., Poon, O., & Nakanishi, D. T. (2007). *Beyond myths: The growth and diversity of Asian American college freshmen, 1971–2005.* Los Angeles: Higher Education Research Institute, UCLA.

Coomes, M. D., & DeBard, R. (Eds.). (2004). *Serving the Millennial generation: New directions for student services.* San Francisco: Jossey-Bass.

Gladwell, M. (2000). *The tipping point: How little things can make a big difference.* Boston: Little Brown.

Leong, F. T. L., & Lau, A. S. L. (2001). Barriers to providing effective mental health services to Asian Americans. *Mental Health Services Research, 3*, 201–214.

Li, G., & Wang, L. (Eds.). (2008). *Model minority myth revisited: An interdisciplinary approach to demystifying Asian American educational experiences.* Charlotte, NC: Information Age Publishing.

Museus, S. D., & Kiang, P. N. (2009, Summer). Deconstructing the model minority myth and how it contributes to the invisible minority reality in higher education research. *New Directions for Institutional Research, 142*, 5–15.

National Commission on Asian American and Pacific Islander Research in Education. (2008). *Asian Americans and Pacific Islanders: Facts, not fiction: Setting the record straight.* New York: College Board.

Park, J. J., & Chang, M. J. (2010). *AAPI serving institutions: The motivations and challenges behind seeking a federal designation. AAPI Nexus: Asian Americans & Pacific Islanders Policy Practice and Community, 7*(2), 107–125.

Pryor, J. H., Hurtado, S., Saenz, V. B., Santos, J. L., & Korn, W. S. (2007). *The American freshman: Forty-year trends, 1966–2006.* Los Angeles: Higher Education Research Institute, UCLA.

Silva, M. (2009, August 4). Obama hails new GI Bill as "an investment in our own country." *Los Angeles Times*, p. A10.

U.S. Government Accountability Office. (2007). *Higher education information sharing could help institutions identify and address challenges some Asian Americans and Pacific Islander students face, GAO-07-925.* Retrieved from http://www.gao.gov/new.items/d07925.pdf

Wu, F. H. (2002). *Yellow: Race in America beyond Black and White.* New York: Basic Books.

5

ASIAN AMERICAN MILLENNIAL COLLEGE STUDENTS IN CONTEXT

Living at the Intersection of Diversification, Digitization, and Globalization

Samuel D. Museus

I n the second half of 2008, Paramount Pictures began advertising a forth-coming movie, titled *The Last Airbender*. The fictional film is based on an animated cartoon, many aspects of which are heavily informed by Asian history and culture. Moreover, the cartoon's characters were originally Asian. The cast of heroes in the Paramount film, however, was all White, with the only main Asian actor playing the role of the antagonist. Consequently, during the summer of 2009, widespread protests concerning the film erupted—both on the streets and on the Internet. These included well-known Asian American bloggers expressing their views that the White casting of the film is racist, and a website was created titled "Racebending," which was designed to solicit participants in a boycott of the upcoming movie. A Facebook group called "People against Racebending," designed to garner support in protest of the movie, also emerged. The organizers of the Facebook group explained that racism was manifested in the casting of the film in three ways: the failure to recognize the contributions of Asians to the making of culture and history that influenced the movie, the prioritization of White actors over actors from other racial groups, and the reinforcement of stereotypes of dark-skinned people as evil. By September 2009, over 4,600 protestors—many of them Chinese, Hmong, Indian, Japanese, Korean, and

Vietnamese American college students—were members of the Facebook group.

I do not intend to argue whether the behavior of the Paramount producers is acceptable or whether the views of the protestors are correct. Rather, I offer this example as a tool for understanding the characteristics of Asian American college students in the Millennial generation. It is an example of a diverse group of Asian American Millennial students coming together with non–Asian Americans and using digital technology to address the perpetuation of racism in Western media. Thus, evident in this example are the diversity of Asian American Millennial students, their understanding and utilization of digital technology, and their awareness of and activism around a global social and political issue. This chapter discusses the importance of understanding these characteristics of Asian American Millennials and their implications for postsecondary educators.

This chapter is based on a few assumptions. First, it is founded on the assumption that Asian American Millennial students deserve the attention of postsecondary educators. Indeed, several scholars have now provided evidence that, although many Asian American students are succeeding in higher education, many others are struggling academically, culturally, psychologically, and socially (Kiang, 2002, 2009; Lewis, Chesler, & Forman, 2000; Maramba, 2008; Museus, 2008a, 2009a; Museus & Kiang, 2009; Museus & Truong, 2009; Teranishi, 2007). Second, this chapter is based on the assumption that educators are best equipped to serve Asian American Millennial college students—or Millennial students from any racial or ethnic background, for that matter—if they understand and adapt to that population. Regarding this point, many researchers have offered evidence that college educators are better equipped if they engage minority students' racial and ethnic backgrounds (Kiang, 2009; Museus, 2008b; Museus & Quaye, 2009; Tierney, 1999) and argued that educational practices are most effective when they incorporate knowledge of the characteristics of the Millennial generation (Tapscott, 2008). Third, the chapter is also based on the assumption that Asian American Millennials represent an asset to educators and the college experience. By way of their unique racial and ethnic backgrounds and experiences, they constitute a valuable form of diversity, and such diversity has been associated with positive developmental college outcomes for all students (Chang, Denson, Sáenz, & Misa, 2006; Chang, Witt, Jones, & Hakuta, 2003; Hurtado, Milem, Clayton-Pedersen, & Allen, 1999).

It is also worth noting that, throughout this chapter, I make generalizations, but I also recognize that the assertions contained herein are not equally applicable to *all* Asian Americans. Just as there is vast ethnic and socioeconomic diversity within this population (Hune, 2002), there are disparities in the extent to which various Asian American Millennials have access to technological resources and are connected to global society. Nevertheless, I assume that the following ideas are relevant, albeit to varying degrees, for all Asian American Millennials.

Asian American Millennials in the Context of Societal Transformations

Asian American Millennials in college have grown up in the context of three major transformations in U.S. society: rapid diversification, widespread digitization, and increased globalization. The following sections underscore these three trends as a lens through which educators can better understand Asian American Millennials and, in doing so, be better equipped to effectively serve Asian American college students and utilize those undergraduates as an asset to enhance the educational experiences for all students in higher education. The concluding sections of this chapter include a discussion of the implications of this discussion for postsecondary educators who hope to transform undergraduate education to effectively meet the needs of Asian American Millennial college students.

Unprecedented Diversification: The Contribution of Asian Americans to Racial and Ethnic Diversity

The U.S. Census Bureau (2008) has projected that racial minorities will make up over 50% of the U.S. population by 2050, highlighting the growing diversification in U.S. society and the increased importance of recognizing and responding to that diversity. In February 2009, the policy and advocacy manager at the Center for American Progress, Erica Williams, underscored the racial diversity of the Millennial generation and the need to respond to it when she asserted that "our generation is going to be the most diverse generation this nation has ever seen. That does not mean we're post-racial. It means we have more races to deal with" (Hudson, 2009). Although it is debatable whether the number of recognized races in U.S. society will change in the foreseeable future, Williams was correct in her assertion that the increased presence and visibility of racial minority populations in the Millennial and future generations, as well as the unprecedented ethnic heterogeneity that exists within them, means that more people in society will inevitably have to interact and function effectively with people from other racial and ethnic groups. In this section, I discuss two trends that highlight this growing diversity as it relates to Asian American Millennials in college: the increased visibility of Asian Americans in public and higher education discourse and the growing diversity within that population.

Increased Visibility in Public Discourse

Asian Americans are becoming increasingly visible in U.S. society and higher education. Moreover, this trend will likely continue in the years to come. Although just over 5% of the U.S. population self-reported as Asian American in 2010, U.S. Census Bureau projections indicate that almost 1 in 10 U.S. citizens will be of Asian descent by the year 2050 (U.S. Census Bureau, 2008). This means that, in the near future, the number of Asian American Millennials entering U.S. colleges and universities will most likely continue to rise. Despite the increasing presence of Asian Americans in society and higher education, it has been noted that this population is often excluded from discourse in the general public and the field of higher education (Museus, 2009a; Museus & Kiang, 2009; Teranishi, Ceja, Antonio, Allen, & McDonough, 2004; Wu, 2002). This is changing, however, and recent events reflect the increased voice that is accompanying the growing numbers of Asian Americans in society. For example, Asian Americans are becoming increasingly visible in local and national government (see chapter 4, this volume). In addition to the recent rise in representation of Asian Americans in government, President Barack Obama recently signed an executive order establishing an advisory commission to oversee efforts to facilitate increased participation of Asian Americans in federal programs. Although it is uncertain what the result of this commission will be, the executive order serves as a symbol of the increasing visibility of Asian Americans in society, as well as the recognition that they can no longer be excluded from public discourse.

Asian Americans are also becoming increasingly visible in higher education. As a result in the increasing number of Asian Americans in postsecondary education and the need to better understand this population, high-profile policy reports have underscored the diversity that exists within this population and the need to move past conceptualizations of Asian Americans that are based on stereotypes to develop a more complex understanding of this group (Chang, Park, Lin, Poon, & Nakanishi, 2007; National Commission on Asian American and Pacific Islander Research in Education, 2008; U.S. General Accounting Office, 2007). In addition, the federal government has allocated public monies for support programs at Asian American– and

Pacific Islander–serving institutions—postsecondary institutions with large numbers of economically disadvantaged and underserved Southeast Asian Americans—and scholars have produced and are producing multiple recent and forthcoming edited volumes focused on developing an increased understanding of the issues faced by and needs of Asian American students in postsecondary education (e.g., McEwen, Kodama, Alvarez, Lee, & Liang, 2002; Museus, 2009b; Museus, Maramba, & Teranishi, forthcoming). One factor, however, that complicates efforts to develop such an understanding is the vast diversity that exists *within* the Asian American Millennial generation and will only continue to expand.

Growing Diversity Within the Asian American Population

Popular understandings of Asian Americans have historically been dominated by racial stereotypes. Specifically, the model minority myth—the assumption that Asian Americans all achieve unparalleled educational and occupational success—has dominated conceptualizations of this group. Scholars have noted that this myth is alive and well and has contributed to the exclusion of Asian Americans from discourse in both the general public and higher education (Chang, 2008; Museus, 2009a; Museus & Chang, 2009; Museus & Kiang, 2009; Suzuki, 2002). My colleagues and I have discussed the negative effects of this stereotype (Museus, 2008a; Museus, 2009a; Museus & Chang, 2009; Museus & Kiang, 2009), so I do not intend to rehash those consequences at length here. Rather, I mention the myth because educators must move beyond such simple preconceived notions and develop a more intricate understanding of the diversity that exists within this population if they are to understand Asian American Millennials and effectively serve and utilize them as an educational asset.

Several researchers have highlighted the vast diversity that exists within the Asian American population (Chang et al., 2007; Hune, 2002; National Commission on Asian American and Pacific Islander Research in Education, 2008; Museus, 2009a; Museus & Kiang, 2009; Teranishi, 2007). Although Asian Americans have always been characterized by diversity of ethnic origins, cultures, histories, languages, and economic conditions, this diversity changed drastically in the second half of the 20th century. Over the past three decades, many Southeast Asian Americans have arrived in the United States as refugees and have drastically increased the diversity within the Asian American race. Scholars have noted that these Southeast Asian groups are distinct from other Asian American ethnic populations and one another in many ways (Hune, 2002; Museus, 2009a; Teranishi, 2007; Uba, 1994). For instance, their families originate from homelands that are economically underdeveloped compared to their East Asian counterparts, have immigrated due to dislocation from war and experienced accompanying trauma, and come from some of the most poorly resourced communities in their nations. The presence of these groups might be the most obvious characteristic that distinguishes Asian American Millennials from previous generations of Asian Americans.

Moreover, U.S. Census data suggest that this within-race diversity is increasing. Table 5.1 displays the percentage of each Asian American ethnic group falling within three different age ranges. It underscores the ethnic diversity within the Asian American race, but it also suggests that a large portion of Southeast Asian Americans are young and will be making their way through the educational pipeline in the years to come. For example, over 34% of Cambodian, Laotian, and Hmong Americans are under 18 years old, while that figure is under 25% for Asian Indian, Chinese, Filipino, Korean, and under 16% for Japanese and Thai Americans. As rising numbers of Asian American Millennials and Asian Americans in future generations pursue college, higher education scholars and practitioners should hold themselves accountable for learning about and addressing the needs of Asian

TABLE 5.1
Proportion of Asian American Ethnic Population by Age

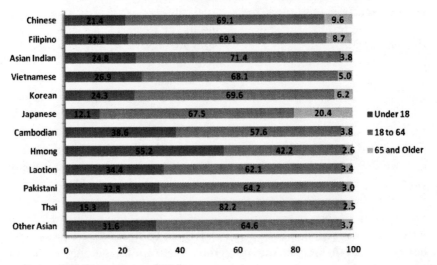

Source: U.S. Census Bureau (2004).

American Millennials in general and Southeast Asian American Millennials specifically.

Moreover, postsecondary educators should understand and appreciate the value that these students bring to undergraduate education. As previously mentioned, this chapter is based on the assumption that Asian American Millennials represent an asset to educators and the college experiences of all students. Similarly, Southeast Asian Americans, by way of their unique historical and cultural backgrounds and experiences, can enhance undergraduate experiences for all students. Indeed, it has been noted that a better understanding of Asian Americans can contribute to increased knowledge of how to shape policies and practices for both Asian American and non–Asian American students most effectively (Museus & Chang, 2009).

Unparalleled and Widespread Digitization: Asian Americans in the Net Generation

Asian American Millennials, like other Millennials, have grown up in the era of an unparalleled digitization of U.S. and global society. Some would argue that, if there is one characteristic that most clearly defines the Millennial generation, it is their affinity for and knowledge and skills in using the Internet and digital technology. In fact, Donald Tapscott (2008), who has conducted one of the most extensive inquiries into the characteristics of this generation, referred to it as the "net generation" and asserted that Millennials view technology as a natural part of the environment and that "technology is like air" for members of this generation (p. 18). Of course, like previous generations, a digital divide exists within the Millennial generation, and many students come to college with limited access to technological resources. Nevertheless, technology use is higher among Millennials—including Asian American Millennials—than it has ever been in America and around the globe.

Asian Americans and the Internet

Although Tapscott (2008) did not provide disaggregated analyses to explain how various racial and ethnic groups are growing up in the digital age, evidence suggests that Asian Americans, especially Asian American Millennials, are using the Internet at relatively high rates compared to the rest of the U.S. population. In 2001 the Pew Internet and American Life Project released the results of a national survey of Internet usage. Their results show that Asian Americans use the Internet regularly more than any other racial group (Table 5.2). However, these results can be somewhat misleading because the Pew Project defined Asian Americans as people who self-identify as Asian American and speak English, meaning that immigrants and refugees who are residents of the United States and might currently be learning English were excluded from these figures. The results also indicated that a larger proportion of Asian Americans are under 35 years of age (63%) compared to the general population (41%) (Table 5.3). Thus, an understanding of Asian American Millennials requires knowledge of the role of digital technology in shaping their identities and lives.

Characteristics of the Net Generation

Tapscott (2008) conducted a survey of over 11,000 Millennials and identified eight norms of this generation. I believe that these norms are important for educators to consider if they are to understand and most effectively serve Asian American and other Millennials students. Moreover, I discuss them in this section about the digitization of American society because Tapscott highlights the fact that they are characteristics of Millennials that are intertwined with their connectedness to the Internet and affinity for digital technology.

First, Tapscott argues that the net generation has grown up with *freedom* as a natural part of their environment. For example, the freedom afforded

TABLE 5.2
Proportion of Races That Report Using the Internet Regularly by Gender

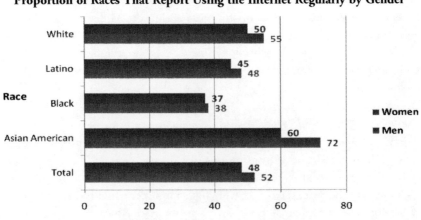

Source: Pew Internet and American Life Project (2001).

TABLE 5.3
Proportion of Asian Americans and Total Population Using Internet by Age

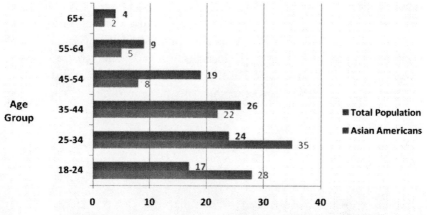

Percentage of Asian Americans Internet Users Falling into Specific
Age Groups Compared to the Total Population

Source: Pew Internet and American Life Project (2001).

by the Internet permits Millennials to consider an endless array of options regarding purchasing goods and when to do work or talk to their friends. Second, this generation is used to *customization*, or personalizing, their experiences as well as their belongings, such as cell phones and Facebook pages. Third, the net generation views their environment with high levels of *scrutiny*, and they use the Internet to assess the quality of commercial products, business practices, and the like. Fourth, *integrity* is important to this generation, and they use the Internet to communicate with the world about violations of integrity. Fifth, the Millennials have grown up as a generation of collaborators who want to be engaged in collaborative activity. Sixth, this generation values *entertainment* and expects the work they do to be satisfying and emotionally fulfilling. Seventh, because the flow of information that Millennials can access via the Internet is characterized by *speed*, this generation expects things to be done quickly. Lastly, Tapscott asserts that the net generation has grown up in a culture of *innovation* and expects new ways to collaborate, learn, and work.

Although these Millennial generation characteristics are not specific to Asian Americans, they can help postsecondary educators better understand how to serve this population. In his book, Tapscott (2008) asserts that the net generation is not only changing education, but is also transforming other social institutions, such as commerce and politics, as well. This argument implies that Millennials are changing the way society functions and, if higher education is to keep up with those changes, it must adapt accordingly. As previously mentioned, this chapter is also founded on the assumption that understanding and adapting to the backgrounds and characteristics of Asian American Millennials is important in efforts to effectively serve this population in the future. I will return to these net generation norms later in the chapter.

Unparalleled Globalization: Connections to National and International Communities

Related to the increased digitization of U.S. society are the heightened levels of connectedness of individuals to national and global society. In 2005 Thomas Friedman wrote his best-selling book, *The World Is Flat*, in which he argued that the decrease in trade barriers and advances in technology have resulted in a world in which people are more connected across the globe than ever before. He also explained, however, that the most recent acceleration of globalization is not a consequence of the actions of large corporations and trade organizations, but it is instead a product of innovative individuals. Thus, according to Friedman, Asian American Millennials have grown up in this environment of increasing globalization at an individual level. Indeed, they are connected in numerous ways to communities across the nation and around the world. Of course, people of Asian ancestry have always been connected to Asian American communities and Asian communities around the world, such as some of the first Chinese immigrants to America who sent money back or returned to visit their homelands (Takagi, 1998). However, the various ways in which Asian American Millennials are connected to communities across the globe are expanding rapidly.

There are at least three salient ways that Asian American Millennials are connected to a wide range of Asian American and Asian communities around the country and the world. First, they are connected to those communities by way of their traditional cultural heritages. Asian immigrants come to this nation with cultural values, norms, and customs that vary substantially from Western cultures (Uba, 1994), and some of these cultural characteristics are handed down through generations via processes of enculturation or the maintenance of norms of indigenous Asian American cultures (Kim, 2009). This is important, particularly for Asian American Millennials, because scholars have shown that college educators who understand and engage racial and ethnic minority students' cultural backgrounds can provide positive educational environments Asian Americans (Kiang, 2009; Museus & Quaye, 2009). Thus, a greater understanding and incorporation of Asian American and Asian issues into the educational experience can contribute to enhanced learning environments for Asian American Millennials.

Second, Asian American Millennials are connected to other Asian American and Asian communities via the Internet. For example, the Pew Project (2001) reports that a greater percentage of Asian Americans get their daily local and international news online than any other racial group (Table 5.4). And, in addition to U.S. online news outlets, Asian American Millennials have widespread access to online daily newspapers from Asian countries and other foreign nations. Asian American Millennials also have instant access to news that is specifically relevant to Asian American communities. Many of them also regularly read blogs, such as Angry Asian Man and APA for Progress, which provide daily news about national and international social political issues that affect Asian American communities. In addition, Asian American Millennials have unprecedented access to information about their homelands, histories, and cultures via the Internet (see, for example, www.cuturalprofiles.net). Of course, all Asian American members of the Millennial generation might not take advantage of these resources, but it is clear

TABLE 5.4
Proportion of Each Race Getting Their Daily News Online

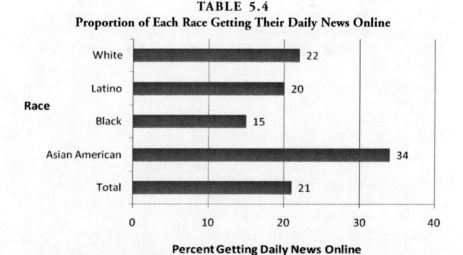

Source: Pew Internet and American Life Project (2001).

that they have access to such resources that is unparalleled by previous generations of Asian Americans.

Finally, Asian American Millennials are connected to Asian American and Asian communities around the country and the world by experiences that afford them the opportunity to interact with those communities. Many Asian American Millennials travel to Asian American communities around the country and Asian countries abroad to visit family and learn about their cultural heritages. It is important to note that colleges and universities can play a major role in expanding the opportunities for Asian American and other Millennial students to take advantage of such learning experiences. Indeed, some institutions of higher education are making efforts to support study-abroad experiences for students to learn about the countries and cultures from which their families come. Also, as I discuss in the following section, college educators can shape educational practices that connect Asian American Millennials with Asian American and Asian communities and address important social and political issues.

Meeting Asian American Millennials at the Intersections of Diversification, Digitization, and Globalization

In the preceding sections, I discussed how Asian American Millennials in college have grown up in an era of unprecedented diversification, widespread digitization, and unparalleled globalization. Underlying this discussion is the belief that Asian American Millennial college students live at the intersections of these transformations. Thus, an understanding of Asian American Millennials in college requires a comprehension of these trends and how they shape the lives of Asian American Millennial college students. In this concluding section, I outline a few recommendations regarding how educators can employ knowledge of these three trends and their relationship to Asian American Millennials to enhance learning environments on campus for Asian American and other undergraduates.

- *Recognize the Diversity of Asian American Millennials as an Asset.* As previously mentioned, Asian American Millennial students bring to college a diverse array of distinctive histories, cultural heritages, and experiences. Kiang (2009), for example, has discussed how Southeast Asian American students bring unique histories and perspectives to the classroom as a result of their immigrant, refugee, and racial minority backgrounds. It is important for college educators to recognize and engage those backgrounds and perspectives to both provide positive learning environments for those students, as well as to take advantage of the rich learning opportunities that accompany those unique experiences and viewpoints.

- *Enhance the Asian American Millennial College Experience With Digital Technology.* If college educators are to most effectively serve Asian American Millennial students, then some consideration of digital technology and the Internet is warranted because they play a fundamental role in the lives of many Asian American Millennial students. Although some Asian American Millennials do not come to college with advanced knowledge of digital technology, incorporating technology into educational practices is equally important for these students, as they too must develop technological skills to succeed in the increasingly knowledge-based economy after college.

- *Nurture Net Generation Norms Among Asian Americans.* Postsecondary educators serving Asian American Millennials in college should also intentionally consider the characteristics and norms of the Millennial generation and incorporate an understanding of those traits into educational practices. They can begin by offering Asian American Millennial students freedom to customize their work and academic programs, infuse entertainment and integrity into academics, and provide Asian American students with opportunities to create personalized projects with the help of digital technology.

- *Apply Asian American Diversity, Digital Technology, and Net Generation Norms to Address Local and Global Issues.* Finally, college educators must consider engaging the diversity of Asian American Millennials, digital technology, and knowledge of net generation norms to address local and global social and political issues. Indeed, as Mitchell Chang notes in chapter 4 of this volume, trends indicate that Asian American Millennials are and will be more civically minded and politically active than previous Asian American generations. Moreover, many Asian American Millennials are already using their knowledge of an affinity for digital technology to address social and political realities that are affecting communities across the United States and throughout the world. These include Asian American students who maintain blogs, engage in online discussions, organize protests, and create and disseminate videos addressing social and political issues. College educators, therefore, should think about how they can incorporate the diversity and technological knowledge and skills of

Asian American Millennials to tackle real local and global social and political issues relevant to Asian American and other communities.

Some educators are already incorporating these ideas into their work. Faculty members in the Asian American studies program at my own institution, for example, utilize social networking technology to plan and execute projects that are designed to serve diverse local Asian American communities in the surrounding area, have facilitated students' creation of videos to teach university community members about lessons they learned during trips to their homeland, and incorporated projects into their courses that allow students to create digital stories that address personal and global political issues. Yet the extent to which these types of innovative ideas are incorporated into mainstream curricula at college and universities across the country is limited. If higher education is to effectively serve Asian American Millennials and nurture them as valuable assets who can enhance learning environments for all students, they must seriously consider how to engage the diversity of Asian American Millennials, as well as their knowledge and skills with digital technology, and their connections to communities around the nation and the world.

References

Chang, M. J. (2008, May 15). Asian evasion: A recipe for flawed solutions. *Diverse Issues in Higher Education.* Retrieved from http://diverseeducation.com/article/11135/

Chang, M. J., Denson, N., Sáenz, V., & Kimberly, M. (2006). The educational benefits of sustaining cross-racial interaction among undergraduates. *Journal of Higher Education, 17*(3), 430–455.

Chang, M. J., Park, J. J., Lin, M. H., Poon, O. A., & Nakanishi, D. T. (2007). *Beyond myths: The growth and diversity of Asian American college freshmen, 1971–2005.* Los Angeles: Higher Education Research Institute.

Chang, M. J., Witt, D., Jones, J., & Hakuta, K. (2003). *Compelling interest: Examining the evidence on racial dynamics in colleges and universities.* Stanford, CA: Stanford University Press.

Friedman T. L. (2005). *The world is flat: A brief history of the twenty-first century.* New York: Picador.

Hudson, K. (2009). What the post-election "service" rhetoric really means [video]. Retrieved from http://www.millennialgeneration.org/

Hune, S. (2002). Demographics and diversity of Asian American college students. In M. K. McKewen, C. M. Kodama, A. N. Alvarez, S. Lee, & C. T. H. Liang

(Eds.), Working with Asian American college students. *New Directions for Student Services* No. 97, 11–20.

Hurtado, S., Milem, J. F., Clayton-Pedersen, A. R., & Allen, W. R. (1999). *Enacting diverse learning environments: Improving the campus climate for racial/ethnic diversity in higher education.* ASHE-ERIC Higher Education Reports Series, 26(8). San Francisco: Jossey-Bass.

Kiang, P. (2002). Stories and structures of persistence: Ethnographic learning through research and practice in Asian American Studies. In Y. Zou and H. T. Trueba (Eds.), *Advances in ethnographic research: From our theoretical and methodological roots to post-modern critical ethnography.* Lanham, MD: Rowman & Littlefield.

Kiang, P. N. (2009). A thematic analysis of persistence and long-term educational engagement with Southeast Asian American college students. In L. Zhan (Ed.), *Asian American voices: Engaging, empowering, enabling* (pp. 59–76). New York: NLN Press.

Kim, B. S. (2009). Acculturation and enculturation of Asian Americans: A primer. In N. Tewari & A. N. Alveraz (Eds.), *Asian American psychology: Current perspectives* (pp. 97–112). New York: Taylor & Francis.

Lewis, A. E., Chesler, M., & Forman, T. A. (2000). The impact of "colorblind" ideologies on students of color: Intergroup relations at a predominantly White university. *Journal of Negro Education, 69*(1–2), 74–91.

Maramba, D. C. (2008). Understanding campus climate through the voices of Filipina/o American college students. *College Student Journal, 42*(4), 1045–1060.

McEwen, M. K., Kodama, C. M., Alvarez, A. N., Lee, S., Liang, C. H. T. (Eds.). (2002). Working with Asian American college students. *New Directions for Student Services* No. 97.

Museus, S. D. (2008a). The model minority and the inferior minority myths: Inside stereotypes and their implications for student involvement. *About Campus, 13*(3), 2–8.

Museus, S. D. (2008b). The role of ethnic student organizations in fostering African American and Asian American students' cultural adjustment and membership at predominantly White institutions. *Journal of College Student Development, 49*(6), 568–586.

Museus, S. D. (2009a). A critical analysis of the exclusion of Asian American from higher education research and discourse. In L. Zhan (Ed.), *Asian American voices: Engaging, empowering, enabling* (pp. 59–76). New York: NLN Press.

Museus, S. D. (Ed.). (2009b). Conducting research on Asian Americans in higher education. *New Directions for Institutional Research* No. 142.

Museus, S. D., & Chang, M. J. (2009) Rising to the challenge of conducting research on Asian Americans in higher education. In S. D. Museus (Ed.), *Conducting research on Asian Americans in higher education. New Directions for Institutional Research* No. 142, 95–105.

Museus, S. D., & Kiang, P. N. (2009). The model minority myth and how it contributes to the invisible minority reality in higher education research. In S. D. Museus (Ed.), *Conducting research on Asian Americans in higher education: New Directions for Institutional Research* No. 142, 5–15.

Museus, S. D., Maramba, D. C., & Teranishi, R. T. (forthcoming). *The minority within the minority: Asian Americans in higher education.* Sterling, VA: Stylus.

Museus, S. D., & Quaye, S. J. (2009). Toward an intercultural perspective of racial and ethnic minority college student persistence. *Review of Higher Education, 33*(1), 67–94.

Museus, S. D., & Truong, K. A. (2009). Disaggregating qualitative data on Asian Americans in campus climate research and assessment. In S. D. Museus (Ed.), *Conducting research on Asian Americans in higher education: New Directions for Institutional Research* No. 142, 17–26.

National Commission on Asian American and Pacific Islander Research in Education. (2008). *Asian American and Pacific Islanders: Facts, not fiction: Setting the records straight.* New York: College Board.

Pew Internet and Life Project. (2001). *Asian Americans and the Internet: The young and connected.* Washington, DC: Author.

Suzuki, B. H. (2002). Revisiting the model minority stereotype: Implications for student affairs practice and higher education. In M. K. McKewen, C. M. Kodama, A. N. Alvarez, S. Lee, & C. T. H. Liang (Eds.), *Working with Asian American college students: New Directions for Student Services* No. 97, 21–32.

Takagi, R. (1998). *Strangers from a different shore: A history of Asian Americans.* Boston: Little, Brown.

Tapscott, D. (2008). *Grown up digital: How the net generation is changing your world.* Columbus, OH: McGraw-Hill.

Teranishi, R. T. (2007). Race, ethnicity, and higher education policy: The use of critical quantitative research. In F. K. Stage (Ed.), *Using quantitative data to answer critical questions: New directions for institutional research* No. 133, 37–49.

Teranishi, R. T., Ceja, M., Antonio, A. L., Allen, W. R., & McDonough, P. M. (2004). The college-choice process for Asian Pacific Americans: Ethnicity and socioeconomic class in context. *Review of Higher Education, 27*(4), 527–551.

Tierney, W. G. (1999). Models of minority college-going and retention: Cultural integrity versus cultural suicide. *Journal of Negro Education, 68*(1), 80–91.

Uba, L. (1994). *Asian Americans: Personality patterns, identity, and mental health.* New York: Guilford.

U.S. Census Bureau. (2004). *U.S. interim projects by age, sex, race, and Hispanic origin.* Washington, DC: U.S. Government Printing Office.

U.S. Census Bureau (2008). Projections of the population by sex, race, and Hispanic origin for the United States: 2010 to 2050. Retrieved from http://www.census.gov/population/www/projections/summarytables.html

U.S. General Accounting Office. (2007). *Information sharing could help institutions identify and address challenges that some Asian American and Pacific Islander students face.* Washington, DC: Author.

Wu, F. H. (2002). *Race in America beyond Black and White.* New York: Basic Books.

PART FOUR

LATINA/O MILLENNIALS IN COLLEGE

6

LA NUEVA GENERACIÓN

Latina/o Millennial College Students at Four-Year Institutions

Victor B. Saenz, Manuel Gonzalez, and Sylvia Hurtado

I n early 2003, the U.S. Census Bureau released new population figures confirming that Latina/os[1] had officially become the nation's largest racial or ethnic minority group, edging past African Americans (U.S. Census Bureau, 2006). This was a symbolic and long-anticipated moment in the demographic history of this country, a moment with repercussions that continue to be digested and explicated. Though this was a historic moment, it has raised questions about the true nature of the Latina/o experience in the United States, especially since some regard the category of Latina/o or Hispanic as nothing more than a convenient tool for policymaking instead of a signifier of a true cohesive ethnic block (Garcia, 2003). Nonetheless, it is an interesting coincidence that this historic moment occurred not only at the turn of a new millennium, but also at the dawn of a generational shift that has given rise to the latest generational category, the Millennial student (Howe & Strauss, 2000).

Our colleges and universities have been bracing for the arrival of the Millennial student for years, a generation made up of the most culturally, ethnically, and racially diverse college students than ever before. Latina/o college students are emblematic of this diverse and emerging Millennial generation of students making their way onto 4-year U.S. college campuses (i.e., students who entered a 4-year institution in 2000 and beyond). In fact, Latina/o college students are increasingly making up the ranks of Millennial students enrolling in our institutions, yet much remains unknown about how best to serve the evolving needs of this critical and fast-growing student population.

Data from the 2010 U.S. Census show that Hispanics now total over 50.5 million, or about one of every six Americans (16.3%) (Pew Hispanic Center, 2011). One of every two people added to the U.S. population are Latina/os, a trend driven largely by immigration patterns and also by the disproportionate share of young people within this fast-growing population (Tienda, 2009). One example of this Latina/o youth movement is evident in the dramatic changes in the profile of public school enrollment over the past four decades. In 1972 Latina/o students composed only 6% of all students enrolled in public schools (K–12), and by 2009 that proportion was up to 22.3% and growing fast (U.S. Census Bureau, 2009). The proportion of Latina/o origin college students has also multiplied during this time, rising from 3.5% of all college enrollees in 1976 to 12.5% in 2009 (NCES, 2010). Moreover, these enrollment trends for Latina/os are only accelerating, and by 2030 Latina/o students are projected to represent over 30% of the school-age population, which includes ages 5 to 24 (Tienda, 2009).

The future prosperity of our country will be increasingly dependent on enrolling more Latina/o Millennial college students and also in supporting them through their higher education pathways. Facilitating the success of Latina/o college students is a complex task because it necessitates a strong grasp of the various dynamics that work to define the U.S. Latina/o experience, dynamics related to language, immigration and class status, national origin, and cultural norms. So, how does a generational theory framework (Howe & Strauss, 2000) help us to explain or better understand this growing generation of Latina/o students coming into our colleges and universities?

The Arrival of Millennials on Campus

Millennials began arriving at our colleges and universities in 2000. This "next great generation" is made up of more diverse college students than ever before, and they are also more embracing of diversity and accepting of the notion that they are a part of a global community. The trademark character traits of Millennial college students as suggested by Howe and Strauss (2000) include their high levels of motivation and self-efficacy, the pressure they bring on themselves to perform and excel, their civic mindedness and engagement with the world around them, their assertiveness and collaborative spirit, and their technologically infused ways of communicating and living. In light of the increasing racial or ethnic diversity within the college-age population, another emerging trend among Millennials is their strong predisposition toward embracing multiculturalism and engaging in groups composed of a diverse population of college peers.

Although tragic events such as the Columbine High School shootings, the terrorist attacks on September 11, 2001, and Hurricane Katrina have left a lasting impact on the lives of today's Millennial college students, other cultural influences have equally contributed to their development (e.g., the rise of the Internet, access to 24-hour news media outlets, etc.; Coomes & DeBard, 2004; Howe & Strauss, 2000). Conversely, some observers note that Millennials have also developed a strong sense of entitlement and a decrease in their sense of responsibility, traits that some attribute to their parents being overly indulgent and involved in their lives (Zemke, 2004). This greater parental involvement has also led to Millennials becoming a more family-oriented generation, a stark contrast to their Generation X peers (i.e., students who entered college from 1981–1999).

Indeed, many of these Millennial student characteristics stand in contrast to the characteristics of generations of college students that preceded them, especially the Generation X crowd. Generation X college students were likely to exhibit more individualistic, nomadic, and apathetic tendencies (Howe & Strauss, 2000). As children, many witnessed an increase in divorce rates among families and the growth of equal rights for women in the workplace. These events had large cultural implications for this group of students as they became "latchkey children" with no central parental figure in their lives (Howe & Strauss, 1991). Often growing up in households without much parental supervision, these students raised themselves as their parents or guardians were at work. Furthermore, Generation X was influenced by Black Monday, the economic crisis of the late 1980s, and the dot.com boom of the mid- to late 1990s, all representing enormous economic swings that left a lasting impression on their educations and career values. Generation X students typically attended school, worked hard academically, and accepted the best offer for college or work. Higher education was a "process" rather than a "journey" for Generation X, and these students were pragmatic, practical, individualistic, and self-reliant young women and men due to the life experiences they had earlier in life (Sacks, 1996).

In light of these and many other defining traits put forth through a generational theory perspective, the key question posed by this edited volume is whether these archetypes are helpful or relevant at all in describing today's students of color, or in this case the modern Latina/o college student.

If generational theory (Howe & Strauss, 2000) is too simplistic or broad for categorizing a group of people, then perhaps its utility in describing a community as diverse as Latina/o college students is even more misguided.

Latina/o Millennials on Campus

Confounding the use of a generational theory framework to describe Latina/o college students are the multiplicity of background, social, and cultural factors that embody the richness and the pan-ethnic identity of Latina/os in the United States. Where generational theory suggests a generalized set of characteristics and behaviors, factors such as Latina/o students' immigrant status, language of origin, family structure, and cultural norms demand a much richer, nonuniversal, and more nuanced understanding of this diverse community of college students. Considering demographic forecasts pointing to more Latina/o college students in the foreseeable future, it is even more important for higher education institutions to better understand the unique experiences of the growing population of Latina/o Millennials within their ranks.

To that end, this chapter employs historic survey data to spotlight key longitudinal trends among two distinct subgroups of entering 4-year college students: Latina/o Millennials and Latina/o Generation X students. We also reviewed trends for White (non-Hispanic) students to provide a comparative perspective, but only on a limited basis. The focus of this chapter is centered on the observed generational differences between Latina/o Millennials entering college and their Generation X Latina/o counterparts.

CIRP Freshman Survey Trends

To accomplish this we employed survey trends data from the Cooperative Institutional Research Program (CIRP) Freshman Survey, an instrument that has been administered to entering college students at hundreds of institutions across the country since 1966 (Pryor, Hurtado, Saenz, Santos, & Korn, 2007). The CIRP Freshman Survey offers a unique series of historical snapshots focused on the changing face of entering college students, a task that is accomplished by asking the same (or similar) questions across different cohorts of entering college students over the years.

Since the first survey was administered, over 13 million entering college students at over 1,900 colleges and universities have participated, making for a rich and diverse profile of entering college freshmen (Pryor et al., 2007). Each year, these surveys are administered during summer orientation and are collected according to an institutional sampling strategy (based on selectivity, control, and type of institution) that ensures broad representation of 4-year institutions to reflect a national, normative profile of the entering college freshman population at all 4-year public or private colleges and universities (see Pryor et al., 2007, for a complete explanation of the methodology). Thus, the trends data employed in our analysis were drawn from a weighted national sample of first-year, full-time freshman students attending 4-year institutions across the United States.

CIRP Freshman Survey trends data were ideal in helping us explore generational differences between Latina/o Millennials and their peer groups. Although the survey has also collected information from community college students over the years, we limited our analysis to trends of entering students at 4-year colleges and universities in order to be consistent with prior national norms reports that have utilized these trends data (Hurtado, Saenz, Santos, & Cabrera, 2008). We acknowledge that it is a limitation to only examine Latina/os at 4-year institutions in light of the fact that the majority of Latina/os in higher education are enrolled at community colleges, but this does not negate the importance and utility of examining trends for students at 4-year institutions. Another limitation was our inability to disaggregate the Latina/o category even further or to consider the immigrant dimension, as the trends data have inherent limitations in the subcategories available for further analysis.

Analytic Strategy

The two primary groups for comparison were Latina/o Millennial college students and their Generation X Latina/o counterparts. Although other comparison groups were certainly possible (e.g., with other racial or ethnic groups or even with generational cohorts preceding these two groups), we decided it was more efficient to focus on the two most contemporary Latina/o generational cohorts. This would allow us to maximize the relevant insights that could be gleaned from this cohort comparison as well as provide sufficient evidence to ascertain the utility of using Millennial generation characteristics to describe the Latina/o Millennial college student.

The trends data offered us an opportunity to examine year-to-year changes in specific survey items, yet for purposes of this analysis we chose to compute moving averages and to focus on a subset of years that targeted each of these generational cohorts. For Latina/o Millennial students we chose survey items from the 2006–2008 trends data, and for Latina/o Generation X students we chose the years 1990–1992. The Millennial cohort had an average unweighted sample size of 20,083, and the Generation X cohort had an unweighted sample size of 6,035. We also reported trends for a comparison group of White (non-Hispanic) Millennial students, although these figures are only cited on a limited basis within this chapter. Analysis of group differences on the trends data were conducted with a difference in proportions test for two independent samples, and we utilized a 95% confidence interval to determine significant difference (Kanji, 1999).

The wide array of content areas encompassed by CIRP Freshman Survey trends allow for an exhaustive examination of students' precollege behaviors as well as their college expectations, academic and extracurricular activities, their career and major aspirations, and their goals and values. For our analysis we only spotlighted items that could help us construct a comparative profile of Latina/o Millennial and Generation X college students. Specifically, our trends analysis focused on constructing a profile of the Latina/o Millennial student by exploring background and family trends, factors and motivators for college attendance, precollege activities, major and career aspirations, goals and values, and expectations for college and beyond.

Results

A Profile of Latina/o Millennial College Students and Their Families

One of the most important changes to the demographic profile of Latina/o Millennials in college relative to their prior generational cohorts has been the dramatic rise in the proportion of Latinas enrolling in college and the attendant decline in Latinos enrollment. Even as the overall number of Latina/os going to college has increased steadily over the past few decades, the proportional representation of Latino male enrollees continues to decline relative to their Latina female counterparts (Saenz & Ponjuan, 2009).

Figure 6.1 shows enrollment trends of Latina/o Millennial and Generation X college students, and it is evident in these data that the gender gap has widened significantly from one generation to the next. In general, proportionally fewer college-age males are actually enrolling in college than in years past, and worse yet, the degree attainment gaps between Latino males

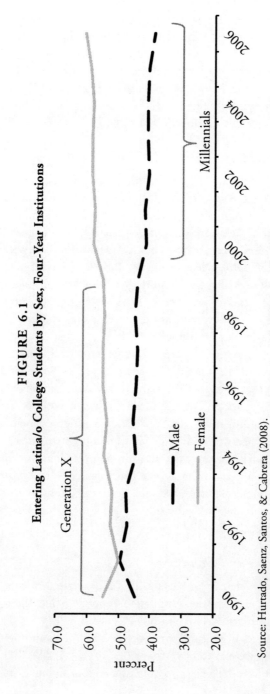

FIGURE 6.1

Entering Latina/o College Students by Sex, Four-Year Institutions

Source: Hurtado, Saenz, Santos, & Cabrera (2008).

Note: These figures represent national normative data collected from entering first-time, full-time college freshmen at 4-year institutions.

and Latina females is widening (Cerna, Perez, & Saenz, 2009). The scope of this gender gap is gaining increased attention among scholars and policy-makers, but its potential impact remains unknown, a point that is all the more disconcerting considering the economic and social consequences that it could portend. One point that is clear is that Latina/o Millennials in college will be increasingly female, and institutions across the country will have to make greater observation of that fact.

Parental Education

A key demographic indicator that also shows a significant proportional dif-ference is the parental education levels of entering Latina/o college students. Latina/o Millennials report that their fathers are slightly more educated as compared to their Generation X counterparts, and the change in their moth-ers' education level is even greater. Table 6.1 examines these parental educa-tion trends for Latina/o college students, and the data demonstrate that a higher proportion of Millennials report that both of their parents have had "some college or beyond" at greater rates than their counterparts. This reported increase in mothers' education is perhaps an artifact of the growing gender gap in educational attainment within the Latina/o population.

The increase in reported parental education for Latina/o Millennials suggests that fewer of them are coming to college as first-generation college students, a point that is further spotlighted in a recent trends report on this critical student population (Saenz, Hurtado, Barrera, Wolf, & Yeung, 2007). Nonetheless, we cannot discount the fact that Latina/os remain most likely among all of their peers to be first-generation college students (Saenz et al., 2007). In short, what we can take away from these trends is that Latina/o Millennials are coming to our 4-year institutions from families that are increasingly educated, although we still need to acknowledge that almost half of these students report that neither their fathers nor their mothers has any college experience.

Divorced Families and Family Size

Another important change in the profile of Latina/o Millennial students' families is the increase in the proportion reporting that their parents are divorced or living apart. Relative to their Generation X peers, Latina/o Mil-lennials are increasingly coming from fractured homes, a finding that appears to mirror broader societal trends. About one-third (32.3%) of Latina/o Mil-lennials reported that their parents were divorced or living apart, up slightly

TABLE 6.1

Parental Education Levels for Latina/o Millennials and Latina/o Generation X College Students

	Latina/o Millennials (avg. 2006–2008)	Latina/o Gen X (avg. 1990–1992)	Actual Difference (%)	Significant Difference
Father: Some college and beyond	49.7	47.3	2.4	*
Mother: Some college and beyond	53.3	43.2	10.1	**

Note: * indicates a significant proportional difference at $p < .05$; ** indicates a significant proportional difference at $p < .01$.

Source: CIRP Freshman Survey Trends Data, 1976–2008. Higher Education Research Institute, UCLA.

but significantly from a generation ago. Interestingly, a much higher proportion of Latina/o Millennials report this family status as compared to their White (non-Hispanic) Millennial peers (21.8%).

Yet another important difference highlighted in Table 6.2 is the changing makeup of their family size, as almost a third more Latina/o Millennials (49.0%) report that they have two or fewer siblings as compared to entering Latina/o college students from a generation ago (36.3%). Indeed, the reported proportion for Latina/os Millennials is even slightly higher than their White (non-Hispanic) peers (46.7%). In sum, Latina/o Millennials are more likely to come to our institutions from broken homes and smaller families than a generation ago. This represents a significant change in the profile of entering Latina/o students at 4-year institutions, perhaps dictating the need to reexamine our understanding of our students' families.

Religion and Spirituality

Perhaps more surprising than the changing makeup of Latina/o families is the shifting trends related to students' religious and spiritual lives. Table 6.3 shows how more Latina/o Millennials report no religious preference (17.7%) than a generation ago (10.9%), and fewer of them frequently attended a religious service in their last year of high school (75.8%) compared to their Generation X peers (85.1%). In spite of this apparent drop in religious activity, a stronger proportion of Latina/o Millennials reported frequently discussing religion (32.5%) when compared to their peers (24.8%), a finding that echoes the tendency of this generation of students to be more engaged with the world around them (Howe & Strauss, 2000).

One other interesting finding spotlighted in Table 6.3 relates to students' spirituality self-rating at college entry. Only 39% of Latina/o Millennials rated themselves "above average" or "highest 10%" among their peers on this self-rating measure, almost 9 points lower than their Generation X peers (47.9%). What these findings may suggest is that Latina/o Millennials are asserting their religious independence more so than their peers from a generation ago, yet they are still drawn to discuss and engage with religion in their own way.

Technology

One of the more conspicuous hallmarks of the Millennial generation is the fact that these students have grown up during a time of fast-paced technological innovation. At the beginning of the 1990s, the Internet was a little used

TABLE 6.2
Changes in Family Structure

	Latina/o Millennials (avg. 2006–2008)	Latina/o Gen X (avg. 1990–1992)	Actual Difference (%)	Significant Difference
Parents both alive and living with each other?	63.8	66.2	−2.5	**
Parents both alive, divorced or living apart?	32.3	27.5	4.8	**
Siblings: Two or fewer[†]	49.0	36.3	12.7	**

Note: * indicates a significant proportional difference at $p < .05$; ** indicates a significant proportional difference at $p < .01$;
[†]Indicates that data for this variable were available only for the 2006 and 1986 CIRP trends data.
Source: CIRP Freshman Survey Trends Data, 1976–2008. Higher Education Research Institute, UCLA.

TABLE 6.3

Religious Practice, Discussion, and Spirituality Self-Rating

	Latina/o Millennial (avg. 2006–2008)	Latina/o Gen X (avg. 1990–1992)	Actual Difference (%)	Significant Difference
Student: No religious preference	17.7	10.9	6.8	**
Frequently attended religious service	75.8	85.1	−9.3	**
Frequently discussed religion	32.5	24.8	7.7	**
Student self-rating: spirituality (above average or highest 10%)	39.0	47.9	−8.8	**

Note: * indicates a significant proportional difference at $p < .05$; ** indicates a significant proportional difference at $p < .01$.

Source: CIRP Freshman Survey Trends Data, 1976–2008. Higher Education Research Institute, UCLA.

network resource that was just becoming widely available, and now its use in our everyday lives is as ubiquitous as the air we breathe. In spite of this innovation, accessibility to technology and information resources has not kept pace, giving rise to a "digital divide" that often pivots along racial and class lines. Nevertheless, it should come as no surprise that when comparing Latina/o students across generations, the Millennials (81.3%) are head and shoulders beyond their Generation X counterparts (33.4%) in their frequent use of computers.

Figure 6.2 demonstrates the enormous growth in the use of computer technology across the past two college student generations. The small but persistent gap in computer usage between Latina/o Millennials and their White (non-Hispanic) peers may be an artifact of the pervasive "digital divide," and it could further indicate the need for more proactive efforts aimed at increasing both usage and technology literacy among all entering college students. The trends data do not offer any other useful indicators that might shed more light on technological behaviors among Latina/o Millennials and their peers, but colleges and universities should nonetheless take note of this difference in computer usage to ensure that Latina/o Millennial students are taking full advantage of the host of technological resources and services that are increasingly at their disposal.

Factors and Motivators for College Attendance

Among the many important factors that drive Latina/o Millennials' decision to go to college are family, financial considerations, and postcollege aspirations. The earlier spotlight on families of Latina/o Millennials focused on their changing makeup, while the trends highlighted in Table 6.4 point to the important role that family can play in influencing these student's decisions to go to college. For example, a larger proportion of Latina/o Millennials (52.1%) as compared to a generation ago (40.0%) report that parental encouragement was a "very important" reason for deciding to go to college. On the other hand, a slightly larger proportion of these same Latina/o Millennials relative to their Generation X peers are choosing their college because they want to live close to home. This may be indicative of the character trait of Millennials wanting to remain closer to their families, but more research would be necessary to further unpack this finding before any definitive conclusions could be drawn.

Financial factors and motivators have also loomed large in Latina/o Millennials' college decision making. Surprisingly, low tuition does not appear

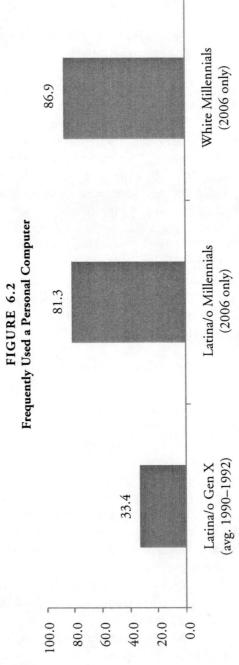

FIGURE 6.2
Frequently Used a Personal Computer

Latina/o Gen X
(avg. 1990–1992)
33.4

Latina/o Millennials
(2006 only)
81.3

White Millennials
(2006 only)
86.9

100.0
80.0
60.0
40.0
20.0
0.0

Note: CIRP trends data was only available for the 2006 survey year for the two Millennial student cohorts.

TABLE 6.4
Family and Financial Factors/Motivators for Going to College

	Latina/o Millennials (avg. 2006–2008)	Latina/o Gen X (avg. 1990–1992)	Actual Difference (%)	Significant Difference
Family				
Very important reason to go to college: My parents wanted me to go	52.1##	40.0	12.1	**
Very important reason in college choice: I wanted to live near home	24.4	20.9	3.5	**
Financial				
Very important reason in college choice: This college has low tuition	22.9!	26.4	−3.5	**
Very important reason in college choice: I was offered financial assistance	47.2	48.9	−1.7	
Very important reason to go to college: To be able to get a better job	71.0##	76.2	−5.2	**
Very important reason to go to college: To be able to make more money	70.8##	70.9	−0.1	

Note: * indicates a significant proportional difference at $p < .05$; ** indicates a significant proportional difference at $p < .01$; ## CIRP trends data from 2006 only; ! CIRP trends data from 2003 only.

Source: CIRP Freshman Survey Trends Data, 1976–2008. Higher Education Research Institute, UCLA.

to be a driving force in students' college choice, as this trend has decreased somewhat among Millennials compared to a generation ago. Similarly, the importance of a financial aid offer in affecting college choice has remained static between the two generational cohorts. Latina/o Millennials report that getting a better job and making more money are still strong reasons to go to college, although these trends have drifted slightly downward. In fact, getting a better job is down significantly as a key reason to go to college from a generation ago; nonetheless, it should be noted that well over two-thirds (71%) of all Latina/o Millennials still report this as a very important reason.

Degree Aspirations

Latina/o Millennials report higher degree aspirations than their Generation X peers. Table 6.5 highlights how a significantly higher proportion of Latina/o Millennials (78.8%) compared to their peers from a generation ago (71.2%) report that a postbaccalaureate degree is their final degree objective. It is worth noting that this proportion is also higher than for White (non-Hispanic) Millennials (71.0%). Hurtado et al. (2008) took a closer look at this trend by gender and found that Latinas appear to be leading the charge toward higher degree aspirations among Latina/o Millennials.

A related trend to degree aspirations explored the role of graduate school in influencing a student's decision to go to college. In fact, preparing for graduate or professional school is a "very important" reason to go to college for Latina/os across both generation groups, and the trend inched slightly upward (although not significantly). We did observe a significant difference in comparing Latina/o Millennials (69.1%) with their White (non-Hispanic) peers (53.0%).

Having high degree aspirations is generally a positive trait for entering college students, especially if educators can find ways to leverage such goals into college success. As Bandura (1991) and others have found, strong self-efficacy can indeed manifest itself in positive academic outcomes when such initial predispositions and aspirations for academic achievement are supported. Moreover, these high aspirations are in line with Howe and Strauss's (2003) claim about Millennials feeling the constant pressure to perform and excel in all they do. Over time, Latina/os have continued to exhibit high degree aspirations, and 4-year colleges should take note of this important trend among their entering Latina/o Millennial populations.

Major and Career Objectives

Changes in students' major and career objectives are another useful set of trends to help explore generational differences. Table 6.6 spotlights the top

TABLE 6.5
Graduate School and Degree Aspirations

	Latina/o Millennials (avg. 2006–2008)	Latina/o Gen X (avg. 1990–1992)	Actual Difference	Significant Difference
Highest Degree Aspiration Post Baccalaureate degree (e.g., MA, PhD, MD, JD)	78.8	71.2	7.6	**
Very important to go to college: to prepare for graduate or professional school	69.1##	67.6	1.5	

Note: * indicates significant proportional difference at $p < .05$; ** indicates significant proportional difference at $p < .01$; ## Data taken from 2006 only.

Source: CIRP Freshman Survey Trends Data, 1976–2008. Higher Education Research Institute, UCLA.

TABLE 6.6
Top 5 Major and Career Objectives

Latina/o Millennials (avg. 2006–2008)	%	Latina/o Generation X (avg. 1990–1992)	%
Top 5 Major Objectives		**Top 5 Major Objectives**	
Business administration (general)	16.9	Business Administration (general)	19.2
Social sciences	11.7	Engineering	10.4
Health professional	11.1	Health Professional	9.8
Biological science	9.5	Education	9.2
Engineering	7.6	Social Sciences	8.1
Top 5 Career Objectives		**Top 5 Career Objectives**	
Business (Exec. or Admin.)	14.2	Business (Exec. or Admin.)	17.0
Doctor (MD or DDS)	8.5	Engineer	8.9
Artist	8.2	Doctor (MD or DDS)	8.8
Education (elementary or secondary)	7.7	Education (elementary or secondary)	8.6
Engineer	6.0	Lawyer	7.4

Note: All common categories for major reported significant differences when compared across generational cohorts (at $p < .01$), and education was ranked sixth at 6.6% but not included for Latina/o Millennials. For the career categories, we observed significant differences across cohorts only for business and engineer (at $p < .01$), and lawyer was ranked sixth at 4.8% but not included for Latina/o Millennials.

Source: CIRP Freshman Survey Trends Data, 1976–2008. Higher Education Research Institute, UCLA.

five major and career objectives of Latina/o Millennials and their Generation X counterparts, revealing an interesting set of differences and similarities between the two generational cohorts. Among the top major objectives, business administration remains the most popular for Latina/o Millennials (16.9%), down slightly from a generation ago (19.2%). Engineering was the second most common major among Generation X students, but it dropped to fifth place among Latina/o Millennials, a persistent downward trend that should raise concerns about the pipeline of Latina/o engineers. Social science majors have taken the second most popular category, followed closely by health professions and then by the biological sciences. There are many programmatic and policy efforts targeting the increase of more students of color in the STEM fields (i.e., science, technology, engineering, and math), and it is somewhat reassuring to see that an increasing proportion of Latina/o Millennials are moving toward some critical science fields in biology and the health professions.

Among the top career objectives, business executive or business administration remained the most popular choice for Latina/o Millennials (14.2%),
although there was a significant decline in this category. Just as we observed
for college major, fewer Latina/o Millennials (6%) reported engineering as a
career choice than their Generation X peers as it dropped from second to
fifth place. Meanwhile, the proportion for medical and education careers
remained relatively static across the generational cohorts. The proportion of
Millennials who reported lawyer as a career choice also declined significantly,
although it still remains among the top five career choices for these students.
The career choice of artist made its way into the top five for Latina/o Millennials, perhaps indicating a growing sentiment among this cohort to express
themselves and embody their community and cultural values through art. In
their review of Latina/o trends, Hurtado et al. (2008) also found much continuity over time in career objectives for entering Latina/o college students, a
finding that is somewhat consistent with our observations.

Volunteerism and Civic Engagement

One of the key characteristics attributed to Millennials is their strong service
orientation and overall engagement, both in terms of service to others as well
as being engaged with the world around them. These values may have been
shaped by key community and world events during their lifetimes (e.g., the
terrorist attacks of September 11, 2001, the war on terror, the Columbine
school shootings, etc.) as well as a heightened sense of urgency and pressure
to excel relative to their peers. In their review of four decades of freshmen
trends, Pryor et al. (2007) noted a steady increase in community service or
volunteer work as well as an increase in students' civic engagement both on
campus and on the national and international scales.

Table 6.7 focuses on Latina/o Millennials and their Generation X peers,
and we found similar increases on some of these same survey trends. At
college entry, a significantly higher proportion of Latina/o Millennials
reported that they performed volunteer work as compared to their Latina/o
peers, and over half (53.2%) reported volunteering at least 1 hour per week.
This amount of weekly volunteer service is even higher than for their White
(non-Hispanic) peers (46.4%), suggesting that Latina/o Millennials are
among the most service-oriented group of Millennials coming to college.
Perhaps even more important for institutions is that they report a higher
expectation than their generational counterparts to continue to participate
in volunteer or community service work.

TABLE 6.7

Volunteerism, Political Engagement, and Social Engagement

	Latina/o Millennials (avg. 2006–2008)	Latina/o Gen X (avg. 1990–1992)	Actual Difference (%)	Significant Difference
Service				
Performed volunteer work	82.6	67.7	14.9	**
Hours per week: Volunteering (1 or more)	53.2	38.3	14.9	**
High expectation: Participate in volunteer or community service work	29.6	21.1	8.5	*
Political Engagement				
Discussed politics (frequently)	30.0	24.8^	5.2	**
Worked in a local, state, or national political campaign	12.5	8.8	3.7	**
Social Engagement				
Hours per week: Student clubs/groups (1 or more)	59.0	61.9	−2.9	**
Socialized with someone of another race/ethnicity	80.7	77.1	3.6	**

Note: * indicates significant proportional difference at $p < .05$; ** indicates significant proportional difference at $p < .01$; ^ indicates that data were taken from 1994 trends year as data are not available from 1990–1992.

Source: CIRP Freshman Survey Trends Data, 1976–2008. Higher Education Research Institute, UCLA.

Two other related trend categories in Table 6.7 included political and social engagement, and on both counts we observed that Latina/o Millennials were dissimilar to their Generation X peers. On the political engagement items, Latina/s Millennials reported a higher frequency of discussing politics (30.0%) relative to their peers (24.8%) and a higher rate of working in political campaigns. These increases are aligned with the broader trends toward increased political activism documented in Pryor et al. (2007). On the social engagement items, Latina/o Millennials reported slightly less time participating in student clubs or groups in high school, although they did report socializing more often with racially or ethnically diverse peers.

When considered alongside their strong service orientation, the emerging profile of Latina/o Millennials is that they are significantly engaged in community, civic, and social spheres. A growing chorus of researchers (e.g., Astin, Vogelgesang, Ikeda, & Yee, 2000; Eyler & Giles, 1999) have established the importance that service and civic engagement opportunities in college can positively impact the cognitive and affective development of college students. Further, many researchers (Chang, 1999; Gurin, Dey, Hurtado, & Gurin, 2002; Saenz, Ngai, & Hurtado, 2007) have long documented the educational benefits than can be derived from diverse learning environments. In light of Latina/o Millennial students' high predispositions toward social, civic, and diversity engagement, colleges and universities should move to fully exploit the learning opportunities that this could present, ultimately helping to improve the academic success for all students.

Goals, Values, and Expectations

One final category of trends that we examined was students' goals, values, and expectations as they entered college. These particular survey items are among the most cited longitudinal trends due to their unique reflection of generational differences among entering college students. Table 6.8 offers a snapshot of some of these trends, and what is certain in observing them is that there have been some important changes in the values of Latina/o Millennials compared to their peers of a generation ago (and also compared to their White non-Hispanic Millennial peers). Sorted by most important value to least, the three top trends suggest that Latina/o Millennials are increasingly pragmatic about their financial livelihoods while also balancing more altruistic goals. Four of five (80.9%) students reported that it was very important or essential to be well-off financially, a significant increase from their Generation X counterparts (76.3%). This value was balanced with an

TABLE 6.8
Goals, Values, and Expectations

	Latina/o Millennials (avg. 2006–2008)	Latina/o Gen X (avg. 1990–1992)	Actual Difference	Significant Difference
Goals and Values (*Very important or essential*)				
Being very well off financially	80.9	76.3	4.6	**
Helping others who are in difficulty	75.2	72.6	2.7	**
Raising a family	74.8	70.5	4.3	**
Becoming an authority in my field	61.5	71.1	–9.6	**
Helping to promote racial understanding	59.3	58.4	0.9	
Obtaining recognition from my colleagues for contributions to my special field	50.2	60.1	–9.9	**
Influencing social values	50.0	50.2	–0.2	
Becoming successful in a business of my own	49.4	48.4	1.0	
Becoming a community leader	41.4	40.3#	1.1	
Keeping up to date with political affairs	39.2	45.5	–6.3	**
Influencing the political structure	27.2	26.6	0.6	
Expectations (*Very likely*)				
Graduate with Honors	16.6^	14.7	1.9	**
Make at least a "B" average	57.6	43.7	13.9	**
Work full time while attending college	10.1	6.2	3.9	**
Seek personal counseling	13.5	6.7	6.8	**

Note: * indicates significant proportional difference at $p < .05$; ** indicates significant proportional difference at $p < .01$; # indicates that data were taken from 2005 trends year as data are not available from 2006–2008; ^ indicates data are from 2001 trends year as data are not available from 2006–2008.

Source: CIRP Freshman Survey Trends Data, 1976–2008. Higher Education Research Institute, UCLA.

increased sense of importance over helping others in difficulty (75.2%) and raising a family (74.8%). Latina/o Millennials' strong predisposition toward helping others in difficulty was also higher than for their White (non-Hispanic) peers (65.8%) as was their commitment to helping promote racial understanding (59.3% to 28.5%). This may suggest that Latina/o college students are even more in sync with the Millennial character trait of being engaged and concerned with the world around them.

Other important values reported by Latina/o Millennials included their goals to become an authority in their chosen field (61.5%) as well as to obtain the recognition of their colleagues (50.5%), although on both counts these trends have dropped precipitously when compared to their Latina/o Generation X cohorts. The fact that a smaller proportion of Latina/o Millennials reported being interested in professional accolades speaks volumes for the changing priorities of this group of students, a value set that is increasingly leaning toward more altruism and activism. About half of Latina/o Millennials reported that it was a very important or essential goal to influence social values or to be successful in their own businesses; fewer still reported that their goals were to become community leaders (41.4%) or to influence the political structure (27.2%), although no significant difference was observed for each of these four trends. One proportional decline that was significant was the trend for keeping up to date with political affairs, as fewer Latina/os reported this was an important goal compared to a generation ago. Although this finding might not agree with prior trends related to increased social and civic engagement, we speculate that Latina/o Millennials are more interested in doing and acting instead of simply keeping up to date, a conjecture that is certainly well evidenced in those same prior trends.

Finally, in reviewing students' expectations for college we identified several trends of special relevance to colleges and universities. First, in keeping consistent with the increased pressure to succeed and expectation to excel, Latina/o Millennials reported a higher likelihood than their peers from a generation ago to graduate college with honors (16.6%) and to make at least a "B" average (57.6%). On a more cautious note, a significantly higher proportion of Latina/o Millennials reported it was very likely they would be working full time while in college (10.1%) or seek personal counseling (13.5%). This latter trend for expecting to seek personal counseling could include academic as well as mental health counseling, and it is more than twice as high for Latina/o Millennials as it is for their White (non-Hispanic) counterparts (6.1%). Although these two trends represent a small proportion of the overall Latina/o Millennial cohort, we nonetheless characterize them as cautious in light of the increasing pressure that students are placing on themselves to succeed. Institutions and their student and academic affairs staff should be prudent in recognizing such signs at college entry, as these are indicators that might place students at risk or in need of additional services.

Conclusion

At the heart of this chapter was the question of how useful it was to employ generational categories such as "Millennial" or "Generation X" to describe and understand the modern Latina/o college student entering our 4-year institutions. Focusing on Latina/o Millennials has yielded insights into the unique challenges and opportunities confronting this emerging group of students on college campuses, and our review of longitudinal survey trends found compelling differences between this generation of students and their immediate predecessors. Our analysis explored trends on students' demographic profile as well as their changing family structure; religious and spiritual activity and independence; technology use; factors and motivators for going to college; degree aspirations as well as major and career objectives; service and civic engagement; and their changing goals, values, and expectations. From these findings we can derive important implications for policymakers and practitioners alike.

Implications for Policy and Practice

At the outset, one of the more important changes to the demographic profile of Latina/o Millennials in college has been the dramatic rise in the proportion of Latinas enrolling in college and the attendant decline of Latinos enrolling. Institutions and policymakers should take note that Latina/o Millennials will be increasingly female. Among some of the family trends that we examined, a higher proportion of Latina/o Millennials that are coming to college have more educated parents than before, although we should acknowledge that these students are still likely to be first-generation college goers. Another family trend suggested that Latina/o Millennials are more likely to come from divorced homes than in the recent past, and yet another trend found that they are coming from families with fewer siblings than a generation ago. Finally, Latina/o Millennial college students were less active in their religious lives than their past predecessors, although they remained spiritual and engaged with religion in their own unique ways.

Other trends highlighted that Latina/o Millennials are way ahead of their Latina/o predecessors in their frequent use of computers, although they still trail their White (non-Hispanic) peers in this category. Also, we noted that Latina/o Millennials are feeling a lot of pressure to perform well and excel in all they do, as evidenced by their increasing postbaccalaureate degree aspirations. We also were somewhat reassured that an increasing proportion expressed greater major and career interests in the critical science fields of biology and the health professions. These findings should be encouraging to policymakers intent on addressing the significant disparity of Latina/o college students in the STEM fields.

One of our key findings noted how Latina/o Millennials are among the most service-oriented group of students coming to college, and they also come with high expectations to continue to participate in volunteer or community service work. Other trends reinforced that these students are also significantly engaged in community, civic, and social spheres. When it came to life goals, Latina/o Millennials are increasingly pragmatic about their financial livelihood while balancing that with more altruistic personal goals. Taken together, these trends speak volumes for the changing priorities of this group of students, as their values lean more toward altruism, activism, and engagement. Practitioners should take note of these important character traits among Latina/o Millennials and perhaps seek ways to cultivate these predispositions among this critical student population.

The Verdict on Latina/os and the Millennial Framework

In returning to our central question, our analysis uncovered trends for Latina/o Millennials that aligned well with some of the key character traits posited by Howe and Strauss (2003), but we also found areas where their generational framework underestimates the potential of these students. For one, we found that Latina/o Millennials come to college for a variety of pragmatic and goal-oriented reasons, and their families play a significant role in guiding their college decision-making process. They also come to college with high expectations to succeed as evidenced by their increased degree aspirations and their plans to prepare for graduate school. All of these trends appear well aligned with the typical Millennial personality profile.

Where the generational framework falls short is in underestimating the commitment to service and civic engagement that Latina/o Millennials exhibit. Although service and global perspectives are certainly included within the Millennial taxonomy, for Latina/o Millennials these traits appear to be encoded in their DNA. Institutions should seize upon this strong value set among Latina/os and recognize the potential to leverage them toward facilitating their academic success. If the modern college or university is indeed retreating to a more holistic and liberal-arts minded educational experience, then—in light of their strong credentials toward civic engagement and service—Latina/o Millennials truly represent a prime group of students to attract and recruit to our institutions.

Another area where the Millennial framework falls somewhat short is in its understanding of the families of Latina/o Millennials. For example, we observed that the parents of Latina/o Millennials are more educated than ever before, but we should not assume that these parents are summarily engaged in all aspects of their children's lives in college. In other words, outreach to the families of Latina/o Millennials needs to be ongoing and consistent, and no assumptions should be made about their information needs. The key is for colleges and universities to understand the diversity that exists within the Latina/o family unit, variances that are driven by immigrant status, socioeconomic status, national origin, regional differences, and a host of other cultural and social differences.

Institutions should also take note of the persistent difference in technology use between Latina/os and their White (non-Hispanic) peers to ensure that these students are taking full advantage of all of the technological resources and services that are increasingly available to them. We also need to acknowledge that while Latina/o Millennials report high degree aspirations and levels of self-efficacy at college entry, such high goals need to be properly nurtured and tended to so that they can be translated into results for students.

Finally, we reiterate that great caution must be taken with respect to the trademark Millennial trait of feeling pressure to succeed, as Latina/o Millennials could be especially susceptible to the external pressures and forces at work that can undermine their college success. Institutions and their staff should be especially diligent in recognizing these warning signs among their Latina/o Millennial students. This spotlight on Latina/o Millennials entering 4-year institutions is sure to inform the work of student affairs and higher education professionals in serving the needs of this emerging and dynamic group of students.

Note

1. Throughout the chapter we employ the term *Latina/os*, but refer to Hispanics when referencing reports or studies that use this category. *Latina/os* describes students that are of Mexican, Puerto Rican, or other Latina/o descent. More specific

Latina/o ethnic and national-origin designations (e.g., Cuban, Dominican, Colum-bian, etc.) are unfortunately not available in the trends data used in this chapter.

References

Astin, A., Vogelgesang, L., Ikeda, E., & Yee, J. (2000). *How service learning affects students.* Los Angeles: Higher Education Research Institute, UCLA.

Bandura, A. (1991). Self-regulation of motivation through anticipatory and self-reactive mechanisms. In R. A. Dienstbier (Ed.), *Perspectives on motivation: Nebraska symposium on motivation* (Vol. 38, pp. 69–164). Lincoln, NE: University of Nebraska Press.

Cerna, O., Perez, P., & Saenz, V. B. (2009). Examining the pre-college attributes and values of Latina/o college graduates. *Journal of Hispanic Higher Education, 8*(2), 130–157.

Chang, M. J. (1999). Does racial diversity matter? The educational impact of a racially diverse undergraduate population. *Journal of College Student Development, 40*, 377–394.

Coomes, M. D., & DeBard, R. (Ed.). (2004). *Serving the millennial generation. New Directions for Student Services* Vol. 106.

Eyler, J., & Giles, D. (1999). *Where's the learning in service-learning?* San Francisco: Jossey-Bass.

Garcia, J. (2003). *Latino politics in America: Community, culture, and interests.* Lanham, MD: Rowman & Littlefield.

Gurin, P., Dey, E. L., Hurtado, S., & Gurin, G. (2002). Diversity in higher education: Theory and impact on educational outcomes. *Harvard Educational Review, 72*(3), 330–366.

Howe, N., & Strauss, W. (1991). *Generations: The history of America's future, 1584 to 2069.* New York: Morrow.

Howe, N., & Strauss, W. (2003). *Millennials go to college.* Washington, DC: American Association of College Registrars and Admissions Officers and LifeCourse Associates.

Howe, N., & Strauss, W. (2000). *Millennials rising: The next great generation.* New York: Vintage Press.

Hurtado, S., Saenz, V. B., Santos, J. L., & Cabrera, N. L. (2008). *Advancing in higher education: A portrait of Latina/o college freshmen at four-year institutions: 1975–2006.* Los Angeles: UCLA.

Kanji, G. K. (1999). *100 statistical tests.* London: Sage.

National Center for Education Statistics (NCES). (2010). Digest of educational statistics, total fall enrollment in degree-granting institutions, by race/ethnicity, sex, attendance status, and level of student: Selected years, 1976 through 2009, Table 235. Retrieved from http://nces.ed.gov/programs/digest/d10/tables/dt10_235.asp?referrer=list

Pew Hispanic Center. (2011). Statistical portrait of Hispanics in the United States, 2009. Retrieved from http://pewhispanic.org/factsheets/factsheet.php?Fact sheetID = 70

Pryor, J. H., Hurtado, S., Saenz, V. B., Santos, J. L., & Korn, W. S. (2007). *The American freshman: Forty year trends.* Los Angeles: Higher Education Research Institute, UCLA.

Sacks, P. (1996). Generation X goes to college. Chicago: Open Court.

Saenz, V. B., Hurtado, S., Barrera, D., Wolf, D., & Yeung, F. (2007). *First in my family: A profile of first-generation college students at four-year institutions since 1971.* Los Angeles: Higher Education Research Institute, UCLA.

Saenz, V. B., Ngai, H. N., & Hurtado, S. (2007). Factors influencing positive inter-actions across race for African-American, Asian-American, Latino, and White college students. *Research in Higher Education, 48*(1), 1–38.

Saenz, V. B., & Ponjuan, L. (2009). The vanishing Latino male in higher education. *Journal of Hispanic Higher Education, 8*(1), 54–89.

Tienda, M. (2009). *Hispanicity and educational inequality: Risks, opportunities and the nation's future.* Paper presented at the American Association of Hispanics in Higher Education (AAHHE), Princeton, NJ.

U.S. Census Bureau. (2006). Facts for features: Hispanic heritage month, September 15–October 14, 2006. Retrieved from http://www.census.gov/PressRelease/www/ releases/archives/facts_for_features_special_editions/007173.html

U.S. Census Bureau. (2009). Current population survey, October supplement, 1989–2009. Table A-5-1. Retrieved from http://nces.ed.gov/programs/coe/tables/ table-1er-1.asp

Zemke, R. (2001). Here come the millennials. *Training, 38*(7), 44–49.

7

MILLENNIAL CHARACTERISTICS AND LATINO/A STUDENTS

Anna M. Ortiz and Dorali Pichardo-Diaz

L atino/as are important when considering the relevance and application of generational theory, as they will likely become the demographic majority of future generations. Media and census scholars frequently report that Latino/a school children will be the single largest ethnic or racial group by the year 2050 (Fry & Gonzales, 2008). Thus, exploring the characteristics of Latino/as who compose the Millennial generation is an important first step for educators in preparing for future generations of students.

As has been stated throughout this volume, diverse Millennials differ in significant ways from the Millennials who were studied in Howe and Strauss's (2000) survey of high school students in Fairfax, Virginia, and in other scholarly works such as Coomes and DeBard (2004). In fact, common characteristics applied to Millennials (such as feeling special, sheltered, or conventional or possessing helicopter parents) are at times quite the opposite of students from non-White ethnic groups (Ortiz & Santos, 2009; Pichardo, 2006). This chapter examines Millennial characteristics through two studies of Latino/a students. In the first study Pichardo (2006) surveyed Latino/a students at a 4-year university and a community college regarding their perceptions of the Millennial characteristics and their applicability to their lives before and during college. The second study by Ortiz and Santos (2009) interviewed 34 Latino/a students at two California universities, primarily asking students about their ethnic identity, its meaning and practice, and how those constructs intersected with the college experience. Throughout the chapter we draw on the data from these studies

- To show ways in which Latino/a students parallel the experiences of students outlined in the Howe and Strauss study
- To suggest ways in which Latino/a students' experiences were divergent from students in the Howe and Strauss study
- To consider how generational theory helps us to project changes in the Latino/a student population, primarily by drawing linkages to generational status from an immigration perspective.

Finally, we close with recommendations for ways in which higher education can better serve this growing population of students.

Precollege Experiences of Latino/a Students

There are a variety of factors that affect Latino/a educational experiences prior to enrollment in higher education. Precollege characteristics that are particularly relevant for Latino/a students include family income, access to quality public schools, parental education, and of course high school attainment. According to the National Center for Education Statistics (2000b), 50% of the Latino population earned an income of $30,000 or less, while only 2% earned $75,000 or more. Latino/a students who come from low socioeconomic backgrounds are at a disadvantage, especially when it comes to attending college. Such students have historically been at risk because of all the negative aspects that poverty entails. For one, students from low socioeconomic status usually attend poorly funded public schools that are not equipped to provide a strong educational foundation for its students (Nora, Rendón, & Cuadraz, 1999).

According to Carnevale and Fry (2000), teenagers whose parents have a college education are more likely to go to college. Though there is a rising trend in the United States of parents with higher levels of education, this trend does not hold true for the Hispanic immigrant population. Many Hispanic students live in families where their parents did not complete high school (Carnevale & Fry, 2000). Among young adults ages 25 to 29, the percentage of non-Hispanic whites who attained at least a bachelor's degree in 2010 was more than three times that of Hispanics (Child Trends, 2011). According to the U.S. Census, individuals with a bachelor's degree earn approximately 77% more than those who only hold a high school degree

(Mortenson, 2002). Although Latino/a parents' educational attainment rates have increased, these rates are still below those of other ethnic groups (National Center for Education Statistics, The Condition of Education, 2001). The percentage of Latino parents earning a high school diploma has increased from about 40% in 1974 to 51% in 1999. Llagas (2003) found that there is a correlation between mothers' education and children's academic achievement. Between 1974 and 1999, the percentage of children ages 6 to 18 whose mother had at least a high school education increased among all ethnic and racial groups. Nonetheless, the gap of White and Latino/a children whose mothers attained a high school diploma or bachelor's degree since 1974 remained the same in 1999.

The majority of Latino/a students attending public elementary and secondary schools are enrolled in schools where minorities compose the majority of the student population. In 2000, 38% of Latino/as were enrolled in schools where minorities accounted for 90% or more of the student population, and 77% were enrolled in schools where minorities accounted for 50% of the student population. In addition, 32% of Latino/a students lived in large urban cities, compared to 6% of White students (National Center for Education Statistics, 2000a). These schools are consistently more poorly funded than their suburban counterparts.

According to Llagas (2003), Hispanic young adults are less likely than Whites and Blacks to complete high school. In 2000, 64% of Latino/as ages 18 to 24 completed secondary schooling compared to 92% of White and 84% of Black students (Kaufman, Alt, & Chapman, 2001). Though completion rates for Latino/as have fluctuated throughout the past decade, there are no consistent trends.

Latino/a College Students

Latino/a students compose 11% of the national student population, which is below parity for the group's proportion within the national population (15.4% according to the Chronicle of Higher Education, 2008). This gap in parity and participation is the highest for all non-White ethnic groups. African American and Native American students participate at parity, and Asian Americans participate at 50% higher than their proportion of the general population. To complicate this parity gap further, Latino/a students are overrepresented in public 2-year community colleges. Nearly 50% of all Latino/a students in higher education are in community colleges, making them

15.5% of the total 2-year college population. Only 8.4% of the student population in 4-year colleges and universities are Latino/as. As one would expect, given these numbers, the proportion of degrees conferred to Latino/a students also falls below parity. Latino/as earned the following degrees in academic year 2005–2006:

- 11.3% of the associate degrees
- 7.2% of the bachelor's degrees
- 5.5% of the master's degrees
- 3.4% of the doctoral degrees
- 5.1% of the professional degrees

In addition, many Latino/as are the first in their families to participate in higher education, with only 12.7% of all Latino/as holding a bachelor's degree or higher, compared to 28.8% of the total population (Chronicle of Higher Education, 2008). More telling is the fact that 22.8% of all Latino/as have an eighth-grade education or less. This number is 17% higher than every other ethnic group in the United States.

Millennial Characteristics Applied to Latino/as

Much of the disparity that is evident in the participation rates and college choices of Latino/a students is also evident when considering the application of Millennial characteristics to this population. For example, the median income in Fairfax County, Virginia, where Howe and Strauss conducted their initial study on Millennials, was $81,050 (Fairfax Department of Systems Management for Human Services, 2001), compared to a median household income for Latino/a families of $37,913 (DeNavas-Walt, Proctor, & Smith, 2009). This is meaningful because students from low-income families usually attend poorly funded public schools that are not equipped to provide a strong educational foundation for their students (Nora et al., 1999). This is compounded by the fact that Latino/a students are often the first in their families to attend college; thus, they encounter difficulty navigating the higher education system without parental role models who understand the process and experience (Nevarez, 2001; Reisberg, 1999). Socioeconomic differences of Latino/a students when compared to majority Millennials, such as those in the Howe and Strauss study, make the application of the Howe and Strauss *characteristics* problematic. Here, we discuss these characteristics and contrast them with the findings from our studies of Latino/a college students to better illustrate *their* experience as Millennials.

Howe and Strauss (2000) proposed that there are seven characteristics common to the Millennial generation. These students are *special, achievers, team oriented, conventional, sheltered, confident,* and *pressured.* If we consider these characteristics and their application to Latino/as we find that there are similarities and significant nuances in their expression. For example, in a study by Pichardo (2006) both statistical and qualitative data revealed the impact of upbringing, socioeconomic status, and college generational status on a Latino/a student's ability to identify with the characteristics of the Millennial generation. Students found that they differed, among other things, due to a lack of access to technology, the need to work instead of participate in extracurricular activities, and unfamiliarity with the college-going process. Each of the Howe and Strauss characteristics will be discussed and contrasted with findings from our studies in greater detail below.

Special

Millennials have been treated as if they are symbols of parental success, vital to the nation and central to their parents' sense of purpose (Howe & Strauss, 2003). In contrast to the Generation Xers, the "slacker" generation who came before them, Millennials are often believed to be better (Lowery, 2001). Others note that they were also treated as special through the care and caution used in child rearing, such as increased health prevention measures and extra care and attention (Coomes & DeBard, 2004). For example, in the early 1980s, parents were raising their children in a consciously child-centered environment (Schwartz, 2003). According to Howe and Strauss (2000), this era depicted a rise in expectant mothers tending to their unborn children through prenatal vitamins, diet, exercise, and Lamaze classes. As children, Millennials had everything "kid-proofed" in their homes and were acknowledged as "babies on board" in vehicles (Howe & Strauss, 2000). According to the study by Pichardo (2006), Latino/as were not in these luxurious "baby on board" vehicles. Throughout focus group interviews conducted by Pichardo, students disclosed the impact of their socioeconomic status and resource availability on their experiences growing up. Students described their inability to afford and be involved in extracurricular activities, working several jobs simultaneously to assist their families with limited resources and to make up for a lack of access to such key accoutrements like computers and the Internet. In fact, she found that socioeconomic status had a negative impact on students' ability to identify with this characteristic.

Sheltered

Similarly, Millennials have experienced more child protection laws, rules, and practices than any other age cohort (Lowery, 2001). They have largely grown up in structured environments where free time is structured into discrete activities (Commes & DeBard, 2004; Howe & Strauss, 2000). These activities often enabled a rule-oriented environment overseen by authority figures.

After being put in day care, after-school programs, and recreational activities by their Baby Boomer parents, Millennials have not had much opportunity to participate in free play (Coomes & DeBard, 2004; Howe & Strauss, 2000). Growing up in structured environments, surrounded by authority figures such as nannies and coaches, in an age of *zero tolerance* has created in Millennials the expectation of structure in all aspects of their lives, and they have conditioned themselves to trust in authority figures.

Ortiz and Santos (2009) found that the term *sheltered* meant something entirely different to Latino/a students than how the term was used in Howe and Strauss's work. For example, many of the women in the Ortiz and Santos study reported that their families were overly protective of them. Their families desired to keep them close to home, which often resulted in pressure to pursue higher education at institutions within driving distance so that their daughters would not have to live in college residences. This extended to an overall ethos that promoted the sanctity of virginity as a characteristic of a good Latina. Parents sought to achieve this goal with strict rules regarding dating and curfews applied before and during college.

Confident

The Millennial generation believes that they will succeed. This may be due to the constant praise and attention they receive from the adults and authority figures in their lives (Zemke, Raines, & Filipczak, 2000). Additionally, they feel a sense of confidence due to the messages of empowerment they are provided (Howe & Strauss, 2000). They are confident that due to their "specialness," their approach to teamwork and collaboration, and their value for community service, they can correct societal ills (Rickes, 2009). Authority figures in the life of Millennials have nurtured this confidence through awards of appreciation for participation that convey the message that their good behavior is continually acknowledged (Coomes & DeBard, 2004). Having been praised throughout their lives, Millennials feel they have mastered acceptable behavior for parents, instructors, and authority figures (Zemke et al., 2000).

In both Pichardo's (2006) and Ortiz and Santos's (2009) studies, Latino/a students also implied confidence in their ability to succeed. However, they encountered various obstacles and struggles throughout their educational journeys as they attempted to accomplish their goals. Ortiz and Santos found that students gained strength and confidence in their ability to overcome obstacles. However, Latino/as did not experience the same kind or level of validation that fosters confidence as described by Millennials. Latino/a parents were not as likely to know how to support their children's achievement in ways that resulted in the social capital that made achievement easier; instead their parents provided emotional support and a strong belief in their children's ability to succeed. Despite not having the constant praise articulated by majority Millennials, Latino/a Millennials were found to be resilient.

Conventional

Howe and Strauss (2003) argued that because parents disclose widely with their children less "psychological" space exists between parents and children, thus making it more likely that children will adopt parents' conservative values. In addition, Coomes and DeBard (2004) claimed that Millennials' thirst for praise and their trust in authorities has increased their desire to follow rules and social conventions. The findings from the Ortiz and Santos (2009) study are similar, though the motivation for trust in authority and rule following is different. Latino/a students were more likely to show deference to authority as a sign of respect for elders, a strong cultural tradition. Additionally, conventional social values among Latino/as are likely to be the result of the relationship between family values and religious values associated with the prevalence of Catholic church membership among Latino/as.

Team Oriented

Our Millennial authors have a variety of explanations for the heightened team orientation of this generation (Coomes & DeBard, 2004; Howe & Strauss, 1991, 2000, 2003; Lowery, 2001, 2004). Team sports is more widespread than in past generations, begins at a younger age, extends beyond the boundaries of school, and includes more girls, though this increase is limited to girls in suburban settings (Sabo, 2009). In addition, Howe and Strauss (2000, 2003) argued that because their parents are individualistic, Millennials are encouraged to be more cooperative and are rewarded for doing so. Although Millennials are widely considered to be highly involved in structured activities outside the home, the Pichardo (2006) study showed that

Latino/a students from lower-income homes were less likely to be involved in structured activities such as sports or clubs.

Team orientation has a close connection to collectivism, a common characteristic of Latino/a cultures. However, there is an important distinction in that collectivism in Latino/a cultures prioritizes the family (nuclear and extended) above the individual (Pedersen, Draguns, Lonner, & Trimble, 2002). The Howe and Strauss (2000) description places the focus of team on peers, rather than within the family. Ortiz and Santos (2009) confirmed that the Latino/as who participated in their study placed the needs of the family before individual needs. Furthermore, students considered success in higher education an act that would serve to elevate the family's status by modeling for younger siblings that college attendance is an achievable and desirable goal. The study also revealed that students perceived the effects of their achievement extended to the ethnic group, positioning the value of collectivism beyond the family. Students also felt their own educational achievement and college success served to elevate the status of the ethnic group.

Pressured

Majority Millennial youth have been pressured to succeed. Parents have made a great investment in their success and have demonstrated this investment by making multiple opportunities for involvement and personal development available to their children. However, this comes with an increased expectation for goal achievement (Schwartz, 2003). In addition, tighter structure in all facets of their lives has created expectations for success with rewards clearly and highly valued (Coomes & DeBard, 2004).

Pichardo's (2006) study highlighted that one major influence on Latino/a students was the role that their parents or guardians played in their lives. In reflecting on their childhood, many students shared how their parents instilled in them a strong work ethic. Many students grew up with parents who worked inordinate hours in order to maintain a decent living, thus having limited time or money to enroll their children in extracurricular activities. Nonetheless, observing their parents' tremendous efforts taught them to value hard work and acknowledge the importance of going to college to improve their quality of life. The study by Pichardo (2006) revealed that despite the fact that many parents were unfamiliar with the educational process and system, they were aware that obtaining an education could improve their children's financial well-being. However, many were unable to afford activities that resulted in enhanced educational opportunities. Though unclear as to how to navigate the educational system, Latino/a parents did not pressure their children to achieve; rather they supported and tried to understand their educational endeavors (Ortiz & Santos, 2009; Pichardo, 2006).

Achievers

The pressure to succeed may be related to Millennials' desire to achieve. They are ambitious and confident in their abilities, aided by their ability to access activities and interventions to help them achieve, such as advanced academic programs, tutoring and other support, and noteworthy extracurricular activities (Atkinson, 2004). Throughout their lives, Millennials have been pushed and challenged to perform in school, extracurricular activities, and sports (Atkinson, 2004). Millennials are programmed by their parents with ambitious schedules of homework and extracurricular activities (Kroft, 2005). For the most part, Millennials have been successful in meeting these challenges. Nonetheless, if problems were encountered, Millennials have been conditioned to believe that Mom and Dad will come through with extra help in the form of extra coaching and tutoring (Atkinson, 2004).

Latino/a Millennials are much like their majority Millennial peers in that they strive to achieve great things and are ambitious. However, this success comes after having gone through a series of barriers and without the luxury of guidance from a parent who understands the U.S. culture, educational system, and, often, the language. Being compared to some of these "high-achieving" Millennials who have family backgrounds that are clearly different from Latino/a Millennials in the sample study revealed added pressures and a sense of an unequal playing field as Latino/as strived to be like their majority Millennial cohort. In this constant race to catch up, students in the study expressed pressure to perform and be above average.

Millennial Parents

Parenting style has been portrayed as a unique Millennial characteristic, primarily through parents' behavior, which has led to the label of "helicopter parents," depicting a high level of parent involvement and oversight (Wills, 2005). However, Latino/a students in the Pichardo (2006) study who reported growing up in a lower-income household stated that parents were not available to help them with academics during their K–12 education experiences nor were they involved in their college experiences. In an effort to adequately provide for their families, often both parents in a Latino/a household worked long hours, leaving them unable to give their children the time and attention that the majority Millennial helicopter parent could afford. Time was not the only factor in preventing parents from being more involved in their children's academic experiences. In Pichardo's (2006) focus groups, students talked about moral support from their parents in going to college to obtain a better way of life. Unfortunately, a lack of knowledge of the higher education system prevented parents from affording the luxuries to hover and to assume the role of helicopter parents. Likewise, Ortiz and Santos (2009) reported that, though students felt a great deal of support from their parents for their educational endeavors, their parents were often unable to provide assistance related to college challenges.

Generational Theory and the Future of Latino/a College Students

The peak of Millennial births was achieved in 1998, meaning that 2016 will be the height of Millennials entering college. Couple this with the rapid growth of the Latino/a population and it is likely that in a relatively short period of time, Latino/as will compose a large percentage of the college Millennial cohort. Generational theory advanced by Howe and Strauss (1991, 2000) and from Twenge (2006) has features that will also characterize future Latino/a college student growth and development. Although these authors may have different descriptions of generational theory, they do agree that age cohorts experience distinct societal cultures and trends, such as technology and world events, that come to define the experience of their generation. The perspective of *generational status*, a term used to describe the distance from the time of the family's move to the United States, shares some features of generational theory, but is not necessarily reliant on specific eras within time. Therefore, generational status related to time of immigration—the immigrant first generation, their children of the second generation, and the third generation—where all in the nuclear family were born in this country, forms the foundation for sharing common values, experiences, and interactions within mainstream society.

Howe and Strauss (1991, 2000) go further to assert that in the United States, generations have four personalities that repeat over time. Sociologists and demographers have found a similar trend among the first, second, third, and later generations when they study how immigrants change once they come to the United States (Alba, 1990; Portes & Rumbaut, 2006). In the case of generational status, the acculturative process produces characteristics that those of the same status share, such as taking on the values and practices of popular culture, the loss of the family's first language, the movement to less segregated living environments, or the tendency to intermarry among successive generations. It is typical that those of second and third generations (and beyond) take on *American* values, while Latino/a cultural values may diminish. Thus, perhaps what is more important than considering generational theory in working with contemporary and future Latino/a students is considering generational status from an immigration point of view.

Implications for Higher Education

The primary implication for higher education is to avoid applying stereotypes associated with Millennials to the Latino/a student population. In Pichardo's (2006) study, students felt significantly different from their generational cohort on nearly all seven of Howe and Strauss's Millennial characteristics. Although some characteristics may appear similar on a superficial level, as evidenced by our discussion in this chapter, a closer inspection reveals that contemporary Latino/a students differ in important ways. The impact of culture on Latino/a students means that family exerts a different influence on their college experiences, that teamwork connects with a cultural value for collectivism, and that experiences related to immigration and socioeconomic class (such as first generation in college status) impact their relationships with knowledge and are key considerations.

Constructivist Pedagogy

As previously mentioned, Millennials favor teamwork and other collaborative approaches. Translated into the learning environment, Carter (2009) and Wilson and Gerber (2008) proposed that constructivist learning activities, such as group projects, problem-centered learning, and active learning, are appropriate for Millennials. Carter argued that the notion of one expert distributing knowledge is contrary to their life experiences where multiple sources of knowledge via interpersonal relationships or the use of electronic media are common. Constructivist and collaborative learning approaches both support the Latino/a cultural value of collectivism and challenge the cultural value of respect for authority.

Activities such as group assignments and activities draw on Latino/a preferences for collaboration and collectivism. They may work well in groups by supporting their fellow students, feeling less of a need to draw attention to individual contributions, and may tend to avoid individual credit for the work of the group. They often find learning and producing in groups enjoyable and are supportive of aspects of their lives as students beyond the specific assignments. However, in our experiences, Latino/as can be hesitant to challenge group members or offer constructive feedback in either an effort to keep peace within the group or in response to differing status of students within the group, such as in working with older students.

Deference to elders and authorities can also contradict basic tenants of constructivist pedagogy. For example, professors who work to position themselves as one of several sources of knowledge or who design assignments or discussions that call students to become knowledge constructers can confuse Latino/a students who have been taught to respect and defer to authority. Care must be taken to assist Latino/as with this transition to new ways of knowing and learning.

Structure in the Learning Environment

Although seemingly contradictory to the notion of constructivist pedagogy, Millennials also have a strong need for structure in the learning environment (Wilson & Gerber, 2008). Assignments need to be structured clearly, with their purposes being made transparent. Syllabi need to clearly state expectations, policies, and procedures. This kind of structure fills a unique need for Latino/a students. Without a family history in higher education, first generation college students are often left to navigate college without experience or guidance. Thus, clear instructions and expectations help students decipher college norms and strive to meet them. Although Carter (2009) noted that Millennials favor trial and error as a learning strategy, Latino/a students who have limited models for college attendance already spend a good amount of time and energy figuring out how to "do college" and thus may feel a sense of relief when faculty take care to structure courses and assignments.

Faculty Accessibility

Faculty play an important roll in the college success of Latino/a students in their role as distributors of college capital that many of these students lack. Latino/a students, like the Millennials characterized in the literature, rely on "adults" to mentor and guide their progress, choosing to perform in ways that please rather than contradict values and conventions. It is important that faculty do not assume that Latino/a students know about the unspoken rules or shortcuts that may be common knowledge to students who come from families and communities with college-going histories. Therefore, it may be helpful to outline strategies to successfully complete assignments, break assignments into smaller pieces to reinforce time management and feedback loops, remind or inform students of important campus resources, and reassure students when content or assignments become difficult.

The last recommendation here is important because Latino/a students may not readily ask questions in class or talk with faculty or peers about their work, leaving them to assume that they are the only ones having difficulty. Laura Rendon's (1994) work on validation presented a key concept. Faculty need to be aware that validating students' work, recognizing the effort and knowledge that they bring to the classroom, is significant for student success. Likewise, they need to also be made acutely aware that harsh criticism without support or subtle messages about underperformance or poor performance can derail a student and ultimately result in attrition.

Support for Pressured Students

As cited earlier, Millennial students feel pressure to succeed and meet the expectations of the adults they desire to please. Latino/a students are also pressured students. Research has shown that Latino/as have experienced greater amounts of suicide ideation and other suicidal behavior (Del Pilar, 2008) compared to other groups, are more likely to have experienced depression, and are more likely to have been medicated for depression (Del Pilar, 2008). Significant for Latino/as is the acculturative stress that they feel as they traverse traditional cultures of their homes and the more Americanized culture of the higher educational systems and universities in particular. The psychological literature (e.g., De Melo & Farber, 2005; Gloria, Castellanos, Segure-Herrera, & Mayorga, 2010; Ishikawa, Cardemil, & Falmagne, 2010) is conflicting in determining if cultural barriers prevent Latino/as from seeking help. In fact, a recent study of community college students showed that enculturated students were more likely to seek help from mental health professionals (Ramos-Sanchez & Atkinson, 2009).

Conclusion

This chapter has illustrated important ways that Latino/a Millennials differ from the Millennial experience that has been more widely reported by studies of predominantly White college students. Although they also share characteristics, the ways in which Latino/s experience these, such as being sheltered, feeling pressured, or desiring to achieve, are unique. We have also discussed how higher education, particularly through faculty work in the classroom, can be more cognizant of how Latino/a students need further support. The lesson conveyed is that our widespread stereotypes of Millennial students may not reflect the predominant experience and needs of Latino/a students.

In addition to the effect of the Millennial stereotype on meeting Latino/a needs, faculty and student affairs personnel need to be aware of the impact of emphasizing Millennial characteristics in their work and vernacular. When Pichardo's (2006) study showed a clip of a focus group of Latino/a students featured on one of the *60 Minutes* stories on Millennials, students universally agreed that the depiction of students in the story showed little resemblance to their own lives, but they also agreed that many of the luxuries and characteristics discussed were ones they aspired to. Many even acknowledged that they were helping to "train" their siblings in this part of mainstream culture. This serves as an important caution. As educators of Latino/a students, it is important that we affirm their cultural background and that we promote the growth and maintenance of their ethnic identity. An abundance of psychological research shows that there are many positive outcomes of a strong ethnic identity. The idealization or promulgation of Millennial generation characteristics, as Pichardo showed, enacts a powerful assimilative pressure on students, one that has the potential to put valued cultural distinctions and important means for college success at risk.

References

Alba, R. D. (1990). *Ethnic identity: The transformation of White America*. New Haven, CT: Yale University Press.

Atkinson, M. L. (2004). *Advice for (and from) the young at heart: Understanding the millennial generation. Guidance and Counseling, 19*(4), 153–158.

Carnevale, A. P., & Fry, R. A. (2000). *Crossing the great divide: Can we achieve equity when generation Y goes to college?* Princeton, NJ: Educational Testing Service.

Carter, T. L. (2009). Millennial expectations and constructivist methodologies: Their corresponding characteristics and alignment. *Action in Teacher Education, 30*(3), 3–10.

Child Trends. (2011). Educational attainment (youth). Retrieved from www.child trendsdatabank.org/?q = node/163

Chronicle of Higher Education. (2008). *Almanac 2008–09*. Washington, DC: Author.

Coomes, M., & DeBard, R. (Eds.). (2004). *Serving the millennial generation. New Directions in Student Services*, No. 106.

Del Pilar, J. A. (2008). Mental health and Latino/a college students: A psychological perspective and new findings. *Journal of Hispanic Higher Education, 8*(3), 263–281.

De Melo, J. A. T., & Farber, B. A. (2005). Willingness to seek help for psychosocial problems among Latino and white American college students. *Psychological Reports, 97*(1), 50–52.

DeNavas-Walt, C., Proctor, B. D., & Smith, J. C. (2009). *Poverty, income, and health insurance coverage in the United States: 2008*. Washington, DC: U.S. Bureau of the Census.

Fairfax County Department of Systems Management for Human Services. (2000) *Demographic Reports 2001: Fairfax county department of systems management for human services*. A Report of the Urban Development Information System. Retrieved from http://www.fairfaxcounty.gov/government/about/

Fry, R., & Gonzales, F. (2008). One-in-five and growing fast: A profile of Hispanic public school students. A report from the Pew Hispanic Center, August 26, 2008. Washington, DC: Pew Hispanic Center.

Gloria, A. M., Castellanos, J., Segura-Herrera, T. A., & Mayorga, M. (2010). Assessing cultural orientation, cultural fit, and help-seeking attitudes of Latina undergraduates. *Journal of College Counseling, 13*(2), 126–140.

Howe, N., & Stauss, W. (1991). *Generations: The history of Americas future, 1584 to 2069*. New York: Morrow.

Howe, N., & Strauss, W. (2000). *Millennials rising: The next great generation*. New York: Vintage.

Howe, N., & Strauss, W. (2003). *Millennials go to college*. Great Falls, VA: American Association of Registrars and Admissions Officers and LifeCourse Associates.

Ishikawa, R. Z., Cardemil, E. V., & Falmagne, R. J. (2010). Help seeking and help receiving for emotional distress among Latino men and women. *Qualitative Health Research, 20*(11), 1558–1572.

Kaufman, P., Alt, M., & Chapman, C. (2001). *Drop out rates in the United States*. NCES 2002-114. Washington, DC: U.S. Department of Education, National Center for Education Statistics.

Kroft, S. (Correspondent). (2005). Echo boomers [Television series episode]. In F. L. Devine (Producer), *60 Minutes*. CBS Broadcasting.

Llagas, C. (2003). *Status and trends in the education of Hispanics*. NCES 2003–2008. Washington, DC: National Center for Education Statistics. Retrieved from http://nces.ed.gov/pubs2003/2003008.pdf

Lowery, J. W. (2001). The Millennials come to campus. *About Campus: Enriching the Student Learning Experience, 6*, 6–12.

Lowery, J. W. (2004). Student affairs for a new generation. In M. D. Coomes & R. DeBard (Eds.), *Serving the millennial generation* (pp. 87–99). San Francisco: Jossey-Bass.

Mortenson, T. (2002). *Higher education as private and social investment.* Presentation to the Key Bank Financing Conference, Feb. 15, Orlando, FL.

National Center for Education Statistics. (2000a). *The condition of education, 2000.* U.S. Department of Education. Washington, DC: Author.

National Center for Education Statistics. (2000b). *Income in the United States, 2002.* Washington, DC: U.S. Department of Education.

National Center for Education Statistics. (2001). Digest of education statistics, 2001 (NCES No. 2002130). Washington, DC: Author. (ERIC Document Reproduction Number ED455275)

Nevarez, C. (2001). *Mexican Americans and other Latinos in postsecondary education: Institutional influences.* Charleston, WV: ERIC Clearinghouse on Rural Education and Small Schools.

Nora, A., Rendón, L., & Cuadraz, G. (1999). Access, choice, and outcomes: A profile of Hispanic students in higher education. In A. Tashakkori & S. Ochoa (Eds.), *Reading of equal education: Vol. 16. Education of Hispanics in the United States: Politics, polices, and outcomes* (pp. 175–199). New York: AMS.

Ortiz, A. M., & Santos, S. J. (2009). *Ethnicity in college: Advancing theory and improving diversity practices on college campuses.* Sterling, VA: Stylus.

Pedersen, P. B., Draguns, J. G., Lonner, W. J., & Trimble, J. E. (2002). *Counseling across cultures* (5th ed.). Thousand Oaks, CA: Sage.

Pichardo, D. (2006). *Do characteristics of the Millennial generation fit Latino college students?* A thesis in partial fulfillment of the requirements for the master's degree. California State University, Long Beach.

Portes, A. P., & Rumbaut, R. G. (2006). *Immigrant America: A portrait* (3rd ed.). Berkeley, CA: University of California Press.

Ramos-Sanchez, L., & Atkinson, D. R. (2009). The relationships between Mexican American acculturation, cultural values, gender and help-seeking intentions. *Journal of Counseling and Development, 87,* 62–71.

Reisberg, L. (1999). To help Latino students, a college looks to parents. *Chronicle of Higher Education, 45,* A43–A44.

Rendón, L. (1994). Validating culturally diverse students: Toward a new model of learning and student development. *Innovative Higher Education, 19,* 33–51.

Rickes, P. C. (2009). Make way for Millennials! How today's students' are shaping higher education space. *Planning for Higher Education, 37*(2), 7–17.

Sabo, D. (2009). The gender gap in youth sports: Too many urban girls are being left behind. *Journal of Physical Education, Recreation and Dance, 80*(8), 35–37.

Swail, W. S., Redd, K., & Perna, L. W. (2003). *Retaining minority students in higher education: A framework for success.* ASHE-ERIC Reader, Vol. 30, No. 2. San Francisco, CA: Jossey-Bass.

Twenge, J. M. (2006). *Generation me: Why today's young Americans are more confident, assertive, entitled and more miserable than ever before.* New York: Free Press.

Wills, E. (2005). Parent trap. *Chronicle of Higher Education, 51*, 46.

Wilson, M., & Gerber, L. E. (2008). How generational theory can improve teaching: Strategics for working with the "Millennials." *Currents in Teaching and Learning, 1*(1), 29–44.

Zemke, R., Raines, C., & Filipczak, B. (2000). *Generations at work: Managing the clash of veterans, boomers, Xers, and nexters in your workplace.* New York: AMACOM.

PART FIVE

NATIVE AMERICAN MILLENNIALS IN COLLEGE

8

INDIGENOUS MILLENNIAL STUDENTS IN HIGHER EDUCATION

Bryan McKinley Jones Brayboy and Angelina E. Castagno

T he status of American Indian and Alaskan Native education is fundamentally different from that of other racialized groups; tribal nations and their citizens are unique in that they are not just a racialized group, but political or legal ones as well (Brayboy, 2005). American Indians and Alaskan Natives (hereafter referred to as Indigenous peoples, or students) are named in the U.S. Constitution twice, and the role of this legal relationship becomes important when examining educational issues (as well as health and other entitlements) for the group. In the process of signing 371 treaties, which were agreements between Indigenous nations and the U.S. government, in addition to over 5,000 congressional acts and executive orders, Indigenous peoples ceded 1 billion acres of land to the United States (Deyhle & Swisher, 1997). Many of these treaties and other laws, executive orders, and acts explicitly address Indigenous education by outlining specific provisions, while others offer broader notions of how the U.S. government would address the educational needs of Indigenous students. Importantly, Indigenous education is still largely connected to and, at least in part, funded by the U.S. government, which makes it fundamentally different from the public education experienced by every other racialized group (Lomawaima & McCarty, 2006).

To better highlight how this U.S.-tribal relationship is conceptualized by the federal government, at least on paper, it may be useful to turn to Executive Order 13336, signed on April 30, 2004, by President George W. Bush (which replaced a similar Executive Order [13096] signed by President Bill Clinton).

The order, in part, reads:

The United States has a unique legal relationship with Indian tribes and a special relationship with Alaska Native entities as provided in the Constitution of the United States, treaties, and Federal statutes. This Administration is committed to continuing work with these federally recognized tribal governments on a government-to-government basis, and supports tribal sovereignty and self-determination. It is the purpose of this order to assist American Indian and Alaska Native students in meeting the challenging academic standards of the No Child Left Behind Act of 2001 (Public Law 107-110) in a manner that is consistent with tribal traditions, languages, and culture.

This executive order goes on to outline how federal monies will be spent, with a focus on improving the academic achievement of American Indian children. It offers insight into the complicated political relationships that influence the academic achievement, at all levels, of Indigenous people in the United States.

This background is important in framing the remainder of the chapter, because it points to the unique relationship that Millennial Indigenous college students have with formal education. This chapter makes a fairly basic point: Many Millennial Indigenous students in higher education who successfully complete their degrees often do so in order to serve their communities and tribal nations (Brayboy, 2004, 2005; Shotton, Oosahwe, Star, & Cintrón, 2007; Waterman, 2004, 2007; Waterman and Arnold, 2010). I am not arguing here that this is exclusively true; rather, I am arguing that there is a continuing trend aimed at service, while recognizing that individuals—even while serving others—personally benefit from this work. The primary motivation appears to be assisting others, although it is clear that there are individual benefits. In the remainder of the chapter, I outline some of the themes found in the literature regarding Indigenous students in higher education, before moving into the political nature of attending higher education. The chapter ends with some potential recommendations for institutions interested in increasing the numbers of Indigenous graduates.

Basic Demographics and Background Information

According to preliminary analyses of the 2010 U.S. Census, American Indian/Alaskan Native peoples, representing over 560 different tribal nations, compose approximately 2% of the U.S. population. About two-thirds of these people now live off of reservation lands, which is a dramatic shift from several decades ago. And while American Indians have been deeply studied and examined at the K–12 level (Castagno & Brayboy, 2008; Deyhle & Swisher, 1997; Tippeconnic & Swisher, 1999), less is actually known about American Indians in higher education (Brayboy, Castagno, & Fann, under contract; Tierney, 1992). This chapter begins to frame what little we do know.

Contemporary Enrollment and Retention Patterns

Reliable statistics regarding Indigenous student participation in higher education are fairly difficult to obtain because of Indigenous students' low overall numbers and infrequent presence in national samples. All estimates agree, however, that Indigenous attendance and persistence in institutions of higher education are still well below the national averages (Brayboy, Castagno, & Fann, 2012; NCES, 2005a, 2005b). Furthermore, many more Indigenous students attend 2-year institutions and require financial aid as compared with White students (NCES, 2005a, 2005b). These conditions are made worse because most states with large populations of Indigenous students are economically poor—Montana, the Dakotas, and states in the Southwest, for example—so Native students are often encouraged through admission requirements and financial aid policies to attend 2-year institutions because they are less expensive than their 4-year counterparts.

It is important to note that generalizations about the achievement levels and experiences of Indigenous students are inherently problematic for at least two reasons. First, although generalizations about any large group of people are subject to error at the individual level, such errors are even more likely for generalizations made about Indigenous students because of significant differences between tribal nations, between urban and reservation communities, and between traditional and less traditional Indigenous students. Second, there is an enormous range and variation in Indigenous populations, with over 560 tribal nations, spread from Maine to Alaska, Florida to California. We recognize these variations, and at the same time, we believe we have some sense of shared characteristics among many Indigenous students in higher education.

This section presents the most recent data available on Indigenous college student enrollment, retention, and graduation rates. Although American Indians and Alaskan Natives compose almost 2% of the total U.S. population, they represent less than 1% of all students enrolled in institutions of higher education, and they earned approximately 0.7% of all associates', bachelor's, and advanced degrees conferred in 2002. Table 8.1 outlines the number of students enrolled in institutions of higher education (IHE) during the 2002–2003 academic year, along with the number of enrolled students who identified themselves as American Indian or Alaskan Native.

Over the past 35 years, the raw numbers of American Indians and Alaskan Natives enrolled in IHE have increased, although the overall percentages of Indigenous student enrollment have largely remained static (NCES, 2005a, 2005b; Pavel, 1998). Indigenous women make up 60.4% (100,200) of all Native students enrolled in colleges and universities, while Indigenous men compose 39.6% (65,700) of all Native students enrolled in colleges and universities in 2008. Although these gender issues cannot be discussed within the size constraints of this chapter, Brayboy has done so elsewhere (Brayboy 2006); the point here is that the college entrance and completion rates of all Indigenous students are in crisis. Researchers and policymakers must begin to address the larger structural issues that serve as barriers to all Indigenous people.

Given the extremely low rates of enrollment and graduation, it should not be surprising that much of the research describing the state of Indigenous students in college centers on either explaining why the graduation rates are low or outlining prescriptions for "fixing" the problem. Most of this research focuses on the individual student. However, there is some work that focuses on both the student and the larger structural barriers that influence the experiences of Indigenous college students (Brayboy, 2004, 2005; Shotton et al., 2007; Waterman, 2007). This research moves away from locating the lack of academic success in the student and instead examines the role of the institution and larger U.S. society in the problems encountered by Indigenous students. In what follows, I review both sets of literature. It is important to note, however, that I give far more credence to structural

TABLE 8.1
Enrollment in Institutes of Higher Learning in 2002–2003

Type of Enrollment	Overall Enrollment	American Indian/ Alaskan Native
Total for all institutes of higher learning	16,611,700	165,900 (0.99% of total)
Undergraduate	14,257,100	151,700 (1.06% of total)
Graduate	2,035,700	11,900 (0.58% of total)
Professional	319,000	2,200 (0.69% of total)

Source: NCES, 2005a.

explanations, even though there are many more studies that rely on individual explanations. I have grouped this discussion under five categories: academic preparation, role models, cultural incongruities, finances, and other institutional barriers

Academic Preparation

The educational pipeline[1] is fraught with perils for Indigenous students. Researchers have argued that a lack of proper academic preparation means that Indigenous students cannot be academically successful in rigorous college environments (Benally, 2004; Greene & Foster, 2003). Unfortunately, much of the research continues to "blame the victim" by highlighting the "failure" of Indigenous students to work hard and prepare themselves for IHE. There is little value in these studies because of their reliance on deficit models and culturally irrelevant and inappropriate research methods and assumptions. Many of these studies also fail to address the fact that many Indigenous students enter college not for themselves, but to serve their community needs. Waterman's (2004, 2007) and Brayboy's (2004, 2005) work highlights the fact that many Indigenous students will not "integrate" into the social or academic contexts in ways that past research says is vital for success, although Shotton et al. (2007) made a compelling case for how students might integrate into institutions. Instead, the students in the Waterman and Brayboy studies are more likely to strategically accommodate—or make adjustments and integrate where it makes sense for their longer-term success and abilities to serve their communities—and make strategic choices in order to "make it through" the institution toward their larger goals of community assistance. Researchers also point to the lack of accessible information about college eligibility requirements and college preparation (Fann, 2005, 2009; Guillory & Wolverton, 2008).

Keeping these themes in mind, we cannot ignore the vast amount of quantitative data that indicate Indigenous students achieve far below their peers on standardized measures of success. Table 8.2 highlights the percentages of youth who have neither a high school diploma nor are currently enrolled in high school. Indigenous students are twice as likely to be out of high school and without a degree as their White peers.

Putting this into stark words, Tierney, Sallee, and Venegas (2007) noted:

> In 2001, about 52 percent of American Indian students graduated from high school as opposed to a national average of about 68 percent. Of those students who graduated, only about 17 percent attended a postsecondary institution—less than half the national average. (p. 16)

TABLE 8.2
Percentages of 16- to 19-Year-Olds Not Enrolled in School and Without a High School Diploma

Racial Groups	Not Enrolled and Without High School Diploma (%)
American Indian/Alaskan Natives	16.1
African Americans	11.7
Latinas/os	21.2
Asian Americans	4.0
Whites	8.2

Source: U.S. Census Bureau, 2000.

These statistics are striking, and it is important to keep in mind that there is significant variation between states and tribal nations. American Indians and Alaskan Natives are at least twice as likely to be considered "below basic" than their White peers, and 5 times less likely to be "advanced" in reading at both the fourth- and eighth-grade levels (Grigg, Moran, & Kuang, 2010); the story is equally distressing for mathematics at these two grade levels. Indigenous students are almost 3 times as likely as their White peers to test "below basic" at fourth-grade and more than twice as likely to test "below basic" in eighth-grade mathematics (Grigg et al., 2010). In 2002, less than 2,000 Indigenous students took an advanced placement exam—a number that is less than one-half a percentage of the total number of students taking these exams (College Board, 2005). Also in 2002, Indigenous students averaged 25 points lower than the national average on the SAT verbal exam and 33 points lower on the SAT math exam (College Board, 2005). These statistics provide further indication of the poor academic preparation many Indigenous students are receiving at the high school level. The pipeline begins to leak early, and it appears to leak often.

By the time most students reach high school, their paths have been laid out for them and the likelihood of their entering college is essentially a foregone conclusion (Fann, 2005). College eligibility requirements vary by state and institutional type; generally, however, minimum eligibility requirements for 4-year colleges and universities require 4 years of college prep English, 3 years of advanced math (Algebra I and above), 2 years of laboratory science, 2 years of a language other than English (and students whose first language is their tribal language do not meet this requirement), and 2 years of social sciences. According to Fann, what is crucial is that Indigenous students have access to the necessary courses for college eligibility and timely access to college counseling and information about what is needed to be eligible. There is evidence that in many states, high schools that serve large populations of students of color, and specifically Indigenous students, do not offer the requisite number of courses to get students college eligible. In California, for example, only 16% of Indigenous students graduate from high school with "college ready transcripts" (Greene & Foster, 2003). Additionally, Indigenous students are, nationally, the least likely group to complete AP courses in high school (Benally, 2004). As a result, many Indigenous students are either prevented from entering into the college pipeline—and, as a result, are diverted to other areas of focus—or they are insufficiently fueled to make it to college.

There are a number of college preparatory programs that have sought to ensure that more students of color receive a postsecondary education. The U.S. Department of Education TRIO programs nationwide serve approximately 4% Indigenous students. This percentage is fairly consistent across all six TRIO programs (Educational Opportunity Programs, Talent Search, Student Support Services, McNair Post-Baccalaureate Achievement, Upward Bound, and Upward Bound Math and Science). It is imperative that more American Indians and Alaskan Natives gain access to these programs. Nationwide, the Gaining Early Awareness and Readiness for Undergraduate Programs (GEAR UP) state-operated programs served 1,483,763 total students during the 2004–2005 year, and American Indians and Alaskan Natives composed 37,976 (James Davis, personal communication, January 9, 2006). In 2006, then, GEAR UP programs served approximately 2.6% American Indian or Alaskan Native students. Both the TRIO and the GEAR UP programs have recently come under scrutiny by the U.S. Congress and their funding appears to be constantly in jeopardy. It continues to be imperative that these programs serve students who need their services and that they meet the needs of more American Indian and Alaskan Native students.

Finances

College Horizons is a precollege workshop specifically for Indigenous students. Over 85% of students participating in College Horizons received their bachelor's degree within 5 years of their high school graduation. According to their website, the 5-day "crash courses" help students select suitable colleges, complete competitive applications, gain test-prep skills, and navigate financial aid and scholarship information. Additionally, according to their director, College Horizons currently serves "1,800 high school students and 500 college/college graduates" (Carmen Lopez, personal communication, November 2, 2010). In 2010, College Horizons served 234 Indigenous students (enrolled tribal members only) who were currently either juniors or seniors in high school; these students came from 26 states and 66 tribal nations. Approximately 47% of the students were first-generation college students and only 36% were men (Carmen Lopez, personal communication, November 2, 2010).

Clearly, the educational pipeline is a major area of concern related to American Indian and Alaskan Native participation in and completion of higher education. Educational policies and practices that only focus on institutions of higher education will not have a significant impact unless they are paired with reform at the K–12 level.

Role Models

Because so few Indigenous students graduate from college and fewer actually attend and graduate from graduate school, there are few Indigenous faculty in institutions of higher education (Bransford, 1982; Brayboy, 2006; Cross, 1991; Edwards, Edwards, Dairies, & Reed, 1984; Haviland, Horswill, O'Connell, & Dynneson, 1983; Hurlburt, Gade, & McLaughlin, 1990; Kleinfield, Cooper, & Kyle, 1987; Shotton et al., 2007; Stein, 1995). Consistent with the changes in enrollment numbers and degrees conferred between Indigenous men and women in recent years, Pavel (1998) reported that between 1983 and 1993, the percentage change for Indigenous full-time faculty was 37%; it was 9% for men and 77% for women. Although Indigenous men and women have a higher representation in the full-time faculty of institutions of higher education than they did 30 years ago, their numbers are still not proportional to their percentage in the overall population of the United States. A 2005 NCES report states that in 2001, Indigenous peoples composed 0.5% of the full-time instructional faculty rank; during that year, they made up .9% of instructors, 0.5% of assistant professors, 0.4% of associate professors, and 0.3% of professors. During this same time, Indigenous peoples composed approximately 1.8% of the total U.S. population.

A number of scholars have noted the important role Indigenous faculty and staff play in the success of Indigenous students in higher education (Shotton et al., 2007; Waterman, 2007). Pavel and Padilla (1993) noted that one crucial factor in Indigenous student persistence is attaining social integration with faculty on campus. Similarly, Jackson, Smith, and Hill (2003) found that Indigenous students identified faculty and staff warmth as an important factor in their success in institutions of higher education. Shotton et al. (2007) added a similar take on peer mentoring, noting that having peer mentors can be useful in the retention of Native students. Tippeconnic Fox (2005) summarized this work well:

> Although acknowledging that students benefit from a good relationship with any teacher, Swisher and Tippeconnic (1999) emphasize that if the teacher happens to be Native American and a good teacher, the relationship is often enhanced. Though they were referring specifically to K–12 teachers, we might extend the thought to higher education as well. Stein (2003, p. 49) on faculty in tribal colleges states, "Indigenous instructors can, in addition to being good teachers, be wonderful role models for the local Indigenous students." In her study of Native American completers in a tribal college, Ness (2002) also found the importance of hiring qualified Native American faculty and staff to promote a welcoming atmosphere and provide role models for Native American students. Bergstrom, Cleary, and Peacock (2003, p. 171) state, "Native teachers have an easier time figuring out what is needed than teachers who are culturally different from the students they teach. What Native teachers have over non-Native teachers is experience with many of the same issues Native youth now confront on a daily basis." Tippeconnic and McKinney (2003) state that one strategy for recruiting and retaining Native American students is to recruit, retain, and promote more Native American faculty because they serve as role models and work with Native American students to ensure academic success. (p. 51)

It remains a truism that in order to have academic role models, there must be individuals who complete their college degrees and advanced degrees that allow them to become faculty members. Keeping the pipeline open and operable is a key component to the process. The lack of role models will continue to persist as long as the college-going and completion rates for Indigenous students suffer. The attainment of advanced degrees is the driest area of the pipeline for American Indians and Alaskan Natives, and it is an area that must be addressed.

Cultural Differences

The differences between life at and in universities and at "home" on reservations, urban areas, or other highly concentrated pockets of Indigenous people can be dramatic (Brayboy 2004, 2005; Waterman, 2007). The differences between these lives is perhaps the most studied area in educational research on Indigenous students (Browne & Evans, 1987; Carroll, 1978; Lin, LaCounte, & Eder, 1988; Scott, 1986; St. Germain, 1995). Many scholars draw on cultural difference theories for understanding the low educational attainment of students of color at predominantly White colleges. Watson, Terrell, and Wright (2002), for example, found that the "notions of the ideal institutional environment" for minority students was "often at odds with many traditional institutional environments" (p. 91). Similarly, a common theme in the literature about Indigenous students in mainstream institutions of higher education is the overwhelming cultural discontinuity that often exists between the Native students and the culture of the institution (Brayboy 2004, 2005; Guillory &Wolverton, 2008; Shotton et al., 2007; Waterman and Arnold, 2010). The stories compiled from Indigenous graduates of Dartmouth by Garrod and Larimore (1997) illustrate the dissonance felt by many students. From learning the "correct" way to make appointments with college administrators (Bray, 1992), to hearing harshly spoken words (Worl, 1992), to setting aside cooperation for individualism and competition (Adams, 1992), there are often multiple and various cultural differences between Indigenous students and mainstream universities. These factors appear to be true with Indigenous students in college post-2000 (e.g., Brayboy & Maughn, 2009; Shotton et al., 2007; Waterman, 2007).

Other scholars focus on the competing worldviews and conceptions of legitimate knowledge and argue that these differences impact how Indigenous students experience college (Brown, 2000; Carney, 1999; Fixico, 1995). Donald Fixico, for example, notes the following:

> In the educational process of American Indian students attending mainstream schools, students are compelled to understand or perceive everything from the mainstream point of view. But the instructor should be cognizant that traditional Indian youths also possess a Native perspective that is likely incongruent with mainstream thinking. For these students, they are learning in an alien culture. This unacknowledged and unaccounted for conflict between perspectives has resulted in many Indian students doing poorly in school and dropping out. (1995, p. 71)

According to Fixico, and others, our schools fail to recognize how Indigenous students' perceptions, values, and worldviews might be different from those of the majority. In a similar vein, Gilmore, Smith, and Kairaiuak

(1997) argued that "the institution views students as individuals; the students, in contrast, view themselves as part of a connected web of family and community" (p. 95). They go on to describe how the incompatible notions about the very nature and purpose of higher education cause clash between Indigenous students and the institution. As an example, they explain how "the need to separate facts from values or feelings and to make decisions on the basis of facts alone" (p. 95) is one of the tenets of the positivism that characterizes Western institutions. Unfortunately, they argued, this epistemology "seriously clashes" with the Alaskan aboriginal society in which they conducted their research.

We learn, then, that multiple and fundamental cultural discontinuities exist between many Indigenous students' cultures and the culture of their college or university (for other discussions see Brayboy, 2004, 2005; Guillory & Wolverton, 2009; Shotton et al., 2007; Waterman, 2007). Some scholars believe that this cultural dissonance is especially prevalent for Indigenous students. Because some Indigenous students come to the university after having spent their entire childhood in a community of Indigenous people separated from the mainstream White community, the likelihood that these students will experience more acute cultural differences is high (Brayboy, 2004). Tierney (1992) explicated the general point of all these arguments well when he stated:

> The point here is straightforward: for Indian students their cultural background frames their understanding and action of education in a manner fundamentally different from that of White students. Their perceptions of home and family create stronger allegiances than that of educational opportunities that appear elusive and contradictory. The opportunities are elusive because of the hurdles Indian students must overcome, and they are contradictory because their perception is that the world they come from, and the one for which education prepares them, are oppositional. Students have dreams, but they do not fit into the framework of mainstream institutions. If students are to survive, then it appears as if they will have to either alter their dreams or look elsewhere to fulfill them. (p. 81)

But who are these studies talking about? Is it really possible that all Indigenous students who attend mainstream postsecondary institutions experience such cultural dissonance with the dominant cultures of their schools?

The majority of the studies on American Indian higher education seem to be based on Indigenous students from rural or reservation communities. The studies talk about the cultural dissonance felt by these students and make it seem as if *all* Indigenous students were coming from these more traditional backgrounds. Although this research is important, it seems to ignore the experiences of students who are from urban or suburban predominantly White communities. In *American Indians and the Urban Experience*, Lobo and Peters (2001) argued that limited information exists on urban Indigenous peoples because of the widespread assumption that Native people reside in rural settings and the tendency of academics (and especially anthropologists) is to focus on rural communities. Lobo and Peters's argument is important to keep in mind in the analyses of Indigenous participation in institutions of higher education because significant numbers of students are coming from these communities and are often more assimilated than the extant literature would have us believe. In two different qualitative studies of Indigenous students in colleges, for example, students indicated a range of identities among Indigenous students—some of whom were very assimilated or less culturally connected, and others who were very much connected to their tribal nations and cultures (Brayboy, 2004, 2005; Castagno, 2003).

In sum, based on the studies examined, there are a number of issues that appear to be commonly cited as potential pitfalls for the successful negotiation of institutions of higher education by Indigenous students. First, Indigenous students are often viewed as placing a premium on cooperation when competition is valued in universities (Brayboy, 2005; Waterman, 2007). Individual-centered students do well at universities, but many Native students are more community centered; hence, they do not perform as well as non-Indigenous students. Indigenous students tend to fare well in small group settings or in one-on-one encounters; at most universities these types of interactions are limited. More recently, Brayboy (2004, 2005) and Waterman (2004, 2007) have found that those students who are focused on completion so that they can give back to their communities are more successful in completing college than their peers who are focused solely on themselves and individual achievement. Those students who are trained to be aggressive and orally combative fare well in some university settings, but when they do so, it appears to be part of the strategic accommodation we noted earlier (Brayboy, 2005). The academic aggression necessary to succeed is anathema to many Indigenous ways of being, so many students resort to silence in the classrooms. Ultimately, the price of silence is great among Indigenous students. There is contradictory evidence that shows that students who are more "traditional" or "bicultural" do worse in college because of the incongruities (Carroll, 1978), and others who argue that these students actually perform better in schools (Barnhardt, 1998; Brayboy, 2004, 2005; Kirkness & Barnhardt, 1991; Shotton et al., 2007; Waterman, 2007).

Institutional Barriers

Although Tierney (1992) and others (Shotton et al., 2007; Waterman, 2007) have criticized the use of Tinto's (1975, 1986) model of student departure in scholarship on Indigenous higher education, the model continues to be relevant among others (Garrod & Larrimore, 1997). But there are at least two alternative models developed to specifically explain Indigenous students' experiences in institutions of higher education. Heavy Runner and DeCelles (2002) developed the family education model (FEM) to explain student retention for Indigenous students better than more traditional models (i.e., Tinto's theory of student departure, Austin's [2005] theory of involvement, and Pascarella's [1991] general model for assessing change). The FEM is Indigenous based and suggests that universities ought to re-create the extended family structure within institutional settings in order to enhance Indigenous students' feelings of belonging and support. McAfee (1997, 2000) offered another model, and her work reminds us that statistics about degrees earned may be unreliable because the majority of Indigenous college students will have at least one "stepping out" experience sometime in their college careers. She uses the concept of "stepping out" rather than "dropping out" because she argues it is more accurate to portray Indigenous college attendance in terms of stepping stones; those who were successful and eventually earned a degree in her study were able to find the needed stepping stones to navigate the institution.

> Each stepping stone is identified with positive factors that kept students in school or brought them back into higher education, and with negative factors that served to pull them out and kept them disengaged from higher education. . . . However, no particular stepping-stone is singularly necessary and sufficient for the participants [in her research] to remain in school. (McAfee, 2000, p. 3)

The stepping-stones she identifies are cultural identity, academic preparation, financial resources, motivation, family support, academic performance, alcohol and drug use, and institutional interface; she notes that cultural identity was the most prominent factor that emerged from her research.

At the heart of these issues is the manner in which institutions operate and the ways in which classrooms are run. Is there room in institutions for students who quietly do their work? Are there different ways to negotiate the institution and maintain a connection to other cultural ways of being? The qualitative studies cited throughout this chapter agree that students can, and do, accommodate and often do so strategically. An important question that arises from an examination of these studies is whether institutions can do thorough, honest assessments of their campus climates. Are the institutions hostile to other ways of thinking and interacting? Is the institution welcoming to divergent viewpoints, and is there a place for Indigenous students to engage in schooling in ways that are comfortable for them? These are questions that institutions must be asking themselves as they work toward recruiting Indigenous students into their ranks.

Conclusion

We cannot ignore the statistics that continue to tell us that Indigenous students are not well served by mainstream institutions of higher education. We believe that institutions of higher education need to do a much better job of recruiting and retaining Indigenous students at both the undergraduate and graduate levels. Success along these paths is critical for the health of tribal nations, the pursuit of self-determination, and the realization of educational equity within the United States. And yet at the same time, institutions of higher education must also come to acknowledge that Indigenous students and communities may not always be interested in pursuing "success" in the same ways or for the same reasons as others. Institutions of higher education, leaders within colleges and universities, policymakers, and faculty and staff must be able to hold these two points in constant, and creative, tension if the goal is to truly better serve Indigenous students and communities. As Austin (2005) noted, if institutions of higher education were more knowledgeable about the unique political status of Indigenous people and nations, they would better understand students and the institution's responsibility toward Indigenous students and communities. She notes:

> Leaders of American Indian tribes have unique expectations when it comes to higher education for their students. They want American Indian students to soak up Western knowledge, place that knowledge within the context of their cultures and languages, and return home to better their

communities. Tribal expectations cannot be fulfilled unless American Indian students remain in college. (p. 43)

Tribal nations can especially benefit from Indigenous students with advanced degrees in medicine, law, education, business, agriculture, administration, engineering, and language and culture preservation. And institutions benefit from the presence of these students because they bring their experiences, and ways of engaging the world, to the classrooms and college campus.

Note

1. We understand that the very use of the concept of pipeline can be problematic, because it can appear to be deterministic, one-way, or too simplistic. And, yet, we know that for Indigenous Millennial students, the earlier years of their academic formation was very important for their academic successes (Brayboy, 2004, 2005; Shotton et al., 2007).

References

Adams, N. (1992). My grandmother and the snake. In A. Garrod & C. Larrimore (Eds.), *First person, first peoples: Native American college graduates tell their life stories* (pp. 93-114). Ithaca, NY: Cornell University Press.

Austin, R. (2005). Perspectives of American Indian nation parents and leaders. *New Directions for Student Services, 109*, 41–48.

Barnhardt, R. (1998). Teaching/Learning across cultures: Strategies for success. *Alaska Native Knowledge Network* (www.ankn.uaf.edu), University of Alaska Fairbanks. http://ankn.uaf.edu/Curriculum/Articles/RayBarnhardt/TLAC.html

Benally, S. (2004). *Serving American Indian students: Participation in accelerated learning opportunities.* Report from the Western Interstate Commission for Higher Education, http://www.wiche.edu/pub/15149

Bergstrom, A., Cleary, L., & Peacock, T.D. (2003). *The seventh generation: Native students speak about finding the good path.* Charleston, WV: AEL.

Bransford, J. (1982). To be or not to be: Counseling American Indian clients. *Journal of American Indian Education, 21*(3), 18–22.

Bray, B. (1992). Refuse to kneel. In A. Garrod & C. Larimore (Eds.), *First person, first peoples: Native American college graduates tell their life stories* (pp. 27–40). Ithaca, NY: Cornell University Press.

Brayboy, B. (2004). Hiding in the ivy: American Indian students and visibility in elite educational settings. *Harvard Educational Review, 74*(2), 125–152.

Brayboy, B. M. (2005). Transformational resistance and social justice: American Indians in Ivy League universities. *Anthropology and Education Quarterly, 36*(3), 193–211.

Brayboy, B. M. J. (2006). Indigenous men in higher education. commissioned by the Dellums Commission and the Joint Center on Economic and Political Studies. Washington, DC. Retrieved June 16, 2011 from http://jc.lux.r2integrated.com/sites/default/files/upload/research/files/FullBrayBoy%20-%2025%20pages.pdf

Brayboy, B. M. J, Castagno, A. E., & Fann. A. (under contract; expected 2012). *Postsecondary education for American Indian and Alaska Native students: Higher education toward nation building and self-determination.* San Francisco: Jossey Bass.

Brayboy, B. M. J., & Maughn, E. L. (2009). Indigenous knowledges and the story of the bean. *Harvard Educational Review, 79*(1), 1–21.

Brown, L. D. (2000). *American Indians in higher education: One student's story.* Unpublished dissertation, Iowa State University, Ames, Iowa.

Brown, D. B., & Evans, W. H. (1987). *Native Americans in higher education.* ERIC Clearinghouse (ERIC Document Reproduction Service No. ED299082).

Carney, C. M. (1999). *Native American higher education in the United States.* New Brunswick: Transaction Publishers.

Carroll, R. E. (1978). Academic performance and cultural marginal. *Journal of American Indian Education, 18*(1), 11–16.

Castagno, A. (2003). *(Re)Contextualizing Indian higher education: A qualitative study of Indigenous women at a predominantly White university.* Unpublished master's thesis, University of Wisconsin, Madison.

Castagno, A. E. & Brayboy, B. M. J. (2008). Culturally responsive schooling for Indigenous youth: A review of the literature. *Review of Educational Research 78(4): 941-993.*

College Board. (2005). *Advanced placement program, National summary report, 1999-2003.* Washington, DC: Author.

Cross, W. T. (1991). Pathway to the professoriate: the American Indian faculty pipeline. *Journal of American Indian Education, 30*(2), 13–24.

Deyhle, D., & Swisher, K. (1997). Research in American Indian and Alaska Native education: From assimilation to self-determination. *Review of Research in Education, 22*, 113–194.

Edwards, D., Edwards, M., Dairies, G., & Reed, S. (1984). Modeling: An important ingredient in higher education for American Indian women students. *Journal of the National Association for Women Deans, Administrators, and Counselors, 48*, 31–35.

Fann, A. (2005). *Forgotten students: American Indian high school student narratives on college access.* Unpublished dissertation. Los Angeles: University of California, Los Angeles.

Fann, A. (2009). The state of the field of American Indian and Alaska Native postsecondary access: A review of data and literature. Prepared for the United States Department of Education Office of Indian Education. On file with authors.

Fixico, D. (1995). American Indians (The minority of minorities) and higher education. In B. Bowser, T. Jones, & G. A. Young (Eds.), *Toward the multicultural university* (pp. 103–124). Westport, CT: Praeger.

Garrod, A., & Larimore, C. (1997). *First person, first peoples: Native American college graduates tell their life stories.* Ithaca, NY: Cornell University Press.

Gilmore, P., Smith, D., & Kairaiuak, A. (1997). Resisting diversity: An Alaskan case of institutional struggle. In M. Fine, L. Weis, L. Powell, & M. Wong (Eds.), *Off white: Readings on race, power, and society* (pp. 90–99). New York: Routledge.

Greene, J., & Foster, G. (2003). *Public high school graduation rates in the United States.* Education Working Paper 3. Manhattan: Center for Civic Innovation at the Manhattan Institute.

Grigg, W., Moran, R., & Kuang, M. (2010). *National Indian education study—Part I: Performance of American Indian and Alaska Native Students at Grades 4 and 8 on NAEP 2009 reading and mathematics assessments* (NCES 2010–462). Washington, DC: National Center for Education Statistics, Institute of Education Sciences, U.S. Department of Education.

Guillory, R. M., & Wolverton, M. (2008). It's about family: Native American student persistence in higher education. *Journal of Higher Education, 79*(1), 58–87.

Haviland, M., Horswill, R., O'Connell, J., & Dynneson, V. (1983). Native American college students' preference for counselor race and sex and the likelihood of their use of a counseling center. *Journal of Counseling Psychology, 30,* 267–270.

Heavy Runner, I., & DeCelles, R. (2002). Family education model: Meeting the student retention challenge. *Journal of American Indian Education, 41*(2), 29–37.

Hurlburt, G., Gade, E., & McLaughlin, G. (1990). Teaching attitudes and study attitudes of Indian education students. *Journal of American Indian Education, 29*(3), 12–18.

Jackson, A., Smith, S., & Hill, C. (2003). Academic persistence among Native American college students. *Journal of College Student Development, 44*(4), 548–565.

Kirkness, V., & Barnhardt, R. (1991). First nations and higher education: The four R's—respect, relevance, reciprocity, responsibility. *Journal of American Indian Education, 30*(3), 1–15.

Kleinfield, J., Cooper, J., Kyle, N. (1987). Postsecondary counselors: A model for increasing Native Americans' college success. *Journal of American Indian Education, 27*(1), 9–16.

Lin, R. L., LaCaunte, D., & Eder, J. (1988). A study of Native American students in a predominantly White college. *Journal of American Indian Education, 27*(3), 8–15.

Lobo, S., & Peters, K. (Eds.). (2001). *American Indians and the urban experience.* Walnut Creek, CA: Altamira Press.

Lomawaima, K. T., & McCarty, T. (2006). *To remain an Indian: Lessons in democracy from a century of Native American education.* New York: Teachers College Press.

McAfee, M. *From their voices: American Indians in higher education and the phenomenon of stepping out.* Unpublished dissertation, Colorado State University, Fort Collins, Colorado.

McAfee, M. (2000). From their voices: American Indians in higher education and the phenomenon of stepping out. *Research News on Graduate Education, 2*(2), 1–10.

National Center for Education Statistics (NCES). (2005a). *Enrollment in postsecondary institutions, fall 2002 and financial statistics, fiscal year 2002.* Retrieved from http://nces.ed.gov/pubsearch/pubsinfo.asp?pubid = 2005168

National Center for Education Statistics (NCES). (2005b). *Enrollment in postsecondary institutions, Fall 2003; Graduation rates 1997 and 2000 cohorts; and Financial Statistics, fiscal year 2003.* Retrieved from http://nces.ed.gov/pubsearch/pubs info.asp?pubid = 2005177

Ness, J.E. (2002). Crossing the finish line: American Indian completers and non-completers in a tribal college. *Tribal College Journal, 13*(4), 36–39.

Pascarella, E. (1991). The impact of college on students: The nature of the evidence. *Review of Higher Education, 14,* 453–466.

Pavel, D. M. (1998). *American Indians and Alaska Natives in postsecondary education.* Washington, DC: U.S. Department of Education Office of Educational Research and Improvement National Center for Education Statistics.

Pavel, M., & Padilla, R. (1993). American Indian and Alaska Native postsecondary departure: An example of assessing a mainstream model using national longitudinal data. *Journal of American Indian Education, 32*(2), 1–23.

Scott, W. J. (1986). Attachment to Indian culture and "difficult situation": A study of American Indian college students. *Youth and Society, 17,* 381–395.

Shotton, H. J., Oosahwe, E., Star, L., & Cintrón, R. (2007). Stories of success: Experiences of American Indian students in a peer-mentoring retention program. *Review of Higher Education, 31*(1), 81–107.

St. Germain, R. (1995). Drop-out rates among American Indian and Alaska Native students: Beyond cultural discontinuity. ERIC Digest. Retrieved from http://www.ericdigests.org/1996-2/indian.html

Stein, W. (1994). The survival of American Indian faculty: Thought and action. *National Education Association Higher Education Journal, 10,* 101–114.

Stein, W. J. (1995). The survival of American Indian faculty. *Thought and Action, 10*(1), 101–113.

Swisher, K. G., & Tippeconnic III, J. W. (1999). *Next steps: Research and practice to advance Indian education.* Charleston, WV: ERIC Clearinghouse on Rural Education and Small Schools. (ERIC Document Reproduction Service No. ED 427 909).

Tierney, W. (1992). *Official encouragement, institutional discouragement: Minorities in Academe—The Native American experience.* Norwood, NJ: Ablex.

Tierney, W., Sallee, M., & Venegas, K. (2007, Fall). Access and financial aid: How American Indian students pay for college. *Journal of College Admission, 197,* 14–23.

Tinto, V. (1975). Dropout from higher education: A theoretical synthesis of recent research. *Review of Educational Research, 45*(1), 89-125.

Tinto, V. (1986). *Leaving college: Rethinking the causes and cures of student attrition.* (ERIC Document Reproduction Service No. ED283416). Illinois.

Tippeconnic Fox, M. (2005). Voices from within: Native American faculty and staff on campus. *New Directions for Student Services, 109*, 49–59.

Tippeconnic, III, J. W., & McKinney, S. (2003). Native faculty: Scholarship and development. In M. K. P. Ah Nee-Benham & W. J. Stein (Eds.), The renaissance of American Indian higher education: Capturing the dream (pp. 241–256). Mahwah, NJ: Erlbaum.

U.S. Census (2010). http://2010.census.gov/2010census/popmap/, last accessed June 21, 2011.

Waterman, S. J. (2004) *The Haudenosaunee college experience: A complex path to degree completion.* Unpublished doctoral dissertation, Syracuse University, Syracuse, New York.

Waterman, S. (2007). A complex path to Haudenosaunee degree completion. *Journal of American Indian Education, 46*(1), 20–40.

Waterman, S.J., & Arnold, P.P. (2010). The Haudenosaunee flag raising: Cultural symbols and intercultural contact. *Journal of American Indian Education, 49* (1&2), 125–144.

Watson, L., Terrell, M., Wright, D., Bonner II, F. A., Caviet, M. J., Gold, J., . . . Person, D. R. (2002). *How minority students experience college: Implications for planning and policy.* Sterling, VA: Stylus.

Worl, R. (1992). A Tlingit brother of Alpha Chi. In A. Garrod & C. Larimore (Eds.), *First person, first peoples: Native American college graduates tell their life stories* (pp. 64–79). Ithaca, NY: Cornell University Press.

9

NATIVE AMERICAN MILLENNIAL COLLEGE STUDENTS

Stephanie J. Waterman

What humankind has done is develop history
and culture, and it becomes incumbent on those
whose work it is to educate to understand both.

(Coomes, 2004, p. 29)

One highly visible way in which Millennial students differ from earlier students is their racial
and ethnic diversity.

(Broido, 2004, p. 73)

istorical events and culture are necessary constructs when discussing Native American college students because of our unique history and distinctive Indigenous cultures. For instance, because of
the Indian Gaming Regulatory Act (IGRA) of 1988, this generation of students has always lived with gaming. Other Millennial students are not subject to this act. A useful way to enter the discussion and gain a broader
understanding about Native American college students is through the historical perspective. Native American history is often overlooked or relegated to
two units in secondary school. Native Americans are also the most diverse
group among the diverse. This chapter uses the framework of history, culture, and diversity to explore the college experiences of Native American
Millennial students.

This chapter does not, however, include Asian Pacific and Alaskan Native experiences. I, as one who lives on the mainland and has not researched Asian Pacific Islanders and Alaskan Natives, do not feel I can speak for them. I apologize for this omission, but I would rather omit than misrepresent. The term *Native American* will be used in this chapter because I come from a region (the northeast) where that is the accepted term. In other parts of the United States, American Indian is acceptable. Most Native people prefer to be called by their nation or tribe name, for example, Apache, Navajo, or Mohawk. For the purposes of this chapter *Native American* will be the term used most often.

The chapter begins with historical factors that impact Native Millennial students today such as the aforementioned IGRA of 1988. Cultural influences such as the importance of family and students' desire to give back to their communities are presented. Next, the sheer diversity of this population is presented, followed by recommendations and a summary and conclusions.

Millennial college students have been defined as those born after 1982 (Coomes & DeBard, 2004), and that is the assumption behind this chapter. However, any discussion of Native American education must begin with the past—an introduction to the boarding school era.

Boarding School Era

Other populations in the United States have experienced oppression and marginalization. But for Native Americans, their forced removal from homelands, by military force or deceptive means; the illness sometimes purposely introduced; the denial of history in textbooks and school curriculums; the hostility often in the form of violence; the high rate of suicide; and the presence, acceptance, and celebration of Native American mascots have contextual implications for these college students regardless of their ages.

Although the boarding school era formally began in the 1800s, the resulting generational trauma lingers today (Hill, 1992). Many grandparents and parents of Native American Millennial students attended a boarding school. By design, the purpose of Native American schooling was to remove the communal and familial strengths of Native communities (Adams, 1988), to assimilate, and to force this population to replace Indigenous values with White values (such as individuality and competitiveness) in an effort to gain land (Adams, 1995; Carney, 1999; Deyhle & Swisher, 1997). Boarding school students worked many hours in hard labor, were taught rudimentary academic skills, engaged in Bible study, and were given vocational training. In a bizarre effort to brainwash, holidays such as July 4 and Washington's birthday were grand celebrations that consisted of parades, pageants, and speeches in support of the United States (Adams, 1995; Lindsey, 1995).

Boarding school survivors have reported shame upon their return, because they did not know their own culture or language, nor did they feel welcome in the White community. Trained to be farmers, they were returned to lands that were typically not farmland (Wilkins, 2004). Confused, lost, and sometimes brainwashed, survivors self-medicated with alcohol, and because they were not parented they in turn struggled to be good parents. This set in motion a generational trauma (Hill, 1992) where one generation passes on the trauma to the next. It certainly set in motion a distrust for European-style formal education (Huffman, 2008). Each subsequent generation works toward healing, learning how to love not only family but to be "Indian," regaining traditions and languages that were literally beaten out of them. This includes the Millennial college student.

Tribal Colleges

Tribal colleges and universities (TCUs) are not to be confused with boarding schools. TCUs have always been available to the Native American Millennial student as a direct result of self-determination efforts of the post–civil rights era. TCU academic goals include providing a foundational education for transfer to a 4-year institution. TCUs are funded by the federal Tribally Controlled College or University Assistance Act, but per-student funding is less than that for a typical nontribal community college (Martin, 2005). The American Indian Higher Education Consortium (AIHEC) "was organized in 1972 to provide an opportunity for tribal college board of directors, administration, faculty, and students to communicate and collaborate with one another to support the mission of tribal colleges" (Martin, 2005, p. 81). In 1978 the Tribally Controlled College Act, Public Law 92-471, was passed providing "core funding." In 1994 TCUs received land-grant status, and 2 years later President Bill Clinton signed the Tribal College Executive Order (Stein, Shanley, & Sanchez, 2003, p. 81). Where land-grant status helps connect TCUs to "mainstream institutions by sharing projects, resources, and information [through] equity-grants," the executive order promotes self-sufficiency and high-quality education through "participation in programs funded by the federal government and to bring more attention to [TCU] 'accomplishments'" (Stein et al., 2003, p. 81).

There are presently 37 tribal colleges in the United States (AIHEC, 2010). Tribal colleges have played a major role in the higher education of geographically isolated tribes. Like Diné College, institutions are culturally centered within the community they serve—service to the tribal community being a major characteristic—as well as language and culture preservation and economic development (AIHEC, 2010). It is interesting to note that TCU attendance is growing (Martin, 2005). In addition to providing higher education in a culturally specific environment, many college students enter higher education there, gaining credits, skills, and the confidence to transfer to 4-year predominantly White institutions (PWIs) (Brown, 2002; Davis, 1992).

Because of the post–American Indian movement's impact on increased pride and acceptance of Native identity, a resurgence in traditional practices, and the outside acknowledgment of Indigenous expertise and knowledge, Native American Millennial students have available traditional educational supports and options as never before. The tribal college movement is one example. Another is Native-based K–12 schooling, which is self-determinant in curriculum, combining federal and state requirements along with traditional community requirements. The community-controlled Rough Rock School in Arizona (McCarty, 2002) and the Onondaga Nation School in New York (George et al., 2003) are two examples. Previous generations did not have this option.

Gaming

Thirty-one states have tribes that operate gaming facilities regulated under the 1988 Indian Gaming Regulatory Act (NIGC, 2009). Native American Millennial college students have always lived with gaming, whether it is located in their own community or a nearby community, and with the assumption of others that all Native people are wealthy because of gaming or that all Native people favor gaming.

Tribes do not operate their gaming uniformly. Some tribes operate large and profitable casinos, while others operate small high-stakes bingo halls. These enterprises encourage business development where little existed before. The profits are handled according to individual tribal governments and IGRA regulations. Gaming profits have allowed tribes to provide services and educational scholarships. Although many of these scholarships are substantial, some are not. These opportunities encourage students to obtain a college education as they provide professional occupations. Yet many tribal members are able to find employment in gaming or business on the territory without having a college degree, discouraging some from attending college. Tribes also vary in their required qualifications for employment, meaning that someone with a college degree can be working side by side with someone who has not graduated from high school.

It is important to note that not all tribes have gaming, and not all that do are highly profitable. Gaming is a contested topic in many Native American communities. Although many of these enterprises are profitable, these businesses are often run by outsiders because the tribe does not have trained personnel. But these enterprises have brought jobs and profits to some tribes in areas where virtually no jobs existed before.

Predominantly White Institution Attendance

Millennial Native Americans are attending 4-year PWIs more than 2-year institutions (DeVoe & Darling-Churchill, 2008). This is the first generation to do so. This does not mean that tribal colleges are in decline nor does it deny the vital role of the tribal college. In addition to this new trend, more Native American women than men are attending and completing college. According to National Center for Education Statistics (NCES) data, in 1976 there was little difference between college participation of Native American men and women. However, by 2005, women outpaced men by over 22% (DeVoe & Darling-Churchill, 2008). In addition, data indicate that college participation of Native American women has doubled since 1976 (DeVoe & Darling-Churchill, 2008). Women of any race bring distinct qualities to college. Native American women, in particular, bring unique experiences with them to college.

Given that women in most Native American societies play central roles in their communities (LaFromboise, Heyle, & Ozer, 1990; White Shield, 2009), women may view their own educations as their responsibility to family and community, incorporating their modern education into traditional roles. Several researchers have found family to be not only important to Native American college success but also the impetus for attending college (J. Guillory, 2008; R. Guillory, 2002; Lindley, 2009; Shotton, 2008; Waterman, 2005/2006). Getting an education to support the family and being a role model for children in the family have also been found to be important (Lindley, 2009; Napier, 1996). Having children was not a barrier for these women, but rather the reason cited for attaining an education. This was especially true for women in recent studies that included Millennial students (e.g., Lindley, 2009; Shotton, 2008; Waterman, 2005/2006).

Historically Native American Fraternities and Sororities

Native American Millennials have taken a unique step that no generation before them has, the establishment of Historically Native American Fraternities and Sororities (HNAFS). HNAFS are Native-founded fraternity and sorority organizations that serve Native American college students and Native American communities. Although these organizations welcome anyone to membership, the focus and commitment is wholly centered on serving the Native American community. The purpose of HNAFS is to fill a gap in *Native American* college student support, providing a cultural support not found at a PWI (S. Oxendine, personal communication, October 1, 2009). Some HNAFS incorporate specific local culture into their rituals, while others are more pan–Native American in their orientation. Activities such as smudging and sweat lodges "serve as a mechanism for the maintenance of cultural practices away from home" (Jahansouz & Oxendine, 2008, p. 14). Table 9.1 lists the HNAFS organizations, origin, and year founded.

Challenges that these organizations face are their newness, small membership, lack of a national umbrella organization, the general misunderstanding, stereotypes, and ignorance about Native American communities (S. Oxendine & D. Oxendine, personal communication, October 1, 2009). Because these organizations are in their infancy, they are still working out policies and establishing a national presence, such as within the Association of Fraternity/Sorority Advisors (AFA).

General fraternal culture has not always been a good fit with Native American culture. Terminology can be an issue. For instance, chapter expansion is referred to as "colonization." Colonization of the Americas was a brutal invasion inflicted upon the Indigenous population. Some HFNAS chapters have challenged the use of this term and have experienced push back from AFA and other dominant fraternal organization (S. Oxendine, personal communication, October 1, 2009). Other terms have been incorporated to reflect Native culture. For instance, Derek Oxendine is on the chief council of Phi Sigma Nu as dean of Ma'enos, a Cheyenne word for turtle, their mascot (D. Oxendine, personal communication, October 1, 2009). Alpha Pi Omega Sorority refers to their intake process as the Honey Process

TABLE 9.1
Native American Fraternities and Sororities, Origins, and Founding Dates

Type	Name	Origin	Founded
Sorority	Alpha Pi Omega, Inc.	University of North Carolina at Chapel Hill	1994
	Sigma Omicron Epsilon, Inc.	East Carolina University	1997
	Gamma Delta Pi	University of Oklahoma	2001
	Omega Delta Psi	University of Northern Colorado	2006
Fraternity	Phi Sigma Nu, Inc.	University of North Carolina at Pembroke	1996
	Epsilon Chi Nu	East Carolina University	1996
	Beta Sigma Epsilon	University of Arizona	2001
	Sigma Nu Alpha Gamma– Society of Native American Gentleman	University of Oklahoma	2004

and their prospective members as Honeycombs (S. Oxendine, personal communication, October 1, 2009).

Role of Elders in HNAFS

Legacies do not exist because these organizations are in their infancy; there were no HNAFS in existence when our elders were in college. However, the organizations do have very active graduate chapters that allow elders the opportunity to join. Reverse legacy refers to the process where parents, with college degrees, join after their children to become members. The graduate chapters of some HNAFS also serve a mentoring or role model function.

Elders in the Native American community have been invited to meetings and have been supportive of HNAFS efforts. For instance, Native American Elders in North Carolina were involved in the development of Alpha Pi Omega and Phi Sigma Nu (D. Oxendine, personal communication, October 1, 2009). On June 6, 2008, the North Carolina Commission of Indian Affairs passed a resolution recognizing Alpha Pi Omega and Phi Sigma Nu as the first Native American fraternity and sorority organizations, respectively, for the work they do in the community and for Native leadership (North Carolina Commission of Indian Affairs, 2008). Given the importance of elders in Native American communities, this is a true honor.

Because Native Americans are so diverse and their population is increasing, we can expect a growth in HNAFS membership and possibly see the development of new organizations (Locklear & Oxendine, 2007). The sheer diversity of Native American cultures warrants expansion because one organization may not meet every college student's cultural and service needs, especially in a PWI environment where Native students experience racism and cultural isolation (Huffman, 2008).

Diversity

Although they compose only 1% of the population in the United States, Native Americans are the most diverse group; there are over 500 federally recognized Indigenous nations, as well as over 200 without federal recognition (Wilkins, 2004). Native people live on reservations and territories, in urban areas, and rural areas. Some identify as traditional, Christian, progressive, or in between. Native American college students are diverse, yet they share many common experiences and traditions.

An approach to understand this diversity is the concept of Native students' "ways of being" (Brayboy, 1999, p. 107). "Ways of being" vary according to cultural and historical contexts. For instance, Eastern Native American nations have been in contact with Whites since their arrival. Eastern Natives may be influenced by White culture and have more experience interacting with Whites, whereas for some Western Natives contact was as late as the 19th century. Ways of being within nations also impact how students behave. For instance, some cultures are very traditional, maintaining their language and remaining steadfast in their culture. For students to negotiate the PWI environment, they have to adapt in ways that are congruent with their own identity as a Native American and those as a college student.

Native American Millennial identity is a complex topic. Native American identity has cultural, legal or political, and personal dimensions (Horse, 2005). Tribal identity is defined by the individual's tribe or nation based on the tribe's criteria. Federal guidelines also exist. Many Native Americans carry Bureau of Indian Affairs Certificate of Indian Blood cards as proof that they have at least one-quarter Native American blood (Garroutte, 2003).

One-quarter Native American blood is the federal threshold to be identified as a Native American and is often the determinant for financial aid specific to Native students. The Haudenosaunee (Iroquois) issue their own "red cards" as proof of identity based on traditional matrilineal kinship. Native American nations and tribes are sovereign nations, hence, the political nature of their identities. Consider the terminology used in this chapter. American Indian, Native American, Indigenous, and tribal designation are all acceptable terms. Individuals prefer certain terms that vary according to region. Reclaiming language and identity includes using Indigenous words for nation and clan, including traditional names for children as opposed to English names. For example, when Diné College was founded, it was founded under the name of Navajo Community College but later changed its name to claim an identity in the Navajo language.

The cultural definition of Native identity is fluid and dynamic. Identifying "traditional" varies from nation to nation, from region to region, and from one generation to another. Where some nations have steadfastly maintained their ceremonies and language, a traditional person may be one who speaks the language, participates in ceremonies, and perhaps conducts ceremonies or holds a position of leadership (in some nations this is called holding a title). In another nation, where language and culture are struggling to survive, learning the language, learning the culture, and thinking "traditionally" may identify a traditional person in that environment. That may change over time as resources change or as life circumstances allow an individual or community the time to pursue traditional teachings and practices. This depends on the existence of elders who pass on the language and traditions, as our elders are our encyclopedias (Shenandoah & Hill, 2006).

Role of Student Groups and Native American Studies

Native American student groups and Native American studies programs play vital roles in helping Millennial students maintain their cultural integrity and negotiate PWIs. Student groups provide venues for support and camaraderie. Many large institutions such as Harvard and Stanford universities hold powwows, allowing for cultural celebration. Other institutions may have traditional dinners or have elder speakers. The national American Indian Science and Engineering Society (AISES) has regional and campus chapters that encourage and support students in the sciences. AISES has seen a large growth in membership and programming (AISES, 2011), which is an indication that Millennial Native students want and use these resources.

Native studies programs combine the academic study of Indigenous issues and topics along with student support (Champagne & Stauss, 2002). Native studies programs are typically interdisciplinary and are located under an umbrella department such as American Studies. The focus of study is the Native American community, but through an Indigenous lens and not through a mainstream lens. Native studies programs offer general Native American history courses, religion, and language classes. Research is expected to benefit the Native community.

Because Native studies programs are interdisciplinary and located within other departments, they can operate at the whim of the umbrella department. Few programs, even those that are departments, have sufficient full-time faculty and staff (Champagne & Stauss, 2002). These struggles continue today with the added burden of the economic struggles of the 2009 financial collapse. Native American Millennial students express an appreciation for these programs (Brown, 2005; Waterman, 2005/2006).

After formal and informal efforts to remove cultural traditions, the strength of families, and the desire to "go back to the blanket" (Adams, 1995, p. 291), to remain Native, is strong. Millennial students want to give back to their communities (Brayboy, 2004; J. Guillory, 2008; Waterman, 2004). Many students experience their college educations through a Native lens, filtering their educations to fit their own traditions and community needs.

Recommendations

Native American Millennial students, like the ones who went before them, continue to report cultural misunderstanding by their classmates, institutional staff, and faculty (Brayboy, 2005; Fox, 2005; Perry, 2002). Colleges need to become familiar with the Native populations from which they draw students. Current issues for Native populations differ from region to region. It is important for college staff to be aware of these issues by staying current with the news media as well as establishing relationships with neighboring Native communities. Not all Native Americans live on reservations, and most large cities have a Native American center. These centers can serve as a resource for educating the local institutions as well as serving as a home away from home for Native students. Some Native students no longer know their cultures. Given the policy of cultural removal, this should be no surprise. Relationships with surrounding Native communities and city cultural centers can be important resources for these students.

Native American Millennial college students strive to maintain their cultural traditions while they use technology such as iPhones, Blackberrys, and social networking tools such as Twitter. From the outside, they may appear as any other Millennial college student. Do not assume that because Native American Millennial students came from a reservation that they are not technologically savvy. Technology has expanded the reach of a formal education and as well the influence of pop culture. This can be an advantage and a disadvantage.

The threat of urban encroachment and the influence of popular culture and technology impact Native culture, especially for Native American Millennial students. There are few positive role models in the media who are Native American. Pop culture in the media is filled with violence and misogyny, and it glorifies youth, not elders. This can be troubling for our youth, especially as gaming brings money and outside dangers directly onto Native American territories. Urban encroachment does mean access to libraries, greater employment, and resources, but it also means gangs and drugs are also accessible.

Because of this self-determination era, Millennial students who attended a Native-controlled secondary school may have a greater sense of pride and cultural understanding when entering college than those who did not. It is also important to know that Native American Millennial students may be transferring from a TCU that was culturally specific and most likely quite rural. Although these students may enter college with confidence in their Native identity, they may experience culture shock (Huffman, 2008). In this case it is very important to have a relationship with the urban Native center or neighboring Native community for resources and support.

Native American Millennial students may also enter college with an Indigenous name as opposed to an English name. Some of these names can be difficult for non-Native people to pronounce. Do not assume that you can shorten the name because this may change the meaning of the name. Take the time to learn how to correctly pronounce the name, and again, having a relationship with the Native community or the Native studies or student support office will be helpful.

Because gaming is handled according to each tribe's individual governance, scholarships and student supports are not uniform. Do not assume Native American Millennial students are fully funded or that they can work in the summer at the casino or that they have access to summer work. Find out what is supported financially and determine possible residency or citizenship requirements.

Summary and Conclusions

The Native population has been increasing, raising the potential for growing numbers of Native college students. At the same time Native American businesses have also increased, heightening the need for a college education for their children. Despite the boarding school era of forced cultural removal, Native Americans have developed tribal colleges and are attending these colleges and PWIs in greater numbers. More Native American women are attending college than Native American men, and for the first time, more are attending PWIs. Historically Native American fraternities and sororities have been developed by Millennials to support students. Gaming provides scholarships, business opportunities, and professional occupations, yet can also discourage college attendance.

Native American Millennial students must negotiate the college way of being with their own indigenous way of being while maintaining their cultural integrity. Family was often reported as the reason to further an education and a major support while gaining that education. Native American student groups provide social and cultural support. Native American studies programs provide social and cultural support along with academic research and intellectual stimulation. Students desire to give back to their communities, not to gain an education to "break away" (Tinto, 1993, p. 96). Native American Millennial students have community and institutional supports that are unprecedented. Still, they experience many of the barriers of the generations before them. It is imperative that college personnel working with Native American Millennial students establish relationships with Native American urban centers and neighboring Native American communities.

References

Adams, D. W. (1988). Fundamental considerations: The deep meaning of Native American schooling, 1880–1900. *Harvard Educational Review, 58*(1), 1–28.

Adams, D. W. (1995). *Education for extinction: American Indians and the boarding school experience: 1875–1928.* Lawrence, KS: University of Press of Kansas.

American Indian Higher Education Consortium (AIHEC). (2010). *Tribal colleges and universities (TCUs) roster.* Retrieved from http://www.aihec.org/colleges/TCUroster.cfm

American Indian Science and Engineering Society. (2011). *About AISES.* Retrieved from http://www.aises.org/who/about

Brayboy, B. M. (1999). *Climbing the ivy: Examining the experiences of academically successful Native American Indian undergraduates at two Ivy League universities.*

Unpublished doctoral dissertation, University of Pennsylvania, Philadelphia, Pennsylvania.

Brayboy, B. M. (2004). Hiding in the ivy: American Indian students and visibility in elite educational settings. *Harvard Educational Review, 74*(2), 125–152.

Brayboy, B. M. (2005). Transformational resistance and social justice: American Indians in Ivy League universities. *Anthropology and Education Quarterly, 36*(3), 193–211.

Broido, E. M. (2004). Understanding diversity in millennial students. In M. D. Coomes & R. DeBard (Eds.), *Serving the Millennial generation. New Directions for Student Services, 106,* 73–85.

Brown, D. L. (2005). American Indian student services at UND. In M. J. T. Fox, S. C. Lowe, & G. S. McClellan (Eds.), *Serving Native American students. New Directions for Student Services, 109,* 87–94.

Brown, D. L. (2002). *The perceptions of selected tribal college transfer students attending the University of North Dakota.* Unpublished doctoral dissertation, University of North Dakota, Grand Forks, North Dakota.

Carney, C. M. (1999). *Native American higher education in the United States.* New Brunswick, NJ: Transaction Publishers.

Champagne, D., & Stauss, J. (2002). *Native American studies in higher education: Models for collaboration between universities and indigenous nations.* Walnut Creek, CA: Altamira.

Coomes, M. D. (2004). Understanding the historical and cultural influences that shape generations. In M. D. Coomes & R. DeBard (Eds.), *Serving the Millennial generation. New Directions for Student Services, 106,* 17–31.

Coomes, M. D., & DeBard, R. (2004). A generational approach to understanding students. In M. D. Coomes & R. DeBard (Eds.), *Serving the Millennial generation. New Directions for Student Services, 106,* 5–16.

Davis, J. (1992). Factors contributing to post-secondary achievement of American Indians. *Tribal College, 4*(2), 24–30.

DeVoe, J. F., & Darling-Churchill, K. E. (2008). *Status and trends in the education of American Indians and Alaska Natives: 2008* (NCES 2008-084). Washington, DC: U.S. Department of Education, National Center for Education Statistics.

Deyhle, D., & Swisher, K. (1997). Research in American Indian and Alaska native education: From assimilation to self-determination. *Review of Research in Education, 22,* 113–194.

Fox, M. J. T. (2005). Voices from within: Native American faculty and staff on campus. In M. J. T. Fox, S. C. Lowe, & G. S. McClellan (Eds.), *Serving Native American students. New Directions for Student Services, 109,* 49–59.

Garroutte, E. M. (2003). *Real Indians: Identity and the survival of Native America.* Berkeley, CA: University of California Press.

George, R., Waterman, D., Jacques, F., Waterman, S. J., Erb, C., & Gibson, M. (2003, November). *Honoring tradition through the Onondaga Nation School.* Paper presented at the National Indian Education Association national conference, Greensboro, North Carolina.

Guillory, J. (2008). *Diverse pathways of "giving back" to tribal community: Perceptions of Native American college graduates.* Unpublished doctoral dissertation, Washington State University, Pullman, Washington.

Guillory, R. M. (2002). *Factors related to Native American students' persistence in higher education: A comparative analysis of student and state and university officials' perceptions.* Unpublished doctoral dissertation, Washington State University, Pullman, Washington.

Hill, D. (1992). *Ethnostress: The disruption of the aboriginal spirit.* Hagersville, ON: Tribal Sovereignty Associates.

Horse, P. G. (2005). Native American identity. In M. J. T. Fox; S. C. Lowe, & G. S. McClellan (Eds.), *Serving Native American students. New Directions for Student Services, 109,* 69–78.

Huffman, T. (2008). *American Indian higher education experiences: Cultural visions and personal journeys.* New York: Peter Lang.

Jahansouz, S. J., & Oxendine, S. D. (2008). The Native American fraternal values movement: Past, present and future. In *Perspectives: A publication for Members of the Association of Fraternity Advisors* (p. 14). Carmel, IN: AFA.

LaFromboise, T. D., Heyle, A. M., & Ozer, E. J. (1990). Changing and diverse roles of women in American Indian cultures. *Sex Roles, 22*(7–8), 455–476.

Lindley, L. S. (2009). *A tribal critical race theory analysis of academic attainment: A qualitative study of sixteen Northern Arapaho women who earned degrees at the University of Wyoming.* Unpublished doctoral dissertation, University of Wyoming, Laramie, Wyoming.

Lindsey, D. F. (1995). *Indians at Hampton Institute, 1877–1923.* Urbana, IL: University of Illinois Press.

Locklear, B., & Oxendine, S. D. (2007, March). *American Indian Greek organizations: A new vehicle for carrying on old traditions.* Presented at the NASPA/ACPA Joint Meeting Educational Program, Orlando, Florida.

Martin, R. G. (2005). Serving American Indian students in tribal colleges: Lessons for mainstream colleges. In M. J. T. Fox, S. C. Lowe, & G. S. McClellan (Eds.), *Serving Native American students. New Directions for Student Services, 109,* 79–86.

McCarty, T. L. (2002). *A place to be Navajo: Rough Rock and the struggle for self-determination in Indigenous schooling.* Mahwah, NJ: Erlbaum.

Napier, M. (1996). Nine Native women: Pursuing the doctorate and aspiring to positions of leadership. In K. Arnold, K. Noble, & R. Subotnik (Eds.), *Remarkable women: Perspectives on female talent development* (pp. 133–148). Cresskill, NJ: Hampton Press.

National Indian Gaming Commission (NIGC). (2009). *Indian Gaming Regulatory Act.* Retrieved from http://www.nigc.gov/Laws_Regulations/Indian_Gaming_Regulatory_Act.aspx

North Carolina Commission of Indian Affairs. (2008, June 6). A Resolution Acknowledging the Contributions made by Phi Sigma Nu, Inc. Fraternity and Alpha Pi Omega, Inc. Sorority to American Indian men and women in Higher Education. Raleigh, North Carolina.

Perry, B. (2002). American Indian victims of campus ethnoviolence. *Journal of American Indian Education, 41*(1), 35–55.

Shenandoah, A., & Hill, S. (2006). *The nation within our midst: Onondaga history, culture, and spirituality.* Onondaga Land Rights and Our Common Future Educational Series [DVD]. Neighbors of the Onondaga Nation. For more information: http://www.peacecouncil.net/NOON/video

Shotton, H. J. (2008). *Pathway to the Ph.D.: Experiences of high achieving American Indian females.* Unpublished doctoral dissertation, University of Oklahoma, Norman, Oklahoma.

Stein, W. J., Shanley, J., & Sanchez, T. (2003). The effect of the Native American Higher Education Initiative on strengthening tribal colleges and universities: Focus on governance and finance. In M. K. Nee-Benham & W. J. Stein (Eds.), *The renaissance of American Indian higher education: Capturing the dream* (pp. 75–98). Mahwah, NJ: Erlbaum.

Tinto, V. (1993). *Leaving college: Rethinking the causes and cures of attrition* (2nd ed.). Chicago: University of Chicago Press.

Waterman, S. J. (2004). *The Haudenosaunee college experience: A complex path to degree completion.* Dissertation, Syracuse University, Syracuse, New York.

Waterman, S. J. (2005/2006). Haudenosaunee (Iroquois) college experiences study. Unpublished raw data.

White Shield, R. (2009). Identifying and understanding Indigenous cultural and spiritual strengths in the higher education experiences of Indigenous women. *Wicazo Sa Review, 24*(1), 47–63.

Wilkins, D. E. (2004). A tour of Indian peoples and Indian lands. In C. A. Gallagher (Ed.), *Rethinking the color line: Readings in race and ethnicity* (2nd ed.; pp. 66–86). Boston: McGraw-Hill.

PART SIX

LGBTQ MILLENNIALS
IN COLLEGE

10

LGBTQ MILLENNIALS
IN COLLEGE

Lori D. Patton, Carrie Kortegast, and Gabriel Javier

This chapter discusses the presence of lesbian, gay, bisexual, transgender, and queer (LGBTQ) Millennial students in college. We draw particular attention to issues and trends at the individual and institutional levels about which student affairs professionals should have knowledge in order to work successfully with Millennial student populations. As the demographics of colleges and universities shift, so too does the population of students at these institutions who openly identify as LGBTQ. Although the demographics consistently change, only miniscule advances have occurred with regard to structuring campus life in ways that are welcoming and inclusive of LGBTQ students. Thus the goal of this chapter is to illuminate the need for student affairs professionals to work consciously toward fostering campuses that are conducive to the needs of LGBTQ students. First, we foreground the centrality of identity to LGBTQ students. Using identity as a springboard to discuss personal identity development, we then broaden our perspective by examining the campus environment- and institutional-level issues that student affairs professionals must be aware of in order to make a positive difference in the college experiences of LGBTQ students.

Who Are LGBTQ College Students? The Complexities of Identity

There are more than 1 million youth who identify as having a same-sex orientation or attraction (Holmes & Cahill, 2005). According to Jennings

(1994), LGBTQ students in the Millennial generation are coming out at much earlier ages than previous generations. Seidman (as noted in Miceli, 2005) added that these students are "quicker to self awareness and self acceptance because of the broader normalizing currents in America, and increasingly choosing to refuse the closet as a social accommodation". As noted in chapter 11 of this volume, conceptualizations of LGBTQ identity for Millennial students are deviating from prescriptive labels toward more fluid concepts in both theory and practice. Seminal psychosocial development models (e.g., Cass, 1979, 1984; D'Augelli, 1994; McCarn & Fassinger, 1996) can no longer succinctly explain the wealth of diversity among LGBTQ people's developmental experiences. Because of the intricate nature of identity and the fluidity of identity development, prescriptive identity development, in particular stage models, "are not adequate to describe all non-heterosexual identity processes" (Bilodeau & Renn, 2005, p. 27). Although there is acknowledgment of the limitation of identity development models, alternative models or perspectives have not yet gained traction within student affairs (e.g., queer theory). The complexities associated with making sense of identity development and the willingness among student affairs educators to address this complexity mirror many of the critical discussions regarding identity that individual LGBTQ students and the communities to which they belong are having among themselves.

Models like that of Cass (1979, 1984), D'Augelli (1994), McCarn and Fassinger (1996), and several others continue to play an important role in understanding and working with LGBTQ Millennial students in their identity development but do not provide a complete picture. For example, many theories fail to consider the intersection of LGBTQ identities with racial and ethnic identities (Holmes & Cahill, 2005). Instead of employing and depending on these models singularly, they are considered as one element in what Savin-Williams (2005) referred to as the "differential development trajectory" of identity development (p. 82). The idea of this trajectory is grounded in the notion that a person's "coming out" is, simultaneously, unique to his or her own life (differential), warrants movements from simplicity to complexity (developmental), and often follows a developmental path illuminated by various psychosocial developmental models (trajectory). Acknowledging coming out in these terms allows student affairs professionals and those who work very closely with LGBTQ students to understand their identity processes as a continuous journey; one in which the process or journey is central rather than solely the destination.

A key aspect of this developmental process involves naming one's own reality and to which community one belongs in a society that emphasizes and thrives on particular labels. A major challenge for LGBTQ Millennial students both internally and externally revolves around the use and groupings of the terms *lesbian, gay, bisexual, transgender,* and *queer.* Collectively, these terms are widely known, recognized, accepted, debated, and eschewed, often in the same conversation. For student affairs educators, an issue regarding what type of labeling is most appropriate may emerge. Thus, the onus is typically placed on an author, presenter, lecturer, or speaker to clarify the context of these words and their particular order. Dilley (2002b) indicated that these various terms could have similar meanings or totally different distinctions based on the context in which meaning of the terminology is being made. Examples of this seemingly sporadic word and letter flip-flopping include:

- Placing "L" before "G"
- Placing "G" before "L"
- Ordering the letter "TBLG," thereby acknowledging levels of privilege and "acceptance" and increasing the visibility of the transcommunity
- Whether to include "I" for *intersex*
- Whether "Q" represents *queer, questioning,* or both
- Whether to include the letter "Q" at all.

The differences between usage, letter inclusion, and letter meaning vary widely, not only across geographic and political lines, but also along socio-economic, ability, and race or ethnicity distinctions. Driver (2007) wrote that "Identifications are constituted within dense intersections of age, geography, sexuality, race, class, ethnicity, and gender, without being reducible to any isolated dimension of experience" (p. 3). For example, in a study focusing on the experiences of African American gay and bisexual men at one historically Black college, Patton (2011) found that participants offered a range of descriptors to refer to their sexual identities. Their disregard for terms such as *gay* and *bisexual* was reflective of expectations in the Black community with regard to manhood. Similarly, Poynter and Washington (2005) indicated that these labels "are often associated with white culture" (p. 45). Terms such as *sexually free, same gender loving, woman who loves women,* or *man who loves men* are all labels that expand beyond the typical

LGBTQ designations. This creative labeling is highly descriptive of Millennial students, particularly given their desire to move beyond the confinement of the popular terms that have been used to characterize their identities without regard for the nuances associated with their individual and collective social locations. For student affairs practitioners and theorists, this means that attempts can be made to succinctly define identity terms, but an understanding must also exist that acknowledges the futility that may potentially emerge upon engaging in the exercise of labeling. The reality is that the LGBTQ designation may only be useful in describing broad commonalities across a multitude of experiences, with the caveat that each person has the agency and right to define him- or herself for him- or herself.

Another trend with regard to LGBTQ identity is the popularity, prevalence, and preference of using the concept of fluid sexual identity or orientation. A parallel concept with regard to gender identity expression might be one's preference to identify as gender-queer or queer. In her book *Queer Girls and Popular Culture*, Driver (2007) discusses how the intersection of gender and sexual identities is expressed among the women in her study:

> Many of the girls I spoke with undo common sense ideas of what it means to be girls, some go so far as to refuse gender categorization altogether. Twenty-one-year-old Lynn says "I'm a female-bodied gender deviant. By appearance, I seem to fit right in the middle of the butch/femme dichotomy, but am nowhere to be found in the polarized identities of girl or else boy. . . ." While all youth in my study were born female and claim to desire other biological females, many actively refuse to label themselves as boy, or girl, lesbian or heterosexual, feminine or masculine. (p. 3)

In general, the increasing use of these terms signifies a turning away from identity terms that feel overly prescriptive. Beemyn (2005) contend that "more college students are rejecting the gender assigned to them and openly exploring other gender possibilities" (p. 111). Where once *bisexual* was used to describe a self-identified man or woman who is attracted to self-identified men or women across varying, intersecting, and complex levels of attraction, the term *pansexual* has emerged as a term to describe one's attraction to types of people—characteristics or traits of a person—rather than focusing on their perceived, actual, or assigned gender identity or expression. Indeed, there has also been movement to use *sexual attractionality* over *sexual orientation* in order to better represent some people's experiences of dynamic attraction versus static orientation. The process of self-identification is hardly new; however, what seems to be true among Millennial populations is that there are newer and developing terms to describe their experiences and identities. In short, LGBTQ identities in and of themselves are not new identities, but the language used to name these identities is increasingly new. Despite these emergent conceptualizations in the naming of identities, we firmly acknowledge that in many ways, the process of labeling lies in a contentious balance with the original intent to disrupt traditional prescriptive labels.

The Role of the Media

It is important to note that the emergent trends in identity labeling hardly exist in a vacuum. As D'Augelli (1994) indicated, external variables are extremely influential in shaping identity processes. Several major influences have played a role in changing how LGBTQ people view themselves as well as how they are viewed by others. For example, the family structure in the United States is constantly shifting. In some states such as Iowa and Massa-chusetts, same-sex couples possess marriage rights and privileges that did not exist a decade ago. In addition, there has been a rise in the number of children raised by same-sex couples (Tasker & Patterson, 2007). Researchers report no statistically significant differences between children raised by same-sex parents and children raised by heterosexual parents. Studies indicate that these children are well adjusted, capable of establishing quality friendships with peers, feel a sense of integration during their adolescent years, and do not experience teasing and bullying at a rate higher than their counterparts raised by opposite-sex parents. These developments indicate a turning point in deficit discourses that once limited what LGBTQ people could do and be. Although a full treatment of these influences is beyond the scope of this chapter, we specifically highlight the media as a major influence in these newer identity conceptualizations among LGBTQ Millennial populations.

Whereas historically LGBTQ individuals and their experiences have been pathologized, negatively stereotyped, and demonized, the Stonewall riots in 1969 ushered in a dramatic shift in public consciousness regarding LGBTQ people and issues that continue presently to shape Millennials. Jennings (1994) reported that "Today's gay youth are much more likely to hear news stories, see films, or read books that depict openly gay people and their concerns" (p. 262). Streitmatter (2009) identified several television shows (*Ellen*, *Will & Grace*, *Queer as Folk*, *Queer Eye for the Straight Guy*, *The "L" Word*) and feature films (*Brokeback Mountain*, *My Best Friend's Wedding*, *Philadelphia*) as major milestones that have unfolded and essentially changed how LGBTQ individuals are characterized in society. Streitmatter asserted that "the media have not merely *reflected* the American public's shift to a more enlightened view of gay people, but they have been instrumental in *propelling* that change" (p. 2). By no means do we intend to promote an overly romanticized idea that LGBTQ populations have gained full societal acceptance. In actuality, there are many populations of LGBTQ people whose experiences are hardly reflective of those depicted in the aforementioned media forms. Many of these positive depictions are likely market driven for capitalistic gain and geared toward only presenting the images most easily digestible in the heterosexual imagination. Despite these drawbacks, Streitmatter's assessment is that the media have masterfully ushered in a certain level of societal comfort and familiarity with LGBTQ communities. It is not uncommon to find themes, storylines, and characters that bring LGBTQ stories to the forefront. Consider the grand wedding between Stanford and Anthony in the movie *Sex in the City 2* (released in 2009); Miss Jay, the infamous male judge and runway coach "diva extraordinaire" on the reality show *America's Next Top Model*; Bianca Montgomery, the self-proclaimed lesbian daughter of *All My Children's* main character Erica Kane; CNN's documentary *Gary and Tony Have a Baby*; *Grey's Anatomy* doctors/lovers Callie and Arizona; and *Glee* character Kurt Hummel who disclosed his sexual identity to his father. Among the most dominant presence of LGBTQ populations in the media has been through MTV's *The Real World*, a reality television series that began in 1992 and continues to feature individuals who are "involved in challenging normative oppressive institutions set by an older generation" and "reveals gay youths as the contemporary pioneers" (Pullen, 2007, p. 117). With such a diverse array of representations filtered through the media, it is not surprising that many Millennials feel empowered to use their agency to define who they are. It is critical that student affairs educators understand this diversity. In other words, while the media provide a glimpse into the experiences of LGBTQ people, it is equally important to understand that the media are incapable of providing a comprehensive story. It certainly has the power to influence how LGBTQ college students are viewed, how they view themselves, and the impact of these mutually shaping views within the campus environment, especially the extent to which they engage in the culture and life of the college campus.

LGBTQ Issues and Student Affairs

Institutions of higher education, as well as the field of student affairs, have had a complicated history of supporting LGBTQ students. Shifts in attitudes, policies, and practices toward LGBTQ students have mirrored changes in societal attitudes toward this population. Campus policies and practices have evolved over the past half century from expelling students for "homosexual or perceived homosexual" behavior[1] to trying to help, treat, and cure LGBTQ students (Dilley, 2002a). Institutional policies continued to suppress the assembly and organization of LGBTQ groups after colleges and university shifted away from suppressing individual acts of "homosexuality" (Dilley, 2002a). Today, changes with policies and practices to support and recognize LGBTQ students, faculty, and staff include "the adoption of equal opportunity policies inclusive of sexual orientation and gender identity, the adoption of domestic partner benefits, inclusion of GLBT issues in campus diversity initiatives, and increased interest in GLBT studies" (Zemsky, 2004, p. 248). Moreover, these changes have given way to the professionalization of LGBTQ student services and the presence of LGBTQ student alliances.

Based on their desire for authentic engagement, comfort level with their sexual identity, and access to opportunities and resources, LGBTQ Millennial students will encounter LGBTQ communities and systems of support in an infinite number of unique ways on campus. Indeed, exposure and experience with LGBTQ adults, parents, elder role models, and peers range on college campus. Where there once were few out and open places on college campuses for LGBTQ students to explore their identities, more institutions are both acknowledging the need to support LGBTQ students and establishing formal systems. These support systems range anywhere from neutral tolerance to institutional recognition of LGBTQ student groups to establishing professionally staffed LGBTQ offices.

Indeed, one constant struggle in Millennial students' journeys to self-identification may be in how many options exist to provide interactions with the LGBTQ community. For example, presuppose that an institution addresses sexual orientation, gender identity, and gender expression in its statement of nondiscrimination, has policies and practices in place ensuring same-sex domestic partner benefits, and has established an office, center, or staff person within the institution who serves as the main contact for LGBTQ students' needs and concerns. Broadly speaking, one might easily consider this to be a campus where a multitude of methods exist to promote support and involvement for LGBTQ students. In theory, while these various resources and opportunities are important, most are sorely lacking on many campuses. On the other hand, these avenues can also pose a barrier for LGBTQ students in their search for a community because these resources, policies, and support mechanisms are assumed to serve "one" LGBTQ community. Since many LGBTQ populations continue to be mis- or underrepresented in mainstream popular culture, there is a false assumption that a unified LGBTQ community actually exists. Millennial students who receive these erroneous messages can become frustrated and disappointed as they seek a space of belonging on the college or university campus. Whether it is a young person who is beginning to come out or an adult who has been out for years, each may likely have difficulties finding a community of support on campus. This struggle is even more pronounced for people of color, individuals of differing ability status, and low-income populations who have identities that do not neatly fit the media-generated image of LGBTQ communities as White, male, able bodied, and middle class. For example, students of color who perceive the office to be a White space that lacks cultural relevance may not frequent the LGBTQ center established on a particular campus. Zemsky (2004) asserted that "GLBT campus organizations that organize around a particular model of coming out and the assumption of the primacy of gay identity may not be viewed as environments within which a young student of color can integrate their sexuality and their racial identities" (p. 259). Thus, when other identity domains are considered, what appears to be a wealth of resources may not be resourceful at all for some students.

Supporting LGBTQ Millennial Students

In response to student and societal changes, colleges and universities have responded in a variety of ways to meet the changing needs of LGBTQ Millennial students as well as educating the larger campus community on LGBTQ issues. Although some LGBTQ students come to college "still secretive" about their sexual identity or orientation, others come to campus open about their sexual and gender identities, expecting that "their worldviews to be embraced . . . their voices heard, their concerns acknowledged, their needs met, and their educational environments welcoming" (Sanlo, 2000, p. 486). That said, colleges and universities should expect that there are and will be LGBTQ students on their campuses and be prepared to meet their needs for community, involvement, and support, regardless of institutional type. Yet most colleges and universities still struggle with how to support LGBTQ students, staff, and faculty because they exist within a societal culture that is homophobic, heterosexist, transphopic, and fixated on gender binaries (Beemyn, Curtis, David, & Tubbs, 2005; Bilodeau, 2005; Love, 1998).

LGBTQ Student Support Services

Offices dedicated to providing services to address the needs of LGBTQ students are relatively new to the field of student services, with most established in the late 1980s (Sanlo, 2000). The creation of centers is typically the result of a campus climate task force recommendation or in response to pivotal incidents of harassment or discrimination against LGBTQ students (Ritchie & Banning, 2001; Sanlo, 2000). Campuses often look to these centers to provide individual, programmatic, and institutional services to meet the needs of LGBTQ students, faculty, staff, and the greater community. In addition to supporting and working with individual students, centers are often responsible for campus-wide educational efforts. Explicitly or implicitly stated, LGBTQ centers often serve as the campus voice and conscience on LGBTQ issues.

Departments of housing and residential life have provided services for LGBTQ students primarily through themed or special interest housing or gender neutral housing options. Students who choose to live in LGBTQ themed housing tend to do so because they have the "freedom to be themselves and the freedom to feel comfortable with their sexual orientations" and because it is a "safe place where they were not harassed" (Herbst & Malaney, 1999, pp. 111–112). While LGBTQ themed housing is attractive to some students, it is not attractive to all LGBTQ students. A growing trend is the gender neutral housing option, which allows students to identify the gender or sex they feel most comfortable living with as roommates.

LGBTQ Programs

Programs such as SafeZone, Speakers Bureaus, Lavender Graduation, Coming Out Week, and Drag Shows are intended to raise awareness and visibility and to educate the campus community about LGBTQ issues. On some campuses, student members of LGBTQ organizations initiate these programmatic efforts; at other institutions, administrators are responsible for these programs. While these programs bring awareness and visibility of the *presence* of LGBTQ students on campus, they often do little to *promote* acceptance or *challenge* the endemic issues of homophobia. Additionally, some awareness programs encourage voyeurism and spectatorship rather than true engagement. Although these programs may bring some level of awareness and visibility, as well as serve as a springboard toward more substantive educational efforts, they may also be criticized as catering to the "come meet a real live gay person" phenomenon for mass consumption, which ultimately could be perceived as offensive to some LGBTQ students.

In addition to bringing awareness, it is important to be mindful of whom the intended audiences are for these programmatic efforts while remaining cautious that many of these efforts are created with the intent to educate heterosexual people rather than truly supporting LGBTQ students. For example, SafeZone is essentially a program that allows individuals to identify as allies to LGBTQ people through stickers, buttons, and a public SafeZone member list. Although SafeZone programs do have a component of publicly identifying individuals that are LGBTQ allies, which raises awareness and visibility of LGBTQ students and allies, they do little to challenge larger systemic issues of safety, acceptance, or the oppression of LGBTQ issues and people. Institutionally approved LGBTQ programs must move toward a more critical, social justice lens that addresses and interrogates systems of oppression.

Lastly, LGBTQ students might begin to feel tokenized should they only be asked to contribute and participate in discussions that have sexual orientation, gender identity, or gender expression at the core. LGBTQ students who decide to participate in efforts such as SafeZone are often placed in the unique predicament of balancing the public transmittal of their sexual orientations, gender identities, or gender expression with their desire for privacy. For example, the student leader for a campus chapter of the Stonewall Democrats (the LGBTQ caucus of the Democratic Party) might be automatically assumed to be LGBTQ. Whether or not this is true, such an assumption can be limiting to an individual who prefers to keep this aspect of identity private rather than open to everyone. Thus, opportunities to be involved in college student activities are likely to be complementary to their LGBTQ identities instead of being a primary focus.

LGBTQ Student Organizations

Millennials have been characterized as having an activist orientation (Broido, 2004; DeBard, 2004; Howe & Strauss, 2000). Jennings (1994) stated:

> Gay youth have often become activists in their own right, building a series of community-based support groups across the nation . . . for older lesbians and gay men, watching gay and lesbian adolescents speaking out on television and at rallies, fighting for their rights in schools and going to the prom

with same-sex dates reveals a generation gap of truly immense proportions, as such actions were simply inconceivable even a decade ago. (p. 262)

Given that LGBTQ students are exploring identities at a younger age, there has been an increasing prominence of gay-straight alliances (GSAs) in high schools to provide a safe space for students. Not only do these organizations provide support, they also provide activist training, organize rallies and protests, and generate awareness (Griffin, Lee, Waugh, & Beyer, 2005). GSAs also create coordinated efforts with surrounding postsecondary institutions to collaborate and host meetings. Miceli (2005) noted that GSAs represent "pockets of youth across the nation asserting positive, proud, and unapologetic self-image; agents of change claiming a space and a voice in schools; and catalysts for a social movement" (p. 13). These students, many of whom will attend college, take these same characteristics to campus. For them, GSAs might be considered the norm rather than a new phenomenon. Thus, they may attend college with the expectation that an LGBTQ organization has already been established. As these Millennial students enter higher education, there is a greater likelihood that they will have had some community service experience or involvement in activism. Thus, they are more likely to have a willingness to continue this type of civic and public engagement while in college. More specifically, these students can play a major role in strengthening the existing LGBTQ student organizations on campus or starting new organizations where one does not exist.

Postsecondary institutions are hardly where they need to be in terms of sufficiently supporting LGBTQ students. Educational, federal, state, and institutional policies are lagging behind the many developments occurring within the LGBTQ population. As a result Millennial college students are positioned to fend for themselves and actively work to support and serve as resources to one another. Galvanizing student voices and commitment to action may actually be what is needed to force college and university campuses to ensure that LGBTQ student needs are met while holding faculty, staff, and students accountable for their roles in creating equitable and safe environments. Certainly the activism that could stem from LGBTQ student organizations on campus along with allies would push institutions to maintain an ongoing examination of homophobia and heterosexism on campus, prompt institutional leaders to firmly decide how students' needs should be met, as well as identify those who are charged with spearheading the efforts, holding them accountable for hiring qualified, committed, and knowledgeable staff and challenging institutions to move beyond awareness efforts toward political engagement and commitment to make the campus environment a welcoming space for all students.

Responsibility for LGBTQ Services

In 2009 the Consortium of Higher Education LGBT Resource Professionals reported that 150 colleges and universities housed an LGBTQ center or office. Although more institutions are establishing LGBTQ resource offices, cumulatively the number of colleges and universities with centers is dismally low given the existence of thousands of campuses in the United States alone. Such numbers beg the question, how are LGBTQ students served on campuses where no formal LGBTQ programs, staffing structures, or offices exist? Responsibilities for serving LGBTQ students should not be relegated to one department or area, but rather all departments need to be prepared and ready to address these students' varying needs. In addition to traditional student affairs departments (i.e., residential life, student activities, career services), student services, including the health center, financial aid, and registrar's office, also need to be sensitive and have protocols in place to be more welcoming of LGBTQ students. Rather than working in isolation, these offices and departments should work collaboratively to establish policies and practices that support LGBTQ students within their respective functional areas as well as across the campus.

One reason for the seeming lack of institutional responsibility is that there are few voices in the upper administrative ranks of colleges and universities to advocate for LGBTQ students. Senior student affairs officers are particularly integral in ensuring that proper services are in place for LGBTQ students. They have the position, power, and voice to promote "the creation of supportive environments for LGBT students" and must "speak articulately and consistently about service to LGBT students as an important dimension of the core mission of the student affairs organization, regardless of institutional context" (Roper, 2005, pp. 83–84). There must also be consistency in tone and language regarding the expectation that individual departments create and provide services that cater to the needs of LGBTQ students.

Another reason that colleges and universities have not provided more services to LGBTQ students is a lack of resources. Many institutions either do not have or are not willing to extend the resources necessary to support a full-time position dedicated to lead LGBTQ student services or an LGBTQ center or office. All colleges and universities need to have dedicated staff members in which the majority, or at least a portion, of their job responsibilities include advocating about and for LGBTQ issues and students. For example, at some institutions, multicultural student centers and departments include LGBTQ student services. However, the primary focus of these units is to provide support for students of color. Thus, there is the potential for great confusion about what the role of multicultural student services should be. Moreover, new issues are ushered in for students who are no longer content with viewing themselves through a compartmentalized lens. In other words, should a bisexual, African American woman seek support from the multicultural center, the LGBT campus coordinator, or the women's center? Institutions must generate enhanced strategies to serve students in a more holistic way, which could include the establishment of liaisons to work together to foster programs and services that promote inclusion of a wide range of identities.

Responsibilities for LGBTQ student services are rarely written into formal job descriptions. Instead, student affairs educators who have a vested interest in the welfare of LGBTQ students perform these responsibilities in informal or voluntary ways often with few rewards and some level of scrutiny. Kortegast (2009) further noted that this type of work tends to be assumed out of personal interest, commitment to LGBTQ issues, or in response to a vacuum of support for LGBTQ students and issues on campus. Providing student services to LGBTQ students is not a prescriptive formula; it is one that takes into consideration institutional type, resources, and student population. A formal center might be the right model for some institutions; however it is not a "fix-it" solution for all institutions. The goals should not be focused on merely obtaining a center, but to have a systematic, inclusive plan to assess and address the needs of LGBTQ students. In the absence of a formal plan, services provided and educational efforts will remain individually driven entities, rather than institutionally enacted efforts (Kortegast, 2009). As a result, a lack of continuity and coordinated efforts for serving today's Millennial college student may result in lower satisfaction, retention, and graduation for these students. There is a clear link between the success of LGBTQ students and the presence of supportive people and spaces on campus (Sanlo, 2000).

Finally, there is a prominent need for trained individuals to work with LGBTQ students as well as access to a professional space for this training and professional development to occur. Most professional organizations for student affairs include statements of practice that encourage members to refrain from discriminating against individuals based on sexual orientation and gender identity. For example, the National Association for Student Personnel Administrators' (NASPA) *Commitment to Diversity, Inclusion, and Equity* (n.d.) statement includes language regarding the need to "recognize" and "appreciate" diversity, including sexual orientation and gender identity. NASPA's *Standards of Professional Practice* (1990) statement asserted that "Members respect individuality and promote an appreciation of human diversity." However, it further stated that "In keeping with the mission of their respective institutions and remaining cognizant of federal, state, and local laws, they do not discriminate on the basis of . . . gender identity, gender expression, affectional or sexual orientation" (para. 7). The organization defers to the institution for professional guidance rather than standards of the field.

Fundamentally, student affairs work should be about inclusion, access, and advocacy for students in higher education (Talbot & Viento, 2005). Illustrating this inclusion is the American College Personnel Association's *Statement of Ethical Principles and Standards* (2006), which not only provides language regarding a nondiscriminatory policy enveloping sexual orientation and gender identity, but also states that members "will actively work to change discriminatory practices" (p. 5).

Certainly new professionals need to be prepared and should expect to work with LGBTQ students upon graduating from a student affairs graduate program. As discussed above, the professional standards and codes of ethics, as well as the Council for the Advancement of Standards in Higher Education (CAS) guidelines mandate that "faculty [are] to attend to diverse issues in developing and delivering their curriculum" (Talbot & Viento, 2005, p. 79). Attending to these diverse issues encompasses addressing the needs of LGBTQ students.

Although scholars in the field recommend that issues surrounding LGBTQ concerns and inclusive practices be present within the student affairs graduate curriculum (Talbot & Viento, 2005), often they are not, given the varying comfort levels and thresholds of knowledge the faculty possess (Talbot & Kocarek, 1997). Furthermore, discussion regarding inclusion should extend beyond student development theories in the curriculum and examining the campus climate for LGBTQ students. Such discussion should move toward actually engaging students with materials and strategies to promote social justice work on behalf of LGBTQ populations on campus (Flowers, 2003; Gayles & Kelly, 2007).

Conclusion

This chapter draws attention to the needs of LGBTQ Millennial college students. We chose identity as a starting point in an effort to describe trends and issues that shape how LGBTQ individuals understand themselves, as well as influences that shape those understandings. In addition, we illuminated some of the characteristics these students bring to postsecondary institutions and the need for student affairs educators to be aware of the unique needs and experiences LGBTQ students bring to campus. The number of developments occurring among LGBTQ individuals and communities is outpacing the rate of change that colleges and universities are prepared to handle. It is crucial for student affairs educators in every functional area, not just in the LGBTQ centers or offices, to learn about and address LGBTQ student concerns. Student affairs educations should foster environments where the voices of these students are heard and incorporated into pertinent decisions regarding programs, policies, and outreach that directly or indirectly shape the campus climate and can affect these students' access, retention, and satisfaction while in college.

Note

1. While it is currently not common practice to expel students for "homosexual behavior," there are still several religious institutions that have policies banning homosexual behavior.

References

American College Personnel Association: College Student Educators International. (2006). *Statement of ethical principles and standards.* Retrieved from http://www .myacpa.org/au/documents/Ethical_Principles_Standards.pdf

Beemyn, B. (2005). Serving the need of transgender college students. In J. T. Sears (Ed.), *Gay, lesbian and transgender issues in education: Programs, policies, and practices* (pp. 105–123). New York: Harrington Park Press.

Beemyn, B., Curtis, B., Davis, M., & Tubbs, N. J. (2005). Transgender issues on college campus. In R. Sanlo (Ed.), *Gender identity and sexual orientation: Research, policy, and personal perspectives. New Directions for Student Services, 111* 49–60.

Bilodeau, B. (2005). Beyond the gender binary: A case study of two transgender students at a Midwestern research university. *Journal of Gay and Lesbian Issues in Education, 3*, 29–44.

Bilodeau, B. L., & Renn, K. A. (2005). Analysis of LGBT identity development models and implications for practice. In R. Sanlo (Ed.), *Gender identity and sexual orientation: Research, policy, and personal perspectives. New Directions for Student Services, 111* 25–39.

Broido, E. (2004). Understanding diversity in millennial students. In M. Coomes & R. DeBard (Eds.), *Serving the millennial generation. New Directions for Student Services, 106,* 73–85.

Cass, V. C. (1979) Homosexual identity formation: A theoretical model. *Journal of Homosexuality, 4,* 219–235.

Cass, V. C. (1984). Homosexual identity formation: Testing a theoretical model. *Journal of Sex Research, 20,* 143–167.

Consortium of Higher Education. (2009). *LGBT resource professionals annual report.* Retrieved from http://www.lgbtcampus.org/about/files/2009AnnualReport.pdf

D'Augelli, A.R. (1994). Identity development and sexual orientation: Toward a model of lesbian, gay, and bisexual development. In E. J. Trickett et al. (Eds.), *Human diversity: Perspectives on people in context* (pp. 312–332). San Francisco: Jossey-Bass.

Debard, R. (2004). Millennials coming to college. In M. Coomes & R. DeBard (Eds.), *Serving the millennial generation. New Directions for Student Services, 106,* 33–45. San Francisco: Jossey-Bass.

Dilley, P. (2002a). 20th century postsecondary practices and policies to control gay students. *Review of Higher Education, 25*(4), 409–431.

Dilley, P. (2002b). *Queer man on campus: A history of non-heterosexual college men, 1945–2000.* New York: Routledge Falmer.

Driver, S. (2007). *Queer girls and popular culture: Reading, resisting, and creating media.* New York: Peter Lang.

Flowers, L. A. (2003). National study of diversity requirements in student affairs graduate programs. *NASPA Journal, 40,* 72–82.

Gayles, J. G., & Kelly, B. T. (2007). Experiences with diversity in the curriculum: Implications for graduate programs and student affairs practice. *NASPA Journal, 44*(1), 193–208.

Griffin, P., Lee, C., Waugh, J., & Beyer, C. (2005). Describing roles that gay-straight alliances play in schools: From individual support to school change. In J. T. Sears (Ed.), *Gay, lesbian and transgender issues in education: Programs, policies, and practices* (pp. 167–183). New York: Harrington Park Press.

Herbst, S., & Malaney, G. D. (1999). Perceived value of a special interest residential program for gay, lesbian, bisexual and transgender students. *NASPA Journal, 36,* 106–119.

Holmes, S. E., & Cahill, S. (2005). School experiences of gay, lesbian, bisexual, and trnsgender youth. In J. T. Sears (Ed.), *Gay, lesbian and transgender issues in education: Programs, policies, and practices* (pp. 63–76). New York: Harrington Park Press.

Howe, N., & Strauss, W. (2000). *Millennials rising: The next great generation*. New York: Vintage.

Jennings, K. (Ed.). (1994). Gay and lesbian youth: Voices from the next generation. In K. Jennings (Ed.), *Becoming visible: A reader in gay and lesbian history for high school and college students* (pp. 262–278). Los Angeles: Alyson Publications.

Kortegast, C. A. (2009, November). *Other duties not assigned: Informal responsibilities of gay and lesbian student affairs professionals*. Symposia presentation at the Association of the Study of Higher Education (ASHE) Conference, Vancouver, B.C., Canada.

Love, P. G. (1998). Cultural barriers facing lesbian, gay, and bisexual students at a Catholic college. *Journal of Higher Education, 69*(3), 298–323.

McCarn, S.R. & Fassinger, R.E. (1996). Re-visioning sexual minority identity formation: A new model of lesbian development and its implications for counseling and research. *Counseling Psychologist, 24*, 508–534.

Miceli, M. (2005). *Standing out, standing together: The social and political impact of gay-straight alliances*. New York: Routledge.

National Association of Student Personnel Administrators. (1990). *NASPA standards of professional practice*. Retrieved from http://www.naspa.org/about/standards.cfm

National Association of Student Personnel Administrators. (n.d.). *NASPA's commitment to diversity, inclusion, and equity*. Retrieved from http://naspa.org/about/diversity.cfm

Patton, L. D. (2011). Perspectives on identity, disclosure and the campus environment among African American gay and bisexual men at one historically Black college. *Journal of College Student Development, 52*(1), 77–100.

Poynter, K. J., & Washington, J. (2005). Multiple identities: Creating community on campus for LGBT students. In R. Sanlo (Ed.), *Gender identity and sexual orientation: Research, policy, and personal. New Directions for Student Services, 111*, 41–47.

Pullen, C. (2007). *Documenting gay men: Identity and performance in reality television and documentary film* (pp. 116–138). Jefferson, NC: McFarland.

Renn, K. A., & Bilodeau, B. L. (2005). Leadership identity development among lesbian, gay, bisexual, and transgender student leaders. *NASPA Journal, 42*(5), 342–367.

Ritchie, C. A., & Banning, J. H. (2001). Gay, lesbian, bisexual, and transgender campus support offices: A qualitative study of establishment experiences. *NASPA Journal, 38*(4), 482–494.

Roper, L. (2005). The role of senior student affairs officers in supporting LGBT students: Exploring the landscape of one's life. In R. Sanlo (Ed.), *Gender identity and sexual orientation: Research, policy, and personal. New Directions for Student Services, 111*, 81–88.

Sanlo, R. (2000). The LGBT campus resource center director: The new profession in student affairs. *NASPA Journal, 37*(3), 485–494.

Savin-Williams, R. C. (2005). *The new gay teenager.* Cambridge, MA: Harvard University Press

Streitmatter, R. (2009). *From perverts to fab five: The media's changing depiction of gay men and lesbians.* New York: Routledge.

Talbot, D. M., & Kocarek, C. (1997). Student affairs graduate faculty members' knowledge, comfort, and behaviors regarding issues of diversity. *Journal of College Student Development, 38,* 278–287.

Talbot, D. M., & Viento, W. L. E. (2005). Incorporating LGBT issues into student affairs graduate education. In R. Sanlo (Ed.), *Gender identity and sexual orientation: Research, policy, and personal perspectives. New Directions for Student Services, III,* 75–80.

Tasker, F., & Patterson, C. J. (2007). Research on gay and lesbian parenting: Retrospect and prospect. In F. Tasker & J. J. Bigner (Eds.), *Gay and lesbian parenting: New directions* (pp. 9–34). Binghamton: Haworth Press.

Zemsky, B. (2004). Coming out of the ivy closet: Improving campus climate for GLBT students, faculty, and staff. In W. Swan (Ed.), *Handbook of gay, lesbian, bisexual, and transgender administration and policy* (pp. 247–283). New York: Marcel Dekker.

11

IDENTITY MAKEOVER
MILLENNIAL EDITION

Using Contemporary Theoretical Frameworks
to Explore Identity Intersections Among
LGBTQ Millennial Populations

Lori D. Patton and Stephanie Chang

But which category addresses which complica-
tion? Should I speak to the history of my black-
ness as a black feminist or as a queer, or do I
identify with both because I am a lesbian of African American descent? . . . I toyed with the possibility of ordering them differently—black queer
feminist, black feminist queer, feminist black
queer—of placing question marks between
them . . . the queer modifies and is modified
by the black which then doubly modifies the
feminism.

(Harris, 1996, p. 4)

Among postsecondary educators and university administrators, identity development models and theories have been used to understand
the overwhelmingly diverse developmental experiences of college
students. Indeed, the field of college student affairs relies heavily on identity
development theories, purporting that theory informs practice. Identity
development models are considered to be central to informing how to support students in their psychosocial, cognitive, and moral development. Such

theories and models are equally important in explaining how individuals come to recognize and actualize their social identities such as sexual orientation, race, and gender.

For decades, theories used to understand college students have treated identity in compartmentalized ways, paying little attention to the manner in which identities intersect, how such intersections are governed by interlocking systems of oppression, and the shifting social locations in which individuals are situated as a result (e.g., Cass 1979, 1984). This chapter contemplates and complicates identity as it relates to Millennial generation college students. Acknowledging that a full treatment of this topic is beyond the scope of this chapter, we focus on diverse Millennial college students, particularly those who occupy multiple oppressive spaces in terms of their sexual, racial, and gender identities. While we engage our discussion with sexual orientation as an entry point, we do not simply examine this category in isolation. As Acker (2006) indicated, "focusing on one category almost inevitably obscures and oversimplifies other interpenetrating realities" (p. 442). Instead, we consider the mutually shaping processes that occur among sexual orientation and other aspects of identity within the context of campus environment and examine sexual identities among populations that are also racialized and gendered on college campuses. In our discussion we summarize some of the existing challenges of using current identity development models and theories and consider what the future of identity development theories might entail if such research were situated in the context of broader frameworks such as queer theory and Black feminism and intersectionality theory. In essence we discuss (re)shifting identity discourses and call attention to the value of placing traditional theories and more critical theories in dialogue with one another. Finally, we explain why such an exercise is necessary for examining identity among Millennial generation college students. To explicate our points we describe how a Millennial generation, African American woman with a nonheterosexual identity might experience her diverse identities.

The Current State of Theories on LGBTQ Identities and Development

A host of scholars have offered theories and models to promote greater comprehension of the processes leading to healthy lesbian, gay, bisexual, transgender, and queer (LGBTQ) identities. Cass (1979, 1984), D'Augelli (1994),

Fox (1995), McCarn and Fassinger (1996), Robin and Hamner (2000), Troiden (1988), and several others have been instrumental in offering theories and perspectives that lend themselves to understanding the developmental processes of LGBTQ individuals. As influential as these models have been, they are not without critique. In an earlier review of lesbian identity theories, Sophie (1985/86) noted that stage theories were too linear in nature, failing to accurately predict significant developmental events and the order in which they occur, if at all. Moreover, she declared that general stage theories may appear to be accurate on the surface, but as the heterogeneity of individuals is considered, they become increasingly inaccurate, making it difficult to understand the complexities associated with sexual identity development among these populations. Stage theories often present the erroneous notion that development among men and women is the same (Edwards & Brooks, 1999). Moreover, such theories assert that a healthy sexual identity can only be achieved through "coming out," a process that may "conflict with the community and family values of many cultures" (Evans, Forney, Guido, Patton, & Renn, 2010, p. 312). Another critique of stage models, broadly speaking, is that they are often generated through research with primarily White or male participants, have low participant numbers, and lack a solid research foundation[1] (Evans et al., 2010; Bilodeau & Renn, 2005). There is also an absence of literature on college students and the development of a healthy LGBTQ identity. Although a few scholars (Beemyn, 2005; Bilodeau, 2005; Dilley, 2002; Poynter & Washington, 2005) have focused on the identities and experiences of LGBTQ college students, the majority of this work is focused on adolescents (precollege) or adults (postcollege), signifying an enormous gap and the need for additional research. Given the significant critique of stage models, later theoretical perspectives attempted to address these issues.

The work of Fassinger et al. (Fassinger & Miller, 1996; McCarn & Fassinger, 1996; Tomlinson & Fassinger, 2003) represents a major contribution to the literature in terms of understanding the contextual nature and cultural caveats that shaped identity. Fassinger and colleagues also challenged limited understandings of the coming out process and argued that public disclosure was not necessarily an indication of a more advanced identity (Evans et al., 2010). D'Augelli (1994) introduced a lifespan model of sexual orientation that acknowledges the complex, interactive, and diverse processes of development. His model is credited with moving beyond the linear nature of earlier theories toward recognition that lesbian, gay, and bisexual identities are fluid and shifting throughout people's lives. However, this theory has also been critiqued for presenting bisexuality as an additive process toward a lesbian or gay identity rather than an actual identity in and of itself.

Given the strides made to understand sexual identity, three key areas remain minimally represented in the literature. The first is an examination of what it means to be heterosexual. Edwards and Brooks (1999) stated "we have frequently asked what causes non-heterosexual orientation and neglected to ask what causes the dominant sexual orientation of heterosexuality" (p. 51). Some higher education literature (Mueller & Cole, 2009; Worthington, Savoy, Dillon, & Vernaglia, 2002) has taken this issue to task, but this line of research remains undertheorized, ultimately resituating heterosexuals as the norm and any identity beyond that as abnormal or a research necessity. The second is a more nuanced understanding of how sexual identities intersect (and at times collide) with raced, classed, and gendered identities. For example, Scholl (2001) stated:

> Queer people of color . . . present particular challenges to educators, in part because they exceed containment within singular, fixed, and categorical-based analyses of identity and community. It is not possible to sum up their identities by analyzing race, then ethnicity, then sexuality, for it is also through the particular ways all these identities intersect and are negotiated that we start to come to terms with the irreducible complexity of our identities. (p. 144)

Third is a need to problematize the use of traditional theories by examining the social locations of individuals about whose experiences these theories were designed to uncomplicate. Hulko (2009) defined social location as follows:

> Social location is a dynamic concept; it is contingent, and its attribution reflects processes of subordination and domination—both contemporary and historical. The ways in which identities intersect and oppressions interlock are fluid and varied because the meanings that are ascribed to identity categories and the power afforded or denied to specific social groups are based on the sociocultural context in which these social processes occur. (p. 52)

In other words, reliance on traditional theories alone represents an incomplete picture of identity development and does not sufficiently account for societal power structures that in many ways dictate what is possible for defining LGBTQ identities in personal and sociocultural contexts. Our intent is not to critique existing theories, but instead to address the "theoretical silence" that is imposed when larger oppressive systems remain unnamed in the process of theory building (Hammonds, 1994; Harris, 1996).

(Re)positioning the Traditional Into the Critical

By way of an example, we present a fictional conversation between Rob, the LGBTQ student organization advisor, and Kima, an undergraduate student:

> Rob: Hi Kima. Long time no see. So, what's going on? I thought you were going to make it to the LGBTQ gathering last week? We really missed you and I think it would have been a great opportunity to meet everyone.
>
> Kima: Rob, thanks for checking on me. I planned to go to the meeting but then changed my mind. I've been doing a lot of thinking lately and I'm just not sure that the organization would be a good fit for me.
>
> Rob: What do you mean? I've been advising this group for several years and find the student members to be very welcoming and committed to providing a supportive space. Membership is open to any student and this would help you to get more involved.
>
> Kima: Well, to be honest, I don't know if it would be a good fit for me for several reasons. First, I noticed that there aren't many students of color involved, let alone African American women, which was the first red flag. I have had interactions with some of the members and the vibe just wasn't positive. By this I mean that they couldn't understand why I wasn't willing to label my sexual identity. I'm at a point in my life where labels simply won't do because they feel so confining. I learned this the hard way when I came out to my roommates two years ago. When I said I was bisexual, one jokingly called me selfish and told me that I needed to choose. The other acted strange around me as if she thought I was attracted to her. Believe me, she wasn't my type [they laugh]. Anyway, she eventually moved out, but the discomfort I felt in those interactions is no different from when I spoke to some of the members. They just didn't get me aside from thinking that my race would add to the group's racial diversity. I think the other thing is that the organization seems to have expectations of me that I am not willing to fulfill. I don't feel the need to "come out" to everybody I meet. I'm not ashamed of who I am. In fact, I'm proud of the person I am and look forward to seeing the person I continuously become, but the members made me feel as if the only way to be proud was through verbally acknowledging my sexual identity, which again would force me to place

a label on it. My experiences are quite different and I can't tease apart my identities. When I look in the mirror, I see me, Kima. It's hard enough to be an African American woman on this campus, especially with our limited numbers, and sometimes I feel pulled to represent my race instead of my sexual orientation. And I'm really not involved with the women's organizations. There just really isn't a comfortable space here for me. No space where I can be me with all of my integrated identities. So, it's not just the LGBTQ organization that I haven't joined. I'm not a member of any group where I feel pressured to rank or choose.

Rob: Kima, thanks for being so honest with me. You've really been contemplating these issues. From a theoretical standpoint I see a few things that might help explain what's going on. One way to think about your experiences is that you may actually be going through a phase in your identity and at some point will be able to name it and profess it proudly, but that will be entirely up to you to name your identity. The other perspective that I can offer is that you are coming to understand how you are situated in our society. That means that you have a lens on how your different identities are interacting and how those interactions are facilitated through oppressive systems. Have I confused you yet?

Kima: No, I think I follow, but could you continue?

Rob: Sure. What I mean is that your racial, gender, and sexual identities, as well as many other identities make you who you are, but who you are is very much dictated by racism, sexism, and heterosexism. The identities that seem to be the most salient or that others assume will be salient to you are highly influenced by the "isms" that I just mentioned and in every instance you may feel the impact of their oppression. It's no secret to me, or you for that matter, that we live in a society where White, male, and heterosexual are the norms and any person or perspective that offers something different is deemed wrong. So it seems like you're really beginning to see the larger systems that are affecting your own identity. Trust me, the issue is not with you, but with these systems and those who benefit from them. So you're really at the crossroads of identity politics and it is something that you're not compelled to engage in.

Kima: You're right Rob. That's a huge part of my hesitation with the LGBT group. I'm thinking about things in a very different way. But it's like they think that everybody develops in the same way give or take a few steps here and there, but that's not the case. For example, with the whole "coming out" thing, everybody doesn't see it the same way. I can't just walk into a Black Student Union meeting and discuss my sexual identity and though my racial identity is evident, I can't go to the women's center and expect that they won't assume that all women have the same experiences or struggles. The moment I say that my experience is different in some way, the differences will likely be minimized for the sake of having a unified voice. I guess what was really taking a toll on me as I thought about joining the group were doubts that I had about whether they could understand how racism or sexism has affected my life. We might share some common aspects in terms of the oppression we face as sexual minorities, but I just didn't feel like they could understand the racism that exists among some LGBT people, the homophobia among some African Americans, and the devaluation of women, especially African American women in society.

Although this conversation is fictional, the concerns raised by Kima are real and significant to how many LGBTQ Millennials are experiencing their multiple identities. Studying sexual identity and sexual orientation in more simplistic and isolated ways may have made the most sense with previous cohorts of students. Indeed the questions and issues raised in the scenario, as well as this chapter, broadly speaking, might not have emerged without earlier models and theories. However, given the newest generation of Millennial students, examining identity using unidimensional approaches is unlikely to be appropriate or productive, particularly given some of the characteristics of LGBTQ students. In particular, these students are more likely to come out at a much earlier age (e.g., middle or high school). Moreover, this is a generation of students who are discontent with the use of generalized labels to define who they are; hence the creation of their own descriptors, words, and language to more accurately represent how they view themselves. Millennial generation students are also disrupting the simplistic binaries (e.g., Black/White, male/female, gay/straight) that regulate not only sexual orientation but also gender and race. Such characteristics of this generation tend to suggest a necessary push toward finding comfort in the midst of complexity and ambiguity. There are no finite, universal answers to the questions that have been proposed to this point, including: What does it mean to identify as a lesbian? What does it mean to be gay? What does a transgender identity entail? Nor has there been an in-depth discussion about whether identity development should be the end goal. As Broido, a colleague, inquired, "What if we didn't presume the development of identity to be one of the central 'tasks' of young adulthood?" (Broido, personal communication, 2008).

Although the traditional perspectives of LGBTQ identities claim inclusivity and acceptance, they often fail to address the complex social systems that are also at play with these populations in higher education. Akerlund and Cheung (2000) noted that traditional theories rarely account for a person's "personal characteristics and their cultural orientation may at the same time affect the direction of his or her identity development" (p. 281). They found that current literature was reflective of five themes (discrimination, oppression, choosing between cultures, rejection, and social support) that shaped the identity development of African American, Latino/a, and Asian American gay men and lesbians. Thus, despite the different eras through which generations pass, systemic issues such as racism, sexism, and heterosexism transcend generational boundaries. Though these systems have manifested themselves in different ways over time, they continue to shape the development of theory, influence how individuals come to understand themselves, and disproportionately affect those most oppressed by their existence. Below we present *queer theory* and *Black feminism* as examples of the types of overarching frameworks that not only would be useful in terms of complicating traditional theories, but could also provide a more complex lens through which identity might be examined.

Queer theory is a postmodern approach to sexuality and gender identities that illuminates issues involving the dichotomizing of sex, sexuality, and gender identities (Ward, 2008; Wilchins, 2004). Similarly, womanist and feminist theorists such as Patricia Hill Collins (2000), Kimberle Crenshaw (1989, 1991), Chandra Mohanty (2006), and Bonnie Thornton Dill (1983; Dill & Zambrana, 2009) have written about intersectionality, the importance of lived experiences, the relevance of standpoints, and meaning making of one's identity. Similar to traditional theories, those that we select for further discussion in this chapter do not present the final say but instead are shared to provide a platform for future discussions regarding identities and oppression. These theories can aid higher education scholars to rethink how identity is experienced for LGBTQ Millennial students, particularly those managing multiple oppressed identities.

Queer and Black Feminist Theories

Though deconstructions of identity regarding LGBTQ populations have been in existence, the term queer theory was first used in the 1990s. At its core, queer theory is concerned with challenging seemingly normal social structures and practices that have dictated the meanings of identities, particularly with regard to sexual orientation and gender. Queer theory moves beyond examining identities as monolithic, fixed states and instead seeks to reveal the fluid, discursive nature of identities and how they are constructed within a heteronormative society. Gamson and Moon (2004) contend that "queer theory has helped set a different sort of agenda . . . in sexualities: to operationalize and then investigate the claims that sexual identities are 'discursively produced' and unstable and that the social order rests on 'heteronormativity' (p. 49). In an effort to explain the power of queer theory, Wilchins (2004) analyzed the problematic nature of labels such as "masculine/feminine, man/woman, top/bottom, butch/femme, and real/artificial" (p. 40). Wilchins's introduction to queer theory presented a deconstructed, postmodern approach to decenter the dominant discourses surrounding sex and gender that rely heavily on binary existences. Furthermore, Wilchins tackled queer theoretical questions about the utility of identification and identity, stating:

> By breaking the links between gender, desire, and sex they become incomprehensible, idiosyncratic, a clever thing to do with words. What does gender identification mean it if doesn't tell us about a person's body, gender expression, and sexual orientation? . . . There is power in naming one's self, being with one's own kind, of breaking into smaller and more homogenous groups. But I am still troubled about making identity the main foundation of our politics. (pp. 131, 150)

Queer theory in this context advocates for redefining the constructed meanings of sex, sexuality, and gender identities. Queer theory is not a developmental perspective. On the contrary, it "has the potential to disrupt and challenge the nature of our cultural assumptions about the development of identity, sexuality and sexual identity" (Edwards & Brooks, 1999, p. 54). Queer theory upsets the status quo of thinking about identity as stable and instead purports that identities are constantly shifting and (re)negotiated. Thus identities are simultaneously created and re-created, representing both present and future. The focus of queer theory is not on an individual's social identity, but instead on the problematic social constructions of identity, the binaries and labels that confine identities, and the disruptive heteronormative regimes of power.

For instance, according to one's birth sex, society assigns a particular sex (female). Based on one's assigned sex, societal expectations enforce a specific gender identity (woman) and expression (feminine). A female birth sex presumes a feminine gender expression and gender identity as woman. There are also a host of stereotypes about what constitutes being a woman and feminine. The association of one identity with another contributes socially normative outcomes that dominate one's sex, sexuality, and gender identification. Such outcomes become problematic and have enormous consequences for a female at birth who identifies with a masculine gender expression. For a woman with a masculine gender expression that expresses attraction to women, the matter becomes increasingly complex. According to Greene (2000), "Lesbians violate a fundamental cultural rule. By crossing the boundaries of gender role expectations, lesbians are deemed defective women who want to be men and are socially subordinate to heterosexual women" (p. 241). Therefore, queer theory becomes highly informative in raising questions and challenging socially normative identity relations with regard to sex, sexuality, and gender.

One issue with traditional models of LGBTQ identity development is the tendency to use labels in an effort designed to simplify the complex. Queer and feminist theories readily complicate the use of labels, which has implications when referring to LGBTQ Millennial students. In using this label, we as authors contribute to the reproduction of sexual categories, reify power structures, and impose limitations on the variety of sexual identities that constitute the Millennial generation (Gamson & Moon, 2004). Mohanty (2006) acknowledged that her focus on women's research and writing can essentialize women's experiences. She used the label "women" as a referent point or category of analysis and states

> women as a category of analysis refers to the crucial assumption that all women, across classes and cultures, are somehow socially constituted as a homogenous group identified prior to the process of analysis. This is an assumption that characterizes much of feminist discourse. (p. 22)

Mohanty astutely recognized that using a homogenous group perspective ultimately renders the diverse and complex nature of women's experiences invisible. As a result, a dominant narrative is generated about a certain type of woman and her experiences. We acknowledge that a similar process of essentializing occurs when using a label such as LGBTQ Millennial students to explore implications of theory and identity. LGBTQ individuals are without question diverse, complex, and underserved in the context of postsecondary research, writing, and practice. However, to initiate and produce written work about LGBTQ Millennial students we have consciously chosen to use LGBTQ Millennial students as a category of analysis and anticipate critique of this decision.

Our acknowledgment about LGBTQ Millennial students as a categorical unit of analysis provides an example of how feminist theory contributes to a more critical perspective of identity. In other words, Mohanty's (2006) recognition of women as a referent is a statement about the inherent paradoxes of studying identity. On the one hand, it is important to identify a unit of analysis, but doing so potentially ignores the nature of intersectional identities. For instance, LGBTQ Millennial students are simultaneously constituted by their sex, sexual orientation, gender, race, ethnicity, class, and a host of other identities. Mohanty's scholarship provides a method of articulating the challenges and contentious relationship between labeling for the sake of analysis, while also attempting to account for diversity and complexity in identity work. Therefore, it is important to read these theoretical frameworks as a way of wading through the inherent complexities of understanding identity and thinking differently about how we understand LGBTQ Millennial students.

As we indicated earlier LGBTQ Millennial college students (and any generation or group of people) represent an array of identities. While queer theory upsets the notion of identities as fixed, the reality is that some individuals feel and experience their identities as if they are fixed. Indeed, the naming of one's identity can have very real political implications. Black feminism employs a similar approach to the deconstruction and analysis of identity, but references the importance of standpoint and intersectionality. Collins (2000) is credited for providing a more nuanced explanation of standpoint theory through examining the lives of African American women. She stated: "Each group speaks from its own standpoint and shares its own partial, situated knowledge. But because each group perceives its own truth as partial, its knowledge is unfinished" (p. 290). For African American women, Black feminism as a standpoint indicates that African American women as a collective experience multiple, intersecting oppressions given their histories in America. Despite a collective experience, how such oppressions are felt and experienced differs substantially, ensuring that there is no monolithic experience. For Collins (2000), the standpoint of Black feminism highlights the struggles Black women have and continue to endure at the various intersections of their identities but is also a location from which these multiple identities and experiences can be properly contextualized. The intent to integrate Collins into the conversation of theory and practice with LGBTQ Millennial students is not to compare Collins's work on Black feminist thought, but to draw on Collins's perspective as a resource for understanding standpoints and subjugated knowledge.

As part of U.S. Black women's standpoint, Collins (2000) brings to light the truths of Black women's experiences in relation to intersectionality. When intersectionality is used as a framework for examining identities, no one identity is ranked higher or more important than another. Instead identities reinforce one another and are mutually constitutive (Wingfield, 2008). Thus, intersectionality becomes very helpful toward understanding identities because of its explanatory power. Few (2007) stated that "Black women exist within an intersectionality matrix . . . a specific location where multiple systems of oppressions simultaneously corroborate and subjugate to conceal deliberate, marginalizing ideological maneuvers that define 'Otherness'" (p. 454). For example, when issues of sexuality and sexual identities are examined, rarely are the experiences of African American women considered. In other words, such examinations tend to obfuscate some raced, gendered, and classed identities as if to indicate they do not affect or change the structural realities of sexual identities (Gamson & Moon, 2004). Collins outlines two possibilities for examining how discourses of sexuality "other" Black women or render them invisible. She noted that sexuality is either "analyzed as a freestanding system of oppression similar to oppressions of race, class, and gender" or "sexualities become manipulated within class, race, nation, and gender distinctive systems of oppressions" (p. 138). With the latter, the effects of sexuality within class, race, nation, and gender contextualize Black women through their bodies. Collins references the objectification and exploitation of Black women through slavery, pornography, and prostitution. Similarly, Greene (2000) raised concerns about the "promulgation of many distorted stereotypes" that permeate and tarnish the images of Black women. In a more contemporary example, Wingfield deconstructed the Don Imus media frenzy that ensued when the radio personality referred to the women of the Rutgers University basketball team as "nappy headed hos." She explains:

> Race, gender, and sexuality overlap conspicuously in Imus's choice of words. Yet, while several prominent African Americans . . . publicly denounced Imus as a racist, many noted feminist voices were conspicuously silent about the sexist assault implicit in his comments. The construction of this insult solely as a racial remark obscures the ways in which racist assaults are also informed by gender and sexuality and how easy it is to prioritize one axis of inequality over others rather than treating . . . them as intersecting phenomena. (p. 89)

Dill (1983) stated that "Black women have felt called upon to choose between their commitments to feminism and to the struggle against racial injustice" (p. 137). Moreover, for Black women oppression becomes more about an interconnection of multiple identities because they are working simultaneously (Dill, 1983; Dill & Zambrana, 2009). Similarly, Crenshaw (1989) proposed that fighting against the oppression of Black women should be a collective struggle on multiple planes as opposed to focused solely on issues pertinent to race. The theory of intersectionality is not an end-all solution, but "The value of intersectionality is not simply that it frames the experiences of frequently overlooked groups but that it reveals systems of power and domination (Wingfield, 2008, p. 89).

Pushing Theoretical Boundaries to Examine LGBTQ Millennials

When attempting to understand LGBTQ Millennial students, context is necessary to access the depth of complexity and richness represented among these populations. Renn (2010) reported that "Higher education is the site of much research on LGBT/queer identities and identity development" (p. 132). Since the environment of investigation for LGBTQ Millennial college students rests largely within postsecondary settings, higher education scholars are perfectly situated to pursue the work necessary to advance this area of study and contribute to knowledge production (Renn, 2010). Knowledge production includes inquiry about which locations on campus hold knowledge about LGBTQ Millennial students, especially those occupying multiple oppressive spaces, who is responsible for distributing knowledge about LGBTQ Millennial students, and how LGBTQ Millennial students are positioned in the classroom and differing academic disciplines to establish a sense of agency and support.

This chapter has identified two overarching theoretical frameworks that have tremendous potential for informing how educators make sense of and research identity. Queer theory challenges what we have come to know about identity and theory development. Given our example of current LGBTQ identity development models, queer theory serves as a framework for re-thinking the meaning of labels to Millennial generation students and questioning the structures in place on campuses and in society that place boundaries on the multiple and rich identities among these populations. Queer theory also complicates methods of using theories to generalize and forces those most interested in researching Millennial student experiences to deconstruct binaries, as well as envision identity from a more critical perspective. In short, identity research needs to be "queered," so to speak, to defy normative, essentialist ways of studying Millennial college students.

Black feminism was also presented as a framework to inform identity theories. As noted, intersectionality is at the core of Black feminism and reveals both the subtle and overt ways that identity discourses are shaped. What Black feminism confirms is that regardless of the identity development theory, it is incomplete in terms of capturing the full identity experience. What Black feminism reveals is a need to examine identity through multiple lenses, always remaining mindful of why some voices remain at the margins while others occupy the center. Black feminism issues a call toward working diligently to center them in the study of Millennial college student identities. Applying Black feminism to the conversation between Rob and Kima also reminds us that racial, sexual, gender, and class identities are mutually shaping and impact people in diverse ways based on their social locations.

Only recently have student affairs scholars begun to complicate traditional theories of identity development by considering multiple identities (Jones & McEwen, 2000; Stewart, 2008). In terms of LGBTQ identities, some scholars (Abes & Kasch, 2007; Bilodeau & Renn, 2005; Renn, 2010) have considered the ways in which queer theory can be an informative framework. Patton and Simmons (2008) and Patton (2011) have also contributed to engaging the issue of race and gender in relation to queer identities, as well considering how the structures within particular institutional types (namely historically Black colleges and universities) shape multiple identities. Similarly, some scholarship has used Black feminism as a framework (Abes, Jones, & McEwen, 2007; Howard-Hamilton, 2003; Patton & McClure, 2009). The use of these frameworks is precisely what is needed to push theoretical boundaries by engaging the "borderlands between theoretical perspectives" (Abes, 2009, p. 143). Doing so has the potential to unveil more critical and innovative ways of examining identity for generations to come.

Note

1. For a fuller treatment of the critiques regarding sexual identity development models see Evans, Forney, Guido, Patton, and Renn (2010).

References

Abes, E. S. (2009). Theoretical borderlands: Using multiple theoretical perspectives to challenge inequitable power structures in student development theory. *Journal of College Student Development, 50*(2), 141–156.

Abes, E. S., Jones, S. R., & McEwen, M. K. (2007). Reconceptualizing the model of multiple dimensions of identity: The role of meaning-making capacity in the construction of multiple identities. *Journal of College Student Development, 48,* 1–22.

Abes, E. S., & Kasch, D. (2007). Using queer theory to explore lesbian college students' multiple dimensions of identity. *Journal of College Student Development, 48*(6), 619–636.

Acker, J. (2006). Inequality regimes: Gender, class, and race in organizations. *Gender and Society, 20*(4), 441–464.

Akerlund, M., & Cheung, M. (2000). Teaching beyond the deficit model: Gay and lesbian issues among African Americans, Latinos, and Asian Americans. *Journal of Social Work Education, 36*(2), 279–292.

Beemyn, B. (2005). Serving the need of transgender college students. In J. T. Sears (Ed.), *Gay, lesbian and transgender issues in education: Programs, policies, and practices* (pp. 105–123). New York: Harrington Park Press.

Bilodeau, B. (2005). Beyond the gender binary: A case study of two transgender students at a Midwestern research university. *Journal of Gay and Lesbian Issues in Education, 3,* 29–44.

Bilodeau, B. L., & Renn, K. A. (2005). Analysis of LGBT identity development models and implications for practice. In R. Sanlo (Ed.), *Gender identity and sexual orientation: Research, policy, and personal perspectives. New Directions for Student Services, 111,* 25–39.

Cass, V. C. (1979). Homosexual identity formation: A theoretical model. *Journal of Homosexuality, 4,* 219–235.

Cass, V. C. (1984). Homosexual identity formation: Testing a theoretical model. *Journal of Sex Research, 20,* 143–167.

Collins, P. H. (2000). *Black feminist thought: Knowledge, consciousness, and the politics of empowerment.* New York: Routledge Classics.

Crenshaw, K. (1989). Demarginalizing the intersection of race and sex: A Black feminist critique of antidiscrimination doctrine, feminist theory and antiracist politics. *University of Chicago Legal Forum,* 139–167.

Crenshaw, K. (1991). Mapping the margins: Intersectionality, identity politics, and violence against women of color. *Stanford Law Review, 43,* 1241–1299.

D'Augelli, A. R. (1994). Identity development and sexual orientation: Toward a model of lesbian, gay, and bisexual development. In E. J. Trickett et al. (Eds.), *Human diversity: Perspectives on people in context* (pp. 312–332). San Francisco: Jossey-Bass.

Dill, B. T. (1983). Race, class, and gender: Prospects for an all-inclusive sisterhood. *Feminist Studies, 9,* 131–150.

Dill, B. T., & Zambrana, R. E. (2009). *Emerging intersections: Race, class, and gender in theory, policy, and practice.* New Brunswick, NJ: Rutgers University Press.

Dilley, P. (2002). *Queer man on campus: A history of non-heterosexual college men, 1945–2000.* New York: Routledge Falmer.

Evans, N. J., Forney, D. S., Guido, F. M., Patton, L. D., & Renn, K. A. (2010). *Student development in college: Theory, research and practice* (2nd ed.). San Francisco: Jossey-Bass.

Fassinger, R. E., & Miler, B. A. (1996). Validation of an inclusive model of homosexual identity formation in a sample of gay men. *Journal of Homosexuality, 32*(2), 53–78.

Few, A. L. (2007). Integrating black consciousness and critical race feminism into family studies research. *Journal of Family Issues, 28*(4), 452–473.

Fox, R. C. (1995). Bisexual identities. In A. R. D'Augelli & C. J. Patterson (Eds.), *Lesbian, gay, and bisexual identities over the lifespan* (pp. 48–86). Oxford: Oxford University Press.

Gamson, J., & Moon, D. (2004). The sociology of sexualities: Queer and beyond. *Annual Review of Sociology, 30*, 47–64.

Greene, B. (2000). African American lesbian and bisexual women. *Journal of Social Issues, 56*(2), 239–249.

Hammonds, E. (1994). Black (w)holes and the geometry of black female sexuality. *Differences: A Journal of Feminist Critical Studies, 6*(2), 126–145.

Harris, L. A. (1996). Queer black feminism: The pleasure principle. *Feminist Review, 54*, 3–30.

Howard-Hamilton, M. F. (2003). Theoretical frameworks for African American women. In M. F. Howard-Hamilton (Ed.), *Meeting the needs of African American women. New Directions for Student Services, 104*, 19–27.

Hulko, W. (2009). The time- and context-contingent nature of intersectionality and interlocking oppressions. *Affilia, 24*(1), 44–55.

Jones, S. R., & McEwen, M. K. (2000). A conceptual model of multiple dimensions of identity. *Journal of College Student Development, 41*, 405–414.

McCarn, S. R., & Fassinger, R. E. (1996). Re-visioning sexual minority identity formation: A new model of lesbian development and its implications for counseling and research. *Counseling Psychologist, 24*, 508–534.

Mohanty, C. T. (2006). *Feminism without borders: Decolonizing theory, practicing solidarity.* Durham, NC: Duke University Press.

Mueller, J. A., & Cole, J. (2009). A qualitative examination of heterosexual consciousness among college students. *Journal of College Student Development, 50*, 320–336.

Patton, L. D. (2011). Perspectives on identity, disclosure and the campus environment among African American gay and bisexual men at one historically Black college. *Journal of College Student Development, 52*(1), 77–100.

Patton, L. D., & McClure, M. (2009). Strength in the spirit: African American college women and spiritual coping mechanisms. *Journal of Negro Education, 78*(1), 42–54.

Patton, L. D., & Simmons, S. L. (2008). Exploring complexities of multiple identities of lesbians in a Black college environment. *Negro Educational Review, 59*, 197–215.

Poynter, K. J., & Washington, J. (2005). Multiple identities: Creating community on campus for LGBT students. In R. Sanlo (Ed.), *Gender identity and sexual orientation: Research, policy, and personal. New Directions for Student Services, 111,* 41–47.

Renn, K. A. (2010). LGBT and queer research in higher education: The state and status of the field. *Educational Researcher, 39*(2), 132–141.

Robin, L., & Hamner, K. (2000). Bisexuality: Identities and community. In V. A. Wall & N. J. Evans (Eds.), *Toward acceptance: Sexual orientation issues on campus* (pp. 245–259). Washington, DC: American College Personnel Association.

Scholl, L. (2001). Narratives of hybridity and the challenge to multicultural education. In K. K. Kumashiro (Ed.), *Troubling intersections of race and sexuality: Queer students of color and anti-oppressive education* (pp. 141–161). Lanham, MD: Rowman & Littlefield.

Sophie, J. (1985/86). A critical examination of stage theories of lesbian identity development. *Journal of Homosexuality, 12*(2), 39–51.

Stewart, D. L. (2008). Being all of me: Black students negotiating multiple identities. *Journal of Higher Education, 79,* 183–207.

Tomlinson, M. J., & Fassinger, R. E. (2003). Career development, lesbian identity development, and campus climate among lesbian college students. *Journal of College Student Development, 44,* 845–860.

Troiden, R. R. (1988). Homosexual identity development. *Journal of Adolescent Health Care, 9,* 105–113.

Ward, J. (2008). *Respectably queer: Diversity culture in LGBT activist organizations.* Nashville, TN: Vanderbilt University Press.

Wilchins, R. (2004). *Queer theory, gender theory: An instant primer.* Los Angeles: Alyson Books.

Wingfield, A. H. (2008). Bringing minority men back in: Comment on Andersen. *Gender and Society, 22*(1), 88–92.

Worthington, R. L., Savoy, H. B., Dillon, F. R., & Vernaglia, E. R. (2002). Heterosexual identity development: A multidimensional model of individual and social identity. *Counseling Psychologist, 30,* 496–531.

PART SEVEN

BI- AND MULTIRACIAL MILLENNIALS IN COLLEGE

12

MULTIRACIALIZATION, "MIXING," AND MEDIA PEDAGOGY

Nana Osei-Kofi

Reality is never experienced directly but always through the cultural categories made available by society.

—Stuart Hall, 1997

Strange to wake up and realize you're in style. That's what happened to me just the other morning. It was the first day of the new millennium and I woke up to find that mulattos had taken over. Playing golf, running the airwaves, opening their own restaurants, modeling clothes, starring in musicals with names like "Show Me the Miscegenation!" The radio played a steady stream of Lenny Kravitz, Sade, and Mariah Carey. I thought I'd died and gone to Berkeley. But then I realized. According to the racial zodiac, 2000 is the official Year of the Mulatto. Pure breeds (at least the black ones) are out and hybridity is in. America loves us in all of our half-caste glory. The president announced on Friday that beige is to be the official color of the millennium. Major news magazines announce our arrival as if we were proof of extraterrestrial life. They claim

we're going to bring about the end of race as we
know it.

(Senna, 1998, pp. 12-13)

"**M**ultiracials are in style" (DaCosta, 2006, p. 184). "Ambiguity is chic" (La Ferla, 2003, para 5). Whether described as "generation mix" (Beltrán & Fojas, 2008), "generation e.a.: ethnically ambiguous" (La Ferla, 2003), "generation remix" or "generation m: multiracial" (Spencer, 2009), multiracialized representations are increasingly present on television, in print, and on the big screen. Fortune 500 companies are using "multiracial" models in their advertisements to represent the new, the exciting, and the cutting edge. Couples made up of differently racialized partners like Heidi Klum and Seal are the darlings of the press, and "mixed race" Hollywood stars like Rosario Dawson and Vanessa Williams are household names and are seen regularly in blockbuster movies and on prime time television.

Despite the powerful influence of the media on our understanding of racialization and on the socialization of Millennials in college (Coomes, 2004; Halter, 2002; hooks, 1997; Shohat & Stam, 1994; Vera & Gordon, 2003), scholarship on multiracialization in the study of higher education has not yet engaged with this subject matter to any great extent. To date, scholarship on multiracialization in the study of higher education has primarily focused on the psychology of identity development, seeking to better understand how "multiracial" Millennials in college make meaning of their identities and how this in turn impacts student affairs practice (e.g., Evans, Forney, Guido, Renn & Patton, 2009; Renn, 2004; Renn & Shang, 2008). DaCosta (2006) suggests:

> In our attempts to understand the social implications of new racial categories and increased interracial intimacy . . . we have ignored one of the most far-reaching and consequential institutions likely to shape new racial identifications and their meanings in the years to come—[that is to say] the marketplace. (p. 183)

We know that Millennials, more than members of any previous generation, rely heavily on the media as a primary source of knowledge, which therefore significantly shapes their attitudes, values, beliefs (Coomes, 2004), and identities (Shohat & Stam, 1994). Much of what is learned about difference today is learned through a media pedagogy, where the market is positioned as a place to both come to understand the Other as well as to participate in contemporary cultural formations (Halter, 2002; hooks, 1997; Vera & Gordon, 2003). Consequently, how multiracialization is constructed by media sources has paramount impact on how Millennials come to understand, construct, and interpret multiracialized identities, whether this pertains to how they understand themselves or others.

It is this subject matter that is the focus of this essay. While recognizing that representations are always subject to interpretation, negotiation, complexity, and contradiction, and thus never totalizing, my interest is in understanding hegemonic representations and their meanings within the context of American culture in the 21st century. Through addressing contemporary media representations of multiracialization, I aim to engage with the role of these representations in shaping racialized constructions of difference, and to explore the implications of these constructions for student affairs research and practice.

Before proceeding, a note on language is in order. Much has been said about the use of language in engaging matters of "race." The main issue concerns how to speak to the issue of "race" and recognize it as a social construction that continues to have real material consequences, and not treat "race" as biology and fall victim to essentialism. Therefore, throughout this essay, I use the language of racialization and multiracialization as these terms signify the acts of constructing individuals and groups in particular ways in relation to power and privilege. More specifically, as Olumide (2005) explains, the language of racialization "place[s] the burden of race thinking at the feet of the race thinker" (p. 132). I also believe, as Spencer (2006) argues, that "race in the United States will not be undermined by movements that collaborate with the race concept, but rather by uncompromising assaults on the belief in race itself, whether biological or social, and by deliberate and unceasing deconstructions of whiteness" (p. 101). Accordingly, I use quotation marks around the term "race" to signify its social construction. However, I leave the language of "race" used by the authors upon whose work I draw unchanged out of respect for accuracy in my utilization of their work.

Multiracialized Media Representations

Multiracialized media representations have been significantly reconfigured over time. Nineteenth century American literature and film introduced the notion of the tragic mulatto, living between two worlds, not fitting in, and therefore psychologically troubled and unstable. The tragic mulatta was portrayed on screen and in literature as a dishonest and loose woman. Similarly, the most recognizable sociological theory of racial mixing during this time period was that of the marginal man. According to Stonequist (1937/1961), the marginal man was maladjusted and unstable, lived between worlds, suffered from a feeling of inferiority, and possessed a victim mentality due to a lack of belonging to any racial group. These constructions of multiracialized identities were exemplified in *Birth of a Nation* (1915), a film credited with laying the foundation for some of the most horrible characterizations of racialization in U.S. consciousness. Silas Lynch, the film's mixed race character, is portrayed as emotionally unstable, immoral, criminal, and rapacious (Beltrán & Fojas, 2008).

Following World War II, a shift in representations is evidenced as Hollywood began to experiment with what Squires (2007) describes as *liberal message films*. These films featured biracial characters and were designed to oppose prejudice and at the same time promote the values and behaviors of White middle class respectability. Played by White actors, the biracial characters in movies such as *Lost Boundaries* and *Pinky* were typically caught seeking to pass as White while real Whites were the true heroes, giving these biracial characters limited access to White middle-class society. In attaining this limited access, these biracial characters were distinguished from the lower class and "real" Blacks, from whom they had to distance themselves to maintain their "status" in the racial and class hierarchy of these films.

In short, historically, representations of multiracialized bodies have been presented as a danger to White society, threatening the integrity and superiority of the White race (Furedi, 2001). More recently, however, multiracialized characters have been presented with more nuances, from neutral to heroic. In fact, Beltrán and Fojas (2008) argue that "multiracial action heroes have [now] become a trend in their own right" (p. 11), featuring actors like Keanu Reaves, Jessica Alba, Vin Diesel and The Rock (Dwayne Johnson).

Whether it is film, advertising, or television, representations of multiracialization seem to be everywhere today. For example, in the 2001 film *The Fast and the Furious*, Vin Diesel plays an ethnically ambiguous leader of a diverse group of individuals involved in different ways with street racing in a racially harmonious Los Angeles (Beltrán, 2005). Diesel is described by a Hollywood executive as "the son of today's diverse audience" (Beltrán, 2005, p. 54); his ethnically ambiguous look reinforces his ability to move in and out of different cultural contexts with ease, at once navigating a diverse context while at the same time dominating it (Beltrán, 2005). We learn from the film that in this world speed is what counts rather than how much money you have or the color of your skin (Beltrán, 2005). To this end, Edwin, an African American racer played by Ja Rule conveys to Brian, a White undercover cop among the speed racers, that "it's not how you stand by your car, it's how you race your car that is important." In this statement, as Beltrán (2005) argues, "the 'raceless' credo of street racing is communicated: racing ability and cultural savvy determine status and leadership, not whiteness or money" (p. 61).

Moving from the big screen to representations of multiracialization in print, in the world of fashion advertising, companies like Calvin Klein, the Gap, Abercrombie and Fitch, and Levi's rely on physical markers such as eyes, hair, and skin color to represent "race" and "mixed race" and to symbolize racial unity and harmony in difference (Streeter, 2003). This trend follows in the footsteps of the now world-famous United Colors of Benetton "two-tone" campaign of the mid-1980s. For example, in an effort to symbolize cosmopolitanism, H&M uses models whose features are described as "racially indeterminate" in the belief that this inspires viewers and at the same signifies neutrality (La Ferla, 2003, para 5). The managing editor for the magazine *Teen People* suggests that what the modeling world is looking for today is "the exotic, left-of-center beauty that transcends race or class" (La Ferla, 2003, para 6). Through these modes of representation, multiracialism is used to attract a mass audience (DaCosta, 2006).

A principal with New American Dimensions, a multicultural marketing firm in Los Angeles, describes the current mass audience—many of whom are Millennials—as having "casual mix-and-match cultural sensibilities" (Tseng, 2008, para 8). Tseng compares the flexibility with which Millennials can choose ethnic and cultural identities to "mashups," such as popular music compositions created from samples of music from a range of genres. Tseng argues that much like an iPod list, this population can customize and personalize their identities to suit their preferences.

This perspective suggests that as a society we have transcended "race" and is consistent with press reports that explain that as a result of the progressive mindset of Millennials, we now live in a post-racial era. According to Madland and Teixeira (2009):

> Millennials support gay marriage, take race and gender equality as givens, are tolerant of religious and family diversity, have an open and positive attitude toward immigration, and generally display little interest in fighting over the divisive social issues of the past. (p. 2)

The ultimate proof of this, it is suggested, was the election of President Barack Obama. If a man with a Black father and a White mother can become president of the United States, then surely as a nation, America has transcended "race." President Obama according to this narrative is someone whom by his very existence and social location symbolizes a fluid "racial" harmony.

These examples demonstrate that multiracialized bodies are being re-signified in contemporary media representations. From being portrayed as tragic mulattas and marginal men, through films, advertising and other forms of mass media, multiracials are now depicted as "living bridges between races" (Spencer, 2009, para 8). They are represented as what Hari-taworn (2009) describes as "super-citizens of the new world" (p. 60), as a new people, whose identities represent individual commodity choices that are fluid in nature. Consistent with much of White America's views of race, what results is a perception of race as "merely . . . a style, symbol, or purchas-able commodity . . . stripped of any coercive or institutional power" (Gal-lagher, 2006, p. 105). In this new era, multiracials are presented as fitting in anywhere and easily navigating and commanding authority in a multicul-tural world. It is as though somehow social recognition has come to equate social justice. To this end, Gallagher (2006) argues:

> The endless stream of racial equality story lines [as exemplified above] delivered from politicians, television dramas, music videos, sporting events, and advertisements, all of which suggest totell, or imply to Americans that racial equality, equal opportunity, and upward mobility are now available to all [are paramount obstacles to racial justice]. (p. 115)

Media Pedagogy: The Meaning of Multiracialization

As I suggested earlier, alongside the notion of a post-racial era, the media puts forth "multiracial" people as a "new" people. Typically, in the U.S. context, this notion of a new people is attributed to the 1967 Supreme Court ruling in *Loving v. Commonwealth of Virginia*, which ended race-based legal restrictions on marriage. This decision resulted in the growth of "interracial" marriages, which set the stage for what is now portrayed as a new "multira-cial" population.

Through this line of reasoning, "multiracial . . . [Millennials] are seen as something 'new' or contemporary, rather than as part and parcel of the historical and sociological development of the U.S." (Spencer, 2006, p. 114).

It is true that more people who identify as belonging to different racialized groups have produced offspring since the *Loving* decision; yet to extend this fact to suggest that these individuals are multiracial while simultaneously viewing African Americans as monoracial (a commonly held view) is to at once construct mulitraciality based on the notion of interracial sex, while at the same time acknowledging yet ignoring centuries of so-called interracial sex (Spencer, 2006).

Media representations of multiracialization are also dependent on racialization, yet seek to portray a world in which "race" does not matter. Multiraciality is made salient through visual and cultural markers as evidence of the insignificance of race, yet the very notion that is being described as being of no consequence is what is being used to substantiate the argument, while the idea of a category of multiracial people itself also depends on the existence of racial categorization (Spencer, 2009). Rather than being a "new" people or representing the existence of a post-racial era, I suggest that critical analyses of media representations of multiracialization reveal that "multiraciality" is presented against a White norm and that recognizing the consequences of these representations have significant ramifications for working with Millennials on issues of racialization in the contemporary era.

In the film *The Fast and the Furious*, White superiority is made salient through the presence of White characters portrayed as having great influence in a subculture where in actuality, they would unlikely be present, or if they were present, would hold marginal positions (Beltrán, 2005). Similarly, Brian, the movie's White undercover cop, is immediately accepted by the leading racing team, while non-White characters fail to receive the same acceptance; when it is time for Brian to prove himself, he easily beats two racers of color, yet in the real world, people of color dominate street racing. Meanwhile, the sister of Dominic (Vin Diesel's character), Mia (played by Jordana Brewster), is portrayed as a bridge builder between the White world and a "multiracial" world; she provides crucial information to Brian, with whom she is romantically involved, making it possible for him to save Dominic when he is in trouble, thereby positioning Brian in the role of White savior. Hence, despite the presence of Vin Diesel as a superhero, traditional racial expectations are reinforced throughout the film as it ultimately centers on whiteness. Mia's role in the storyline is also a reminder of the ways in which representations are not only racialized but gendered as well. Reminiscent of the ways in which colonial powers relied on "native" women to "acclimate" colonizers to the benefit of colonial expansion (Stoler, 2002), Mia is positioned in a romanticized role of native informant and romantic interest.

While the world of advertising glorifies the ethnically ambiguous, Hasinoff (2008) reminds us that not all bodies—in this case, not all multiracial women—are considered to have wide market appeal. In advertising, it is light-skinned women, "brown but not too brown" (Valdivia, 2005, p. 13), typically middle to upper class and heterosexual, who are made to stand in for all racial diversity. Even a face as well-known as Beyoncé's was lightened in an advertisement for L'Oréal cosmetics in 2008 (Rajan, 2008).

Ethnically ambiguous women in advertising could be White women with tans, maybe multiracial, maybe light-skinned Blacks, but not dark-skinned, not Black. Gallagher (2006) describes this practice as the "which drop rule," which essentially functions as a way to continue to center whiteness while purportedly celebrating multiraciality. His point is that the offspring of differently racialized pairings have different meanings and are ascribed different values dependent on a hierarchy that is informed by their relationships to whiteness. For example, it is more likely for the offspring of White/Asian pairings to be identified as White and ascribed higher statuses in the racial hierarchy than the children of White/Black pairings, who are assigned to the bottom of the hierarchy. What this points to is a Black–non-Black divide or hierarchy that is used to ascribe value to different groups (Lee & Bean, 2007), and also suggests that we very much continue to function within a color caste system (hooks, 1997)—only those with the "right" look can distance themselves from "dark skin," which remains stigmatized.

Racial identity as choice and the relationship of choice to Whiteness are also critical to contemporary media representations that use "multiraciality" to signify a post-racial era. Dominant racialized media representations reinforce capitalist discourses of commoditization, individualism, and market choice, much like Bordo's (1990) discussion of "cultural plastic" in *Material Girl*. These representations suggest "a construction of life as plastic possibility and weightless choice, undetermined by history, social location, or even individual biography" (p. 657). This is an ideology whereby in the 1979 film *10*, Bo Derek became the exoticized "other" by wearing cornrows (Bordo, 1990), and White characters in *The Fast and the Furious* become "ethnic" by wearing so-called ethnic clothing (Beltrán, 2005).

Similarly, singer Justin Timberlake is able to create a particular form of hegemonic masculinity by adding and subtracting dominant notions of Black male style as he chooses. The inference here is that this is just about fashion and style, it is politically neutral, and has nothing to do with racialization, class, gender, history, power, or privilege. This suggests, for example, that there is no difference historically or materially between Bo Derek wearing cornrows and Black women straightening their hair (Bordo), or between Justin Timberlake using so-called Black vernacular and young African American men doing the same. I suggest that there are both historical and material differences in these examples that are critical in nature. Relaxing and straightening hair is tied to a history of racism, whereby Black women's hair is not viewed as acceptable or beautiful in its natural state (hooks, 1988/2007); meanwhile, Bo Derek's cornrows in no way compromise her White privilege. Similarly, the use of Black vernacular has been and continues to be used to portray African Americans as uneducated, ignorant, and less intelligent, while Justin Timberlake as a White man can use this type of language without being seen in any of these ways. Through these types of stylistic representations, "race" is made visible as a commodity while concurrently made politically invisible; this adds "value" to dominant identities through appropriation, while concomitantly essentializing and pathologizing identities racialized as inferior (Hasinoff, 2008; Skeggs, 2004).These representations reinforce what Squires (2007) describes as a conservative consensus on race in America, also defined by scholars as "new racism," "modern racism," and "subtle racism."

These examples begin to address dominant media representations of multiracialization that shape Millennials conceptions of multiracialized identities in substantial ways and have serious material consequences. Media portrayals of "multiraciality" convey a notion that racial injustice is an issue that has been resolved, and as such, function to depoliticize racialization. Through the use of multiracial bodies, the media makes racism something of the past in the minds of most White Americans (Gallagher, 2006). In reality however, as several scholars have argued (e.g., Gallagher, 2006; Spencer, 2006; Squires, 2007), rather than transcending racialization and creating a post-racial era, what we are witnessing and what in many ways is reflected in contemporary media representations is a reorganization of America's racial hierarchy.

Conclusion and Implications

In this chapter I have sought to contribute to the discussion of Millennials and multiracialization through the lens of the media by expanding earlier discussions of how "multiracial" Millennials self-identify to incorporate how dominant representations of multiracialization shape hegemonic notions of identity; such notions contribute in important ways to how racialization is understood, how Millennials understand themselves, and how they are viewed by others. This analysis suggests that multiracialized media representations on the surface celebrate difference by putting forth "race" as something that is of the past and that is an apolitical, a historical choice of the individual. In reality, however, the media reinforces "racial" categorization in ways that privilege whiteness and often objectify what are seen as "multiracial" individuals.

In resistance to these media constructions of "race" and "multiraciality," student affairs scholars and practitioners need to consider developing policies, practices and approaches to understanding and engaging with Millennials that interrupt fictions of "multiraciality" as proof of a post-"racial" historical moment and at the same time challenge "racial" categorization; to do so is to refuse to collaborate with the idea of "race," as this invention is at the core of social stratification based on physical human variation (Smedley, 1998). Regardless of intention, to neglect moving away from the concept of "race" perpetuates working in partnership with the ideology of "race" (Bhattacharyya, Gabriel, & Small, 2002; Darder & Torres, 2004; Small, 2004; Spencer, 2006). As Goldberg (1990) contends, in resisting racism not only must we break with the "*practices* of oppression, . . . resistance must oppose also the *language* of oppression, including the categories in terms of which the oppressor (or racist) represents the forms in which resistance is expressed" (p. 314). By focusing on racialization and racism, I believe an assault and critique of the belief in "race" is made possible.

Of course, it will not be enough to simply provide students with the skills to critically analyze media representations and understand racialization; although important, it does not sufficiently engage with the ways in which these media representations and the ideology that informs them (re)produce much broader "common sense" ideas of "race" and "mixedness" that shape society in significant ways in relation to power and privilege. As ideas that are rooted in racism, to critically engage with "race" and multiracialization calls for approaches that at the core are informed by a commitment to fighting racism and working for change at a structural level. As I have attempted to show in this chapter, "multiracial" discourses and related practices that on the surface appear to be progressive, often rearticulate racialization in ways that "help preserve White privilege and the structure of that privilege" (Brunsma, 2006, p. 4).

What engaging with these issues might look like at any given institution will depend on the context. There is no boilerplate answer or single way in which to fight racism, but there are a number of questions student affairs scholars and practitioners can entertain in efforts to shape practices that engage with Millennials and multiracialization as part of fighting racism. Questions may include:

- From a policy and programming perspective, are the ways in which the idea of "race" is engaged historically grounded and informed by an understanding of the processes of racialization, and by extension, multiracialization?
- Are there measures in place to guard against essentializing and objectifying "multiracial" students?
- In what ways is the logic of "racial" categorization being challenged and re-thought?
- Are the multiple forms of White privilege openly recognized and addressed, including the ways they function to categorize "multiracial"students?
- In what ways do policies and programs specifically directed toward "multiracial"students function to fight racism, as well as sexism, classism and homophobia?

Also, as part of this work, it is imperative that student affairs researchers approach multiracialization with critical perspectives that challenge racism. I propose that this requires resisting the idea that any engagement of "multiraciality" is by definition a progressive act. The fact that more people than before, many of them Millennials, might identify as "mixed" in some way, is simply that—it does not in and of itself have self-evident meaning tied to the idea of social progress, nor is it an automatic antidote to racism. Moreover, as I have discussed throughout this chapter, it is imperative to frame scholarship in relation to racialization rather than depend on "racial" categorization that quite easily results in essentialism. Instead of presupposing "multiracial" particularity, one might examine multiracialization as a specific set of practices and relations that produce their own ideologies of body and belonging (Haritaworn, 2009), and ask about the consequences of these ideologies.

Along these lines, I also propose the need for a shift in the micro-level focus on identity that is characteristic of student affairs scholarship; it is important to pay greater attention to how issues such as multiracialization function on a structural level—that is to say, on a macrolevel. This provides for the opportunity to frame these issues of difference as societal issues, rather than problems of the individual. Questions to explore here may include:

- What cultural boundaries and dominant social context make multira-cialization possible? (Owusu-Bempah & Howitt, 2000)
- What interests are served by advancing "multiraciality" as an identity category; what role does this play in the project of racialization; how do discourses of multiracialization shape institutions of higher educa-tion; and how are these discourses shaped by power? (Baez, 2004)

To oppose racism at its core—to destabilize deeply ingrained "race" thinking in American society—is no easy task, and at times it requires going against conventional thinking about how to achieve a socially and economi-cally just society. It challenges us to develop new patterns of thought and new practices to contest unequal social relations and creatively struggle for radical social transformation.

References

Baez, B. (2004). The study of diversity. *Journal of Higher Education, 75*(3), 285–306.

Beltrán, M. (2005). The new Hollywood racelessness: Only the fast, furious (and multiracial) will survive. *Cinema Journal, 44*(2), 50–67.

Beltrán, M., & Fojas, C. (Eds.). (2008). *Mixed race Hollywood.* New York: New York University Press.

Bhattacharyya, G., Gabriel, J., & Small, S. (2002). *Race and power.* London: Routledge.

Bordo, S. (1990). Material girl: The effacements of postmodern culture. *Michigan Quarterly Review, 29*(4), 653–677.

Brunsma, D. L. (2006). Mixed messages: Doing race in the color-blind era. In D. L. Brunsma (Ed.), *Mixed messages: Multiracial identities in the "color-blind" era* (pp. 1–11). Boulder, CO: Lynne Rienner.

Coomes, M. D. (2004). Understanding the historical and cultural influences that shape generations. *New Directions for Student Services, 106*, 17–31.

DaCosta, K. (2006). Selling mixedness: Marketing with multiracial identities. In D. L. Brunsma (Ed.), *Mixed messages: Multiracial identities in the "color-blind" era* (pp. 183–199). Boulder, CO: Lynne Rienner.

Darder, A., & Torres, R. (with R. Miles). (2004). Does "race" matter? Transatlantic perspectives on racism after race relations. In A. Darder & R. Torres (Eds.), *After race: Racism after multiculturalism* (pp. 25–46). New York: New York University Press.

Evans, N. J., Forney, D. S., Guido, F. M., Renn, K. A., & Patton, L. D. (2009). *Student development in college: Theory, research and practice* (2nd ed.). San Francisco, CA: Jossey-Bass.

Furedi, F. (2001). How sociology imagined "mixed race." In D. Parker & M. Song (Eds.), *Rethinking mixed race* (pp. 23–41). Sterling, VA: Pluto Press.

Gallagher, C. (2006). Color blindness: An obstacle to racial justice? In D. L. Brunsma (Ed.), *Mixed messages: Multiracial identities in the "color-blind" era* (pp. 103–116). Boulder, CO: Lynne Rienner.

Goldberg, D. T. (1990). The social formation of racist discourse. In D. T. Goldberg (Ed.), *Anatomy of racism* (pp. 295–318). Minneapolis: University of Minnesota Press.

Halter, M. (2002). *Shopping for identity: The marketing of ethnicity.* New York: Schocken.

Haritaworn, J. (2009). Caucasian and Thai make a good mix: Gender, ambivalence and the "mixed-race" body. *European Journal of Cultural Studies, 12*(1), 59–78.

Hasinoff, A. (2008). Fashioning race for the free market on *America's Next Top Model. Critical Studies in Media Communication, 25*(3), 324–343.

hooks, b. (1997). Cultural criticism and transformation. S. Jhally (Producer). Northampton, MA: Media Education Foundation. Retrieved from http://www.mediaed.org

hooks, b. (2007, April). Straightening our hair. *Z Magazine.* Retrieved from http://www.zcommunications.org/zmag (Original work published 1988).

Jhally, S. (Producer). (1997). *Stuart Hall in lecture: Representation & the media* [filmed lecture]. United States: Media Education Foundation.

La Ferla, R. (2003, December 28). Generation E. A.: Ethnically Ambiguous. *New York Times.* Retrieved from http://www.nytimes.com/2003/12/28/style/generation-ea-ethnically-ambiguous.html?pagewanted=1

Lee, J., & Bean, F. (2007). Reinventing the color line: Immigration and America's new racial/ethnic divide. *Social Forces, 86*(2), 561–586.

Madland, D., & Teixeira, R. (2009). *New progressive America: The millennial generation.* Washington, DC: Center for American Progress.

Olumide, G. (2005). Mixed race children. In T. Okitikpi (Ed.), *Working with children of mixed parentage* (pp. 128–143). Dorset, England: Russell.

Owusu-Bempah, K., & Howitt, D. (2000). *Psychology beyond western perspectives.* Leicester: British Psychological Society.

Rajan, A. (2008, August 8). L'Oreal under fire for "whitewashing" Beyonce. *The Independent,* p. 16.

Renn, K. A. (2004). *Mixed race students in college: The ecology of race, identity, and community.* New York: State University of New York Press.

Renn, K. A., & Shang, P. (Eds.). (2008). Biracial and multiracial students. *New Directions for Student Services, 123.*

Senna, D. (1998). The mulatto millennium. In C. O'Hearn (Ed.), *Half and half: Writers on growing up biracial and bicultural* (pp. 12–27). New York: Pantheon.

Shohat, E., & Stam, R. (Eds.). (1994). *Unthinking eurocentrism: Multiculturalism and the media*. New York: Routledge.

Skeggs, B. (2004). New directions in the study of gender and sexuality. *Gay and Lesbian Quarterly, 10*(2), 291–298.

Small, S. (2004). Mustefinos are White by law: Whites and people of mixed racial origins in historical and contemporary perspective. In P. Spickard & G. R. Daniel (Eds.), *Racial thinking in the United States* (pp. 60–79). Indiana: University of Notre Dame Press.

Smedley, A. (1998). "Race" and the construction of human identity. *American Anthropologist, New Series, 100*(3), 690–702.

Spencer, R. (2006). New racial identities, old arguments: Continuing biological reification. In D. L. Brunsma (Ed.), *Mixed messages: Multiracial identities in the "color-blind" era* (pp. 83–102). Boulder, CO: Lynne Rienner.

Spencer, R. (2009, May 19). Mixed-race chic. *Chronicle of Higher Education*. Retrieved from http://chronicle.com/article/Mixed-Race-Chic/44266/

Squires, C. (2007). *Dispatches from the color lines: The press and multiracial America*. New York: State University of New York Press.

Stonequist, E. (1961). *Marginal man: A study of personality and culture conflict*. New York: Russell and Russell. (Originally published in 1937).

Stoler, A. L. (2002). *Carnal knowledge and imperial power: Race and the intimate in colonial rule*. Berkeley: University of California Press.

Streeter, C. (2003). The hazards of visibility: "Biracial" women, media images, and narratives of identity. In L. I. Winters & H. L. DeBose (Eds.), *New faces in a changing America: Multiracial identity in the 21st century* (pp. 301–322). Thousand Oaks, CA: Sage.

Tseng, T. (2008). Millennials: Key to post-ethnic America?*Newgeography*. Retrieved from http://www.newgeography.com/content/00137-millennials-key-post-ethnic-america

Valdivia, A. (2005). Geographies of Latinidad: Deployment of racial hybridity in the mainstream. In C. McCarthy & W. Crichlow (Eds.), *Race, identity, and representation in education* (pp. 307–317). New York: Routledge.

Vera, H., & Gordon, A. (2003). *Screen savers: Hollywood fictions of Whiteness*. Lanham, MD: Rowman & Littlefield.

13

MIXED RACE MILLENNIALS IN COLLEGE

Multiracial Students in the Age of Obama

Kristen A. Renn

The U.S. Census data predict that the number of mixed race college students will increase substantially over the next several years (Renn, 2009). As mixed race Millennials have become more visible on campus, they have challenged "business as usual" for multicultural student services, ethnic studies curricula, and student data collection and reporting (Kellogg & Niskodé, 2008; Wong & Buckner, 2008). This chapter defines and describes the mixed race population and identifies key areas of student and academic affairs that are affected by the increasing presence, visibility, and voice of students who do not identify in the old "choose one only" racial categories that dominated official postsecondary data and campus identity politics through the late 20th century. I describe changes in peer culture, identity politics, and academic emphases related to the emergence of a visible mixed race Millennial student population.

For the purposes of this chapter, "mixed race" students are defined as having parents from more than one racial category. Mixed race people are also called biracial, multiracial, and a host of heritage-specific terms such as "Hapa" or "Blaxican" (MixedFolks.com, n.d.). The U.S. Office of Management and Budget (OMB, 1997), which among other duties oversees the decennial census, defines race to include five categories: American Indian or Alaska Native, Asian, Black or African American, Native Hawaiian or Other Pacific Islander, and White (OMB, 1997). The two options for ethnicity are: Hispanic or Latino and Not Hispanic or Latino (OMB, 1997). Research with youth and young adults indicates that many view Latino/a identity as racial, and youth with a Latino/a parent and a non-Latino/a parent (of any race) often consider themselves multiracial rather than multiethnic (Brown, Hitlin, & Elder, 2006; Renn, 2004). I therefore place Latino/a heritage on par with the five OMB racial categories in defining mixed race students and clarify definitions when necessary in this chapter.

Emergence of Mixed Race Identity Among College Students

Although there is a long history of interracial relationships and childbearing in the United States, the so-called biracial baby boom began about a decade after the 1967 U.S. Supreme Court case *Loving v. Virginia*, which decriminalized interracial marriages (Loving Day, 2009). In the 2000 U.S. Census, which used the new standard, 2.43% of the total U.S. population, not including those with Latino/a ethnicity, responded with two or more races (Jones & Smith, 2001). When the population is analyzed by age, the biracial baby boom is apparent: 3.95% of people under age 18 are two or more races (excluding Latino/a data), but just 1.9% of those over 18 are. Including Latino/as, the numbers increase to 12.34% (under 18) and 7.7% (over 18).

Educational records for K–12 schools and higher education do not reflect the presence of these mixed race youth because they used a federal standard that required one racial category per person. Although the OMB mandated in 1997 that all federal agencies collect data on race and ethnicity using a "choose all that apply" standard by 2003, higher education data collection has lagged behind (Renn, 2009). The 2010–2011 academic year was the first in which institutions were required to report data in the new format. Only after they have been analyzed will accurate figures on the mixed race student population be available.

Even without data from the census or higher education records, there is evidence of growing numbers of bi- and multiracial students and their college experiences. In the mid-1990s biracial students began organizing on college campuses, forming student organizations first on the West Coast then throughout the country (Ozaki & Johnston, 2008). Capitalizing on communication formats enabled by the Internet (e.g., e-mail, websites, chat forums), students could locate resources for starting groups on their own campuses and share ideas for programming and activism across campuses (Gasser, 2008). Some institutions recognized the needs and interests of mixed race students and established programs and services on par with those offered to monoracial student communities of color (Wong & Buckner, 2008). Multiracial people published narratives of their experiences (O'Hearn, 1998), and social scientists provided empirical evidence of the experiences of mixed race college students (Renn, 2004; Rockquemore & Brunsma, 2002; Wallace, 2001). Self-identified mixed race students became a permanent addition to campus.

Mixed Race Millennial Students

In some sense the emergence of mixed race students as a visible group on campus coincided so neatly with the arrival of the so-called Millennials as to make it impossible to describe mixed race students without also including generational characteristics. As cited throughout this volume, Howe and Strauss (2000) provided the foundational description of Millennials. They claimed that this generation is more racially diverse than any other in U.S. history and is "special," sheltered, confident, conventional, team-oriented, achieving, and pressured. Brooks (2001) described Ivy League Millennials as "Organization Kids," raised in highly structured environments where adults planned and programmed play dates, enrichment lessons, and so forth, raising busy, résumé-building offspring. They are also members of the "net generation" (Tapscott, 1997), raised in a wired, connected environment. The experience growing up multiracial in a largely monoracial society (i.e., guided by norms that assume everyone has one race and one race only) may shape these young people at least as much as generational influences do. And in some ways, their multiracial heritage does not make them different from other Millennials generally or Millennials of color specifically. I describe here those generational traits that mixed race students may experience differently from their Millennial peers.

Diverse

Mixed race Millennials enter higher education in the United States at a time when postsecondary institutions are more racially diverse than ever before, and they are expected to be a growing population within this racial diversity. Naomi Zack (1995) described multiracial people as the embodiment of racial "microdiversity," and Carlos Cortes (2000) wrote about the "diversity within" multiracial college students. In some sense, then, mixed race Millennials would seem to be walking examples of the increasing racial and ethnic diversity in U.S. higher education, a testament to this generational trait. To a certain extent they are, inasmuch as they may bring to campus cultures languages and even physical appearances that contribute to a more heterogeneous student body. A student of Latino/a and Japanese American heritage might speak Spanish, dance salsa, and make sushi for her friends, or a student with a Black mother and a White father might share his love of gospel music with his brothers in the predominantly White fraternity he joined because his father had been a member.

Yet not all mixed race students choose to express their multiple heritages, and not all have access to the cultures of each of their racial backgrounds (Renn, 2004). For example, a multiracial student may have been raised in a monoracial and monocultural community, not learning directly about the other culture. Or societal forces of racism and expectations of monoracial identity may have combined to ensure that a mixed race student who does not "look White" never had the opportunity to identify fully with this aspect of his or her background (Rockquemore & Brunsma, 2002; Wallace, 2001). Some multiracial students choose to identify monoracially with one of their heritage groups, never sharing their other background with peers (Renn, 2008; Wallace, 2001). Evolving perspectives on psychosocial development of mixed race individuals support the right of these students to identify as they choose, even if some multicultural educators might wish that every student shared all aspects of his or her background. Mixed race Millennials are, above all else, not a monolithic group, especially when it comes to experiencing and expressing diversity on campus.

Special

Evidence from studies of multiracial college students indicates that some mixed race students do indeed typify the Millennial trait of feeling "special," *as mixed race people.* In some families, tensions that existed when a son or daughter married someone of another race were eased when children came along (Renn, 2004), giving these mixed race youth a reason to feel special— they brought Grandma and Grandpa back into the family. Media, pop culture, and the advertising industry's fascination with—some say objectification of—people who are "racially ambiguous" and the idea of racial fluidity has leant a certain hipness to mixed race identity among college students, even as it reinforces old ideas about the fixedness of race and racial identity (Renn, 2004).

Especially for those mixed race students whose Baby Boomer parents embraced antiracist values or supported civil rights movements, these young people are "vital to their parents' sense of purpose" (DeBard, 2004, p. 35) and bear high expectations. The idea that these post–civil rights "rainbow babies" would somehow build a bridge to racial harmony has been subject to heavy criticism by biracial young adults who have faced both racism (as people of color) and monoracialism—the bias that everyone is and should be one race and one race only (O'Hearn, 1998)—yet the mantle of specialness and expectations remains in place. Indeed, the election of President Barack Obama reinforced the biracial-people-as-bridge expectation, and there is little reason to believe this expectation will be abandoned any time soon. Inasmuch as this expectation attaches to positive social goals, it lends support to the sense of mixed race Millennials as special.

Sheltered

The degree to which mixed race students fit the generational trait of having been sheltered varies, and there are particular aspects of life in which they have been exposed to potential harm in ways that their monoracial peers, and even their parents, have not been. For example, although monoracial families of color cannot shelter their children from racism, they can offer a buffer of parents, siblings, grandparents, and extended family who can identify with, empathize with, and support responses to discriminatory acts faced by people of color. A White parent of a biracial child may have experienced discrimination directly and through actions directed at his or her partner of color, but typically he or she and a White extended family cannot provide the same kind of buffer. On a more mundane level, mixed race youth are not sheltered from the everyday knowledge that they live in a society that in many ways still does not expect them to exist; filling out online college applications, or even consumer surveys, that provide a choose-one-only button for response is a reminder that they do not fit neatly into society. The "need for structure" (DeBard, 2004, p. 35) that is supposed to be a Millennial trait runs directly counter to mixed race students experience of not fitting into the structure of monoracial identity.

Confident

Although it is easy to imagine how the constant reminder that one does not fit into existing structures could erode confidence, there is also evidence that for those mixed race Millennials who go to college, bucking the racial categorization system may actually boost confidence (Renn, 2004). Whether they buy into the "bridge between the races" philosophy or not, they have been exposed to successful mixed race professionals, be they champion athletes (Tiger Woods, Derek Jeter), award-winning artists (Halle Berry, Mariah Carey), or world leaders (President Barack Obama, former U.S. Secretary of State Colin Powell). Finding a social space in the sometimes-complicated campus racial landscape is, for some, a way to build confidence to take on additional leadership and involvement (Renn, 2004). Knowing from early childhood that they do not fit neatly into dominant categories may also provide a foundation for questioning other social structures and building confidence for self-definition.

Pressured

Mixed race students may experience generational pressure to perform, as other Millennial students of color do, and it may be exacerbated by the tacit—or spoken—expectation that they should lead society into some color-blind, postracial new day. If their parents sacrificed social or familial approval to enter interracial relationships, then this pressure may be further amplified. Yet unlike their monoracial peers who may respond to pressure through conformity and reliance on structure (DeBard, 2004), mixed race students may respond through creative nonconformity. For example, the sizable number of students with multiple heritages who choose to define themselves outside of the system of racial categorization (Renn, 2004; Rockquemore & Brunsma, 2002) is evidence that mixed race Millennials may draw on some reserve of resilience and self-definition to cope with pressure.

Wired

As noted earlier, the coemergence of the mixed race youth movement with the ubiquity of the Internet is no coincidence. Using websites, e-mail lists, chat rooms, and social networking sites to learn about and from one another, mixed race college students are an excellent case study in the ways that "digital natives" (Prensky, 2001) explore and construct identities online. Multiracial Generation Xers paved the way, starting campus organizations and forming an online infrastructure for mixed race identities and organizing that benefited mixed race Millennials (Gasser, 2008). Even those mixed race youth who grow up in predominantly monoracial communities now have access to abundant resources for learning about and connecting with other mixed youth in urban, suburban, and rural locales.

Summary

Mixed race Millennials, then, are in some ways very much like other Millennials of color and in some ways made different by the experience of living as multiracial in a monoracial society. They embody diversity and feel special, confident, and pressured. They are perhaps less sheltered than monoracial peers (White and of color). Being wired provides access to identity exploration and construction in ways that mixed race youth of earlier generations lacked. There is no evidence to support a claim that they are more team oriented or achievement driven than any other Millennial students. Their experiences as multiracial people and the identities they express on campus, however, may prompt changes in peer culture, identity politics, and academic interests, the topic to which I turn next.

Peer Culture, Identity Politics, and Academic Interests

As noted earlier, the 2010 change in campus data collection policies required data collection in a format that permits two or more race reporting, creating a clearer picture of mixed race demographics. But the data collection will be catching up to a multiracial youth movement already changing the face of campus life. The emergence of student organizations for and about multiracial issues provides a window into changes in peer culture and identity politics. Student interest in academic coursework addressing mixed race issues and multiracial experiences spans disciplines from biology to sociology, psychology, literature, languages, and history. In this section, I describe how racial identities and generational characteristics interact for mixed race Millennial students in ways that shape—and are shaped by—campus life.

Peer Culture and Identity Politics

Unquestionably, peer culture is a major force in students' lives. As higher education became more diverse in the 1980s, 1990s, and into the 21st century, identity politics emerged as a substantial component of campus peer culture. Gender, race, sexual orientation, and ability—among others—became identity categories in which minority and majority, "target" and "dominant," oppressed and privileged statuses were brought into open discussion. For students of color, organizations for specific (monoracial) heritage groups (e.g., African American, Latino/a, Asian American, Native American) provide critical sources of academic and social support and networking (Patton, 2006).

These same organizations contribute to an identity politics on campus that emphasizes social, intellectual, and cultural belonging, which while it contributes to student success and retention (Patton, 2006), may also promote an atmosphere in which multiracial students' authenticity and legitimacy are questioned. Multiracial students frequently report being questioned if they do not "look X enough," speak Spanish or another non-English heritage language, listen to the "right" music, or otherwise conform to peer expectations for cultural knowledge and behavior (Renn, 2004; Wallace, 2001). Although Millennial students in general are alleged to be exposed to diversity (DeBard, 2004; Howe & Strauss, 2000), physical appearance plays a critical role in mixed race students' acceptance by peers (Renn, 2004; Rockquemore & Brunsma, 2002). The role of skin color and hair texture may be especially heightened for mixed African American women, who may face racism from White peers and resentment from their darker-skinned Black female peers (Rockquemore, 2002). Some mixed race students report being shut out of or made to feel unwelcome in formal and informal groups of monoracial students of color (Renn, 2004; Wallace, 2001), while peer culture on some campuses promotes a "we don't care how X you are, so long as you're at least partly one of us" attitude. For these students, monoracial student groups become a location for exploring identities and heritages (Renn, 2004).

Partly in response to an identity politics that supports identity-specific organizations for students of color but paradoxically creates a peer culture that questions the legitimacy of mixed race students in these groups, multiracial students on many campuses created their own organizations. In stereotypical Millennial fashion, they said, "Us too!" and used existing administrative and student government structures to form freestanding groups. On some campuses, these groups further proliferated into heritage-specific organizations for, for example, Hapa students (mixed Asian and White) or other locally predominant mixes (Ozaki & Johnston, 2008). Exhibiting their "specialness" and "organization kid" (Brooks, 2001) attributes, mixed race students responded to exclusion by creating their own groups, in which, interestingly, some of the same "not X enough" dynamics—in this case "not *multiracial* enough"—play out as students attempt to balance political, social, educational, and support functions (Ozaki & Johnston, 2008). Identity politics, it seems, is a durable element of peer culture from Generation X to the Millennials.

Academic Engagement

There is evidence that mixed race Millennial students, like their generational peers, are interested in connecting their personal identities to their educational endeavors (Renn, 2004). The curriculum is a site for exploring one's different cultural heritages, through history, literature, sociology, anthropology, language, and visual and performing arts. Opportunities for these explorations occur in ethnic studies majors (e.g., African American studies) and in individual courses within a discipline (e.g., literature of Central America or Chinese history). Students may choose personally meaningful topics for papers and projects in these courses and in others that are not culturally specific (e.g., introductory courses in sociology). Some institutions offer courses that focus on multiracial issues (e.g., the politics of multiraciality or media portrayals of multiracial people), and some students report doing undergraduate theses on mixed race issues (Renn, 2004).

Study abroad programs also provide opportunities for identity exploration. Mixed race students with a parent who immigrated to the United States sometimes choose to study abroad in that parent's home country, seeking immersion in culture and language (Renn, 2004). Even if both parents are U.S. born, mixed race students may, like their monoracial peers, choose to study in the region from which their ancestors came.

The benefits of academic exploration of mixed race generally and component heritages specifically are substantial. For many mixed race Millennials, college presents the first opportunity to join a community of other mixed race people (Wallace, 2001). Academic coursework that addresses race, racial identity, and multiraciality provides conceptual and linguistic tools students can use to communicate about their identities and build a shared sense of history and community (Renn, 2004). Learning culture and language helps some students feel more authentic or legitimate in their identification with a heritage group. Exploring racial identity may provide a motivation for students to engage deeply in academic endeavors or to take a course they might not otherwise have taken. The identity-education connection is thus a mutually reinforcing loop.

Summary

Peer culture and academic engagement constitute a substantial influence within a college student's learning and developmental environment. The ways that mixed race students experience and enact racial identity and identity exploration are both influenced by and exert influence on campus. Identity politics have shifted with the emergence of groups that visibly and vocally identify outside the monoracial categories predominant in the late 20th century. And as students pursue their identity-based interests academically, they create new ways of understanding self and others.

Implications and Future Directions

Shifting U.S. population demographics and generational attributes have converged to create "Generation Mix" (Mavin Foundation, 2006). Self-aware, special, diverse, and accomplished "organization kids," mixed race Millennials engage the curriculum and cocurriculum to create social and intellectual spaces for multiracial identity in a society constructed of monoracial categories. What do they want and need from higher education? How will they change it? And what about the next generation of mixed race students? I address these questions in the following sections.

Adapting the Data Infrastructure

Repeatedly, mixed race students have told researchers that they are frustrated, angered, and alienated by college forms that require them to identify themselves by choosing one racial category (Renn, 2004; Wallace, 2001). The vast majority (98%) of institutions collect data on students' race on only the admissions application (Padilla & Kelley, 2005; Renn, 2009). Beginning in 2010, institutions were required to collect data allowing respondents to choose all that apply and to report the data to the U.S. Department of Education using the five monoracial categories plus a "two or more races" category. Presumably, students' first official contact with institutions—the application form—will no longer present the same racially fraught experience that it has been in the past. An additional benefit to the new data collection and reporting system is that institutional officials can more accurately assess the size of the multiracial population and can, if they choose, use the information to provide outreach to these students (as they might to other identifiable groups of students).

Individuals concerned with student outcomes disaggregated by race, however, may find the transition to the new data system confounding. Cohort analyses (analyses that track an entering class through and beyond matriculation) will be as they have been, with the addition of the new "two or more races" category. But trend analyses, for example, of student graduation rates, choice of major, GPA, or postcollege employment, will be discontinuous across data, because the racial category groups will not share definitions before and after the change. A student with a Black and a White parent, before the change, would have been counted in one category only, either the one she indicated or, if she was given the option of more than one on her application, the one designated for her by the institution. So the group with whom she was aggregated would show an additional student.

Her brother, applying after the change, will be counted in the "two or more races" category. When comparing the two cohorts, membership in the Black, White, and "two or more races" categories differs, and any differences across cohorts in the relationship between racial identity and outcomes cannot be accurately determined. With a small percentage of the overall college population identifying as two or more races, perhaps this confounding is considered unimportant. But in regions where the two or more races groups is already high, the effect could be noticeable.

Millennials have been tracked and tested like no generation before them (Brooks, 2001). Discontinuity in trend data may not concern them at all. But educational leaders trying to assess outcomes and understand differences in achievement by racial categories will need to decide how to account for the change in data systems, on campus and in state-level and national data comparisons. Understanding the educational trajectories and outcomes of the Millennial generation as a whole depends on it.

Supporting Mixed Race Student Organizations

Identity-based student organizations (e.g., Black Student Union, Lesbian/ Gay/Bisexual/Transgender Alliance, Women's Coalition) are a longstanding presence in higher education (Rogers, 2006). There is evidence that they contribute to a campus climate that is welcoming and supportive of students from diverse backgrounds, and studies suggest that they play a role in promoting positive student outcomes, including identity development, engagement, and retention (Patton, 2006). Sometimes rooted in a specific heritage combination (e.g., Hapa, which is a term for someone who is of Asian and White heritage), mixed race student organizations emerged on some campuses in the 1990s as social, networking, support, and educational spaces (Ozaki & Johnston, 2008).

Mixed race groups face challenges common to all student organizations (e.g., leadership, maintaining membership, dealing with institutional bureaucracy), but they face additional, specific challenges. First, they typically operate within the context of established organizations based on monoracial identities of color, some of which see the mixed race group as competition for scarce resources. Leaders of monoracial student groups may worry that mixed race members of the Black Student Union may leave to participate in the mixed student group, or that student activities funds will be shifted from the Asian Pacific Alliance to the Hapa group. Advisors of mixed race groups can help prepare student leaders to deal with this situation by discussing potential roadblocks, campus identity politics, and the broader context of these fears. They can also work with individuals responsible for allocating funds to student groups to advocate for additional resources, not a "zero sum game" in which resources for multiracial student groups really are taken from those resources that would have been allocated to monoracial groups.

A second challenge for mixed race groups occurs when group leaders and members do not share a common sense of identity. Researchers have observed at least five distinct patterns of identity among mixed race Millennials in college: (a) identification with one of their heritage groups; (b) identification with multiple heritage groups; (c) identification with a separate, multiracial group; (d) opting out of identification in the racial categorization system of the United States; and (e) situational identification, moving among two or more of the preceding patterns (see Renn, 2008, for a summary of biracial and multiracial identity development). When group leadership and membership hold fast to different patterns—believing strongly that their way of identifying is the *right* and *only* way—conflicts can evolve that destroy the student organization (Ozaki & Johnston, 2008). Leaders and members may enact measures of "being multiracial enough" or "in the right way" with one another, replicating the experiences some of these same students had in monoracial student organizations. Advisors and mentors to these students and their organizations should be aware of this potential conflict and prepare leaders through frank discussion of identity politics, diversity of mixed race identities, and clarification of the leaders' values and priorities (which might, in fact, be set on leading from a certain pattern of identity, regardless of the outcome for the student organization).

Mixed race Millennials are likely to seek structured opportunities for involvement, such as student groups, when they come to college. Even while they may challenge systems of racial categorization, these "organization kids" are likely to trust authorities and seek guidance from advisors (DeBard, 2004). Educators can use students' proclivity for organized activity, willingness to listen to mentors, and interest in exploring personal identities to cultivate leadership and engagement.

Academic Initiatives

Just as interest in exploring personal identities might be a useful "hook" to involve mixed race students in extracurricular activities, it could serve as motivation to pursue academic goals. Educators might leverage students' interest in their own identities into class projects, courses, independent study projects, and cross-disciplinary explorations of mixed race in the United States and around the world. Evidence suggests that students of color are less likely than White students to study abroad (Comp, n.d.), but some mixed race students choose study abroad opportunities in order to develop cultural knowledge of one or more of their heritage groups (Renn, 2004). Online resources (e.g., Mixed Heritage Center, 2009) make academic pursuit of topics easier than ever. Incorporating the topic of mixed race in class discussions—or questioning why it has not been included in, for example, epidemiological studies—could be done in courses as diverse as literature, language, medicine, law, biology, sociology, history, anthropology, education, business marketing, communication, and graphic design. The Millennials' preference for structure and deferral to authority may make it especially easy to introduce what was once, in some circles, considered controversial material.

Generation Next: What Will the Next Generation of Mixed Race Students Be Like?

It is difficult to predict generational trends, but it may be possible to see how the emergence of mixed race identity in the Millennial generation influences campus life for their peers in the subsequent generation. Students who entered college beginning in 2010 will have completed college applications that asked them to check all races that applied to them. For these students, the data structure of higher education will always include them, yet they may remember a time when their parents were asked to identify them in one group or another for K–12 school records. And although the 2010 U.S. Census indicated that the two or more races population is increasing, it is still a small fraction (about 3%) of the nation (US Census, 2011); mixed race youth will still be raised in a society that expects entire families to be of one race only, and all the same race. Perhaps education—K–12 and college—will seem like something of a buffer from monoracial society, like places that are designed, officially at least, with the expectation that not everyone fits in one racial group.

Peer culture may expand to embrace more fully—or at least not to reject out of hand—the concept of mixed race. The next generation of youth will grow up in a nation where a mixed race man can be elected president, and his mixed heritage children will be their age-mates. While much is made in the popular media of the "Obama Effect" on race relations in the United

States, it is not yet clear what that effect ultimately will be. It is undeniable, however, that the election of a biracial man born a few years before the Supreme Court's *Loving v. Virginia* decision elevates the visibility of mixed race people in the United States. Exposure to the panoply of mixed heritage celebrities, athletes, and political leaders, along with more everyday experiences with friends, neighbors, and classmates, may prepare youth across the generation to embrace more easily their mixed race peers.

Intellectual and creative exploration of the ideas of "race" and "mixed race" are robust and growing. The next generation of mixed race youth will benefit from the substantial output from scholars, writers, and artists who have been working on new ways to describe, explain, and portray the mixed race experience in the United States and globally. Following the Millennials, these young people will not have to search as hard to find representations of themselves on campus or in research, narrative, and popular literature.

The effect of this more ready recognition of self on campus and in the public eye cannot be known in advance. Generation Next may be less about activism and visibility than it is about getting on with the business of being part of increasingly diverse higher education in an increasingly diverse society. A day may come, as it has for many female students vis-à-vis campus activism and feminism, when mixed race students do not understand what all the fuss was once about. The country they know has always included visible biracial people, the campus they know has always acknowledged mixed race identity, and families like theirs have always been, if not common, then at least unsurprising. How Generation Next and mixed race Millennials will view one another remains to be seen, though they will be closely linked through both a common experience of being multiracial in a largely monoracial society and family ties, as mixed race Millennials will by definition have mixed race offspring. If history is a guide, Gen Next will form its characteristic traits partly in reaction to Millennial characteristics and partly in response to larger sociocultural forces and events. These kids of the Organization Kids—Gen Next—will no doubt influence higher education in their own ways, just as mixed race Millennials have and will continue to do.

References

Brooks, D. (2001). The organization kid. *Atlantic Monthly, 287*(4), 40–54.

Brown, J. S., Hitlin, S., & Elder Jr., G. H. (2006). The greater complexity of lived race: An extension of Harris and Sim. *Social Science Quarterly, 87*, 411–431.

Comp, D. (n.d.). Study abroad information. Retrieved from http://www.globaled. us/plus/study_abroad.asp

Cortes, C. (2000). The diversity within: Intermarriage, identity, and campus community. *About Campus, 5*(1), 5–10.

DeBard, R. (2004). Millennials coming to college. In M. D. Coomes & R. DeBard (Eds.), *Serving the Millennial generation. New Directions for Student Services, No. 106,* 33–45.

Gasser, H. S. (2008). Being multiracial in a wired society: Using the Internet to define identity and community on campus. In K. A. Renn & P. Shang (Eds.), *Biracial and multiracial college students: Theory, research, and best practices in student affairs. New Directions for Student Services, No. 123,* 63–72.

Howe, N., & Strauss, W. (2000). *Millennials rising: The next great generation.* New York: Vintage.

Jones, N. A., & Smith, A. S. (2001). *Two or more races population: 2000.* Census 2000 Brief. Washington, DC: U.S. Census Bureau.

Kellogg, A., & Niskodé, A. S. (2008). Student affairs and higher education policy issues related to multiracial students. In K. A. Renn & P. Shang (Eds.), *Biracial and multiracial college students: Theory, research, and best practices in student affairs. New Directions for Student Services, No. 123,* 93–102.

Loving Day. (2009). The Loving story. Retrieved from http://www.lovingday.org/ the-loving-story

Mavin Foundation. (2006). Generation Mix. Retrieved from http://www.mavin foundation.org/projects/generation_mix.html

MixedFolks.com. (n.d.). *Representing multiracial people. Names for mixed folks.* Retrieved from http://www.mixedfolks.com/names.htm

Mixed Heritage Center. (2009). Welcome to the Mixed Heritage Center. Retrieved from http://www.mixedheritagecenter.org/

Office of Management and Budget (OMB). (1997). Revisions to the Standards for the Classification of Federal Data on Race and Ethnicity. Retrieved from http:// www.whitehouse.gov/omb/fedreg_1997standards

O'Hearn, C. C. (1998). *Half and half: Writers on growing up biracial and bicultural.* New York: Random House.

Ozaki, C. K., & Johnston, M. (2008). The space in between: Issues for multiracial student organizations and advising. In K. A. Renn & P. Shang (Eds.), *Biracial and multiracial college students: Theory, research, and best practices in student affairs. New Directions for Student Services, No. 123,* 53–72.

Padilla, A., with Kelley, M. (2005). *One box isn't enough: An analysis of how U.S. colleges and universities classify mixed heritage students.* Seattle: MAVIN Foundation. Retrieved from http://www.mavinfoundation.org/news/news_100905_ed compliance.html

Patton, L. D. (2006). The voice of reason: A qualitative examination of Black student perceptions of the Black culture center. *Journal of College Student Development, 47*(6), 628–646.

Prensky, M. (2001). Digital natives, digital immigrants. *On the Horizon, 9*(5). Retrieved from http://www.marcprensky.com/writing

Renn, K. A. (2004). *Mixed race college students: The ecology of race, identity, and community.* Albany: State University of New York Press.

Renn, K. A. (2008). Research on bi- and multiracial identity development: Overview and synthesis. In K. A. Renn & P. Shang (Eds.), *Biracial and multiracial college students: Theory, research, and best practices in student affairs. New Directions for Student Services, No. 123,* 13–21.

Renn, K. A. (2009). Education policy, politics, and mixed heritage students in the United States. *Journal of Social Issues, 65*(1), 165–183.

Rockquemore, K. A. (2002). Negotiating the color line: The gendered process of racial identity construction among Black/White biracial women. *Gender and Society, 16*(4), 485–503.

Rockquemore, K. A., & Brunsma, D. L. (2002). *Beyond Black: Biracial identity in America.* Thousand Oaks, CA: Sage.

Rogers, I. (2006). Celebrating 40 years of activism. *Diverse Issues in Higher Education, 23*(10), 18–22.

Tapscott, D. (1997). *Growing up digital: The rise of the net generation.* New York: McGraw-Hill.

U.S. Census. (2011, March 24). 2010 Census shows America's diversity. Retrieved from http://www.census.gov/newsroom/releases/archives/2010_census/cb11-cn125.html

Wallace, K. R. (2001). *Relative/outsider: The art and politics of identity among mixed heritage students.* Westport, CT: Ablex.

Wong, M. P. A., & Buckner, J. (2008). Multiracial student services come of age: The state of multiracial student services in higher education in the United States. In K. A. Renn & P. Shang (Eds.), *Biracial and multiracial college students: Theory, research, and best practices in student affairs. New Directions for Student Services, No. 123,* 43–52.

Zack, N. (1995). *American mixed race: The culture of microdiversity.* Lanham, MD: Rowman & Littlefield.

PART EIGHT

VOICES OF MILLENNIALS IN COLLEGE: A DIVERSITY OF PERSPECTIVES

14

MOVING UP AND OUT

Students of Color Transitioning From College to the Workforce

Lonnie Booker, Jr., Tonya Turner-Driver, Tammie Preston-Cunningham, Theresa Survillion, and Mattyna L. Stephens

I n recent years, colleges and universities have seen an influx of younger and more eager groups of students who are different from those who entered college in the past two decades (Broido, 2004). This group of young adults currently entering into the workforce has been called the Millennials (Howe & Strauss, 2000; McGlynn, 2005). According to the National Center for Education Statistics (2011), it is estimated that 9.3 million Millennial students were enrolled in colleges and universities as of fall 2009. Hussar and Bailey (2009) estimated there would be an increase of total student enrollment in colleges and universities from 9 to 17% by the year 2018. According to Howe and Strauss (2002), the Millennials are individuals who were born since 1982 and who share common characteristics unlike those of previous generations (Elam, Stratton, & Gibson, 2007). Many of these individuals have recently graduated from college and have since entered into the workforce. Howe and Strauss (2000) proposed seven characteristics that Millennial's possess, which include being special, sheltered, confident, conventional, team oriented, achieving, and pressured. Therefore, while these characteristics provide a brief description of Millennials, they also serve as an indicator of future employees' behavior.

Although Howe and Strauss (2000) provided descriptors for the Millennial generation, there are many nuances within the population, particularly in relation to the diversity of this group. Broido (2004) asserts that the greatest difference in the Millennial generation from previous generations is their racial and ethnic diversity. According to the 2002 U.S. Census, 31% of the U.S. population are people of color under the age of 18. People of color, as defined by the U.S. Census (2002), are Black, Asian, Hispanic, and Native American. Moreover, a recent report by Hussar and Bailey (2009) details that between 1993 and 2003, African American college enrollment rose by 42.7%, Hispanic enrollment rose by 68.8%, and Asian American enrollment rose by 43.5%. With this increased growth of students enrolling in college, there has been a change in the diversity of employees entering into the workforce. According to the U.S. Department of Labor Bureau of Labor Statistics (2009a), there were 83 million people employed in the workforce in 2007. The racial and ethnic diversity within the workforce continues to grow, with the greatest growth being within the Hispanic and Asian population (U.S. Bureau of Labor Statistics, 2009b). Additionally, the U.S. Bureau of Labor Statistics (2009b) projected an increase of Blacks entering the workforce as well.

In addition, racial and ethic diversity research has shown the socioeconomic status of parents has an effect on the education and job choices of their children (Bosco & Bianco, 2005). As more parents of Millennials become better educated and obtain higher family incomes, their children are more likely to attend college (Gohn & Albin, 2006). Gohn and Albin (2006) further indicated that as the demand has grown for more highly skilled employees, a college education is required.

There are a number of issues Millennials will face upon entering the workforce, including demographics (e.g., age, race, ethnicity, etc.) of the workforce, diversity, technological advances, global economy, and the lack of experienced leaders due to mass retiring of executives. As a result, many graduates could have difficulty entering the workforce successfully due to a gap between what society's expectations are of higher education and how students are prepared to responded to those expectations (Newman, Couturier, & Scurry, 2004). This could be largely caused by schools' efforts to improve institutional prestige and revenue instead of working to improve graduates' skills and knowledge (Newman et al., 2004). There is significant disconnection between the skills students need to be successful at work and their expectations of being successful in their careers (Smith, 2006). As a result, new graduates are underprepared and unable to think long term, handle details, or delay gratification (Levine, 2005).

This chapter provides insight on the critical areas of Millennials and their transition into the workforce from college. Individual employee performance in the workforce will be addressed by using the concept of human performance as a theoretical framework. In addition to explaining the basis of our framework, we will also address relevant limitations. Various expectations of Millennials as employees in the workforce will also be discussed. The chapter includes a case study illustrating an anecdote about how characteristics of the most recent generation might function in the workforce. The chapter closes by providing recommendations for employers to decrease the incongruence between their Millennial employees' expectations and organizational practices.

Performance Improvement: A Theoretical Framework

The mindset of business organizations is to always remain ahead of competitors. Rothwell, Sullivan, and McLean (1995) pointed out that the foundational concept of "only the strong do and should survive" has dominated business thinking since the late 19th century. According to Bing, Kehrhahn, and Short (2003), the factors influencing business and industry organizations in relation to their competitors surround increased shareholder value given external factors, such as making better use of technology to deliver just-in-time solutions, an increasingly global economy, and the need for sound leadership and knowledgeable and talented workers. These external factors are not considered temporary, but rather permanent elements of how work is viewed. Organizations must monitor and address these factors by adapting and responding with practical theories or face being overwhelmed and consumed by competitors.

Human Performance Theoretical Lens

Theories describe a phenomenon's main concepts and explain how the phenomenon works (Torraco, 1997). Specifically, business theory helps explain organizational alignment, as well as factors involved and associated with best practices in managing organizations. The results of theory, as powerful and practical explanations, provide principles and models for carrying out work in organizations. The concept of individuals performing work duties at a certain level, thus yielding higher profits for business organizations, is a traditional business framework identified as human performance (Sambrook, 2004).

Human performance, according to Chermack and Lynham (2001) and Holton (2002), involves the explanation and demonstration of specific behaviors designed to accomplish specific tasks and produce specific outcomes among individuals, groups, processes, and systems. The theoretical framework of human performance has a focus on "the valued productive output of a system in the form of goods and services" (Swanson & Holton, 2001, p. 89). According to Swanson (1999), there is a demand for high performance in organizations, so a focus on improving human performance is vital to business organizations. The human performance improvement concept, first introduced by Gilbert (1978) and derived from human capital theory (Becker, 1964), assumes educating workers increases employee productivity and future business earnings. These types of theories can be defined as "descriptions and explanations of how the allocation of scarce resources among a variety of human wants affect technologies and processes designed to optimize individual performance in the business organization context" (Chermack & Lynham, 2001, p. 375).

This concept was introduced as a theorem of human capital theory, where "competent people are those who can create valuable results without using excessively costly behavior" (Gilbert, 1978, p. 17). Human capital refers to the "knowledge, expertise, and skill one accumulates through education and training" (Swanson & Holton, 2001, p. 109). Human capital theory, an economic theory explaining and describing managing scarce resources and producing wealth, suggests employee productivity and future earnings can be increased through education of useful knowledge and skills (Becker, 1964). It can be implicitly understood that education enhances or advances the economic potential of people (Schultz, 1971). Education also offers opportunity for a progressive community, which is capable of engaging in independent and lawful due process and pursuing standards such as equal opportunity, organization, and freedom (Swanson & King, 1991). Even though these qualitative benefits seem to showcase the outstanding contributions of education, they are complex to assess in business organizations (Sweetland, 1996). This complexity could explain why economic development has overshadowed other educational benefits and surfaced as the chosen benefit for determining the power of education (Woodhall, 1987).

Application of Human Performance

Gilbert (1978) introduced human competence "as a function of worthy performance (expressed as W), which is a function of the ratio of valuable accomplishments (expressed as A) to costly behavior (expressed as B)" (p. 18). A short way of expressing the theorem is $W = A/B$, communicating:

1. The way to achieve human competence is to increase the values of our accomplishments while reducing the energy we put into the effort.

2. Great quantities of work, knowledge, and motivation, in the absence of at least equal accomplishments, are unworthy performance.
3. Great accomplishments are not worthy if the cost in human behavior is also very great.
4. Money, energy, or time invested in reducing required behaviors of performance can pay off splendidly.
5. A system that rewards people for their behavior (work, motivation, or knowledge) encourages incompetence. A system that rewards people only for their accomplishments, and not for the net worth of their performance, is an incomplete system that fails to appreciate human competence.
6. Human capital can be best achieved through worthy performance only if we measure and respond directly to human competence.

This framework allows performance factors to be manipulated with the intent of improving performance of individuals, groups, and organizations (Weinberger, 1998). Gilbert (1978) contributed to a focus on the performance of individuals, which involves systematic interventions, and focused on learning experiences, work assignments, and assessment activities for developing knowledge and expertise in people to move them beyond their current performance levels (Swanson & Holton, 2001).

Theories focused on improving the performance of individuals, most of which are informed by Gilbert's (1978) human capital theory, are considered fundamental in the workplace, just as theory is deemed critical to any discipline (Weinberger, 1998). As business organizations look for development and growth of employees to gain economic advantage, employees must understand "opportunities for higher wages, greater economic security, and increased employment prospects" are dependent on their abilities to help businesses reach or maintain their desired targets (Swanson & Holton, 2001, p. 81). With human performance being seen as a tool toward reaching and maintaining industry position, organizations target people in efforts to improve the organization. Those organizations on the cutting edge invest in improved methods to avoid becoming overwhelmed and consumed by competitors (Bing et al., 2003).

Limitations of Human Performance

Human performance is a central element of industry and a priority to organizations. If salaries are seen in "supply-and-demand" terms and "skills and abilities are a form of capital," organizations are only as viable as their position in the world of industry (Swanson & Holton, 2001, p. 81). With this in mind, a focus on human capital theory and improving human performance falls short of individual worker developmental needs when addressing the market position of the organization. Although Gilbert's (1978) theory has degrees of soundness, it appears to have contributed to a business movement without addressing issues surrounding how individual performance is viewed (Swanson & Holton, 2001). A focus on performance improvement has been identified as a limitation of human capital theory (Holton, 2002), although the business organization literature is "dominated by performance orientation" (Sambrook, 2004, p. 613). The focus on performance improvement is seen as a means of "control and dehumanization," where behaviors are "demanded or coerced from individuals in return for compensation" (Holton, 2002, p. 62). The identified need for performance improvement has been "driven by organizational needs to perform" and has caused us to see human beings as resources (Fenwick, 2004, p. 199).

> The human being is more than an economic being; we are social, aesthetic, cultural, sexual beings, and we have many selves, many intelligences, and many rationalities. There is more to life than work that has been commoditized and is defined by commodities. In fact, if we look critically at our lives, we realize that we even must be programmed to desire these commodities and other desires must be obliterated in the process and made dormant. (Cunningham, 2004, p. 226)

The focus on organizational productivity is "driven by organizational needs to perform," not meaningful human growth, so the reason and rational for traditional business approaches toward performance are inadequate (Fenwick, 2004, p. 199).

Human performance improvement's theoretical approaches do not reflect the multilayered elements of individuals, such as belief systems, cultural dimensions of individual development, and defining boundaries, which are becoming more relevant in the workplace (Egan, Upton, & Lynham, 2006; Garavan, O'Donnell, McGuire, & Watson, 2007). Additional theory-building research on performance improvement has been identified as being needed to debunk traditional business theoretical frameworks, validating individual worker experiences and revealing more "radical re-educative approaches" that aim to support and satisfy workers' needs (Fenwick, 2004, p. 199; Fry, 2003).

Millennials Expectations of the Workforce

Over the past 10 years, Millennial students have been entering the workforce in large numbers, giving them power to reshape the rules of play at work (Smola & Sutton, 2002; Twenge & Campbell, 2008). Due to this influx of new workers entering the workforce, research has been conducted on Millennials and their influences on and expectations of being in the workforce (Macky, Gardner, & Forsyth, 2008). Consequently, much of the research focuses on how organizations can successfully build a relationship and manage the new Millennial employee. Although some career-related research has been conducted by Cennamo and Gardner (2008), Smola and Sutton (2002), and Wong, Gardiner, Lang, and Coulon (2008), for the purposes of this chapter we are highlighting a recent study completed by Ng, Schweitzer, and Lyons (2010). This study posited four career-related themes including: work–life balance, meaningful work experiences, opportunities for advancement with pay benefits, and a nurturing work environment.

Work–Life Balance

According to Ng et al. (2010), Millennials entering the workforce are expecting more from their careers in shorter lengths of time in comparison to their parents' generation. After witnessing the impact of organizational downsizing on their parents and families, Millennials are making a choice of whether to work for a living or work to maintain their lifestyle (Lindquist, 2008). Researchers assert the Millennial generation is the best educated and has the highest achievers in history (Howe & Strauss, 2000; Landcaster & Stillman, 2002; Lindquist, 2008), which should correlate to excelling. However, Millennials' inherent desire to achieve self-imposed stress coupled with workforce expectations aids in their struggle for workplace balance. Therefore, to address work–life balance for this generation, organizations should provide these employees with work that is meaningful to them.

Meaningful Work Experiences

Millennials are not just looking for a paycheck from their jobs, but rather jobs that are meaningful and fulfilling to them as well (Landcaster & Stillman, 2002). As a result, Millennials look at potential employers' values and mission before they apply or accept work for certain business organizations (Lindquist, 2008). For example, prior to and during the interview process, many Millennials are checking the background and financial obligations of the organization, as well as asking what the organization can do to help them to lead more purposeful and meaningful lives (Sujansky, 2009). Millennials bring bright and new ideas to the workforce; however, they also desire to play a role in the growth of the organization as well as their own career development.

Opportunities for Advancement With Pay

The biggest challenges facing Millennials in the workforce are often associated with their characteristics of being special, confident, and feeling a sense of entitlement (Sujansky, 2009; Twenge, 2006). Many Millennial employees feel they provide a set of skills the organization needs, and that they should be compensated for those skills. According to Rawlins, Indvik, and Johnson (2008), while some Millennial employees are willing to work long and hard hours, other are not. According to Landcaster and Stillman (2002), Millennials have been taught to believe in themselves. This confidence is facilitated by the many accolades they received from various activities and behaviors as children and young adults. With the emphasis on rewards, Millennials want to be financially compensated for their efforts (Ng et al., 2010). Nonetheless, Millennials want to be part of a welcoming work environment that fosters their development within the workforce.

Nurturing Work Environment

By being team oriented, Millennials want to work in groups on projects, primarily because this is when they most often feel safe and secure (Howe & Strauss, 2000). Moreover, this enables them to work with a more diverse group than any other generation (Howe & Strauss, 2000). For example, their strengths include multitasking, goal orientation, positive attitudes, and a collaborative style (Oblinger & Raines, 2003; Sujansky, 2009). Thus, working with groups provides Millennials an opportunity to not only work with other employees but also to learn from others. This collaborative process helps to build relationships with their coworkers, as well as with management (Ng et al., 2010). Also working in groups allows Millennials, who desire constant feedback, to receive feedback on their performances. This feedback provides them with support for their work and validates their work as meaningful not only to them, but also to the organization (Sujansky, 2009).

Expectations of Millennials in the Workforce

The human performance concept is infused throughout business organizations and impacts every aspect of the organization, including policies and
protocols, as well as expectations of employees. Three critical areas where
preparation and expectation between Millennials of color and the business
world appear inconsistent reside in the perceptions of culture, leadership to
management roles, and diversity.

Organizational Culture

Rothwell et al. (1995) consider organizations to have their own cultures,
separate and distinct from any other organization. Organizational culture
comprises assumptions and beliefs, "shared by members of an organization,
that define in a basic taken-for-granted fashion an organization's view of
itself and its environment" (Swanson & Holton, 2001, pp. 270–271). An
organization's culture often functions as a formula for determining expectations for decision making, use of resources, supervision and management of
employees, and other organizational responses. This formula has buy-in
from employees in the organization, plays out subconsciously, and is learned
(Rothwell et al., 1995). If employees of the organization plan to advance,
they are expected to adopt, adapt, and operate within the organization's
culture, regardless of the employees' personal, professional, or developmental
positions when entering the organization. In addition employees are
expected to be complicit with organizational mission in order to lessen
employee shortages, increase employee commitment, appropriately allocate
training and development funds, and foster engaged and positive worker
attitudes.

From Leadership to Management Roles

Contrary to popular belief, employees are developing in their abilities to
participate in previously inaccessible organization functions (Rothwell et al.,
1995). In most organizations, work roles have been classified at the employee,
manager, and executive levels, and while each role's duties have evolved,
there are clear expectations from employees at each work level. The employee
role, formally limited to tasks, now has elements of quality improvement.
Attributed by Noe (2002) to the concept of high-performance work teams,
many workers at the employee level are performing managerial-type duties.
As employees reach levels of advancement, they can move into managerial

roles. The role of managers, with the entry of high-performance work practices, is to manage staff alignments, coordinate activities, facilitate decision-making processes, encourage learning, and create and maintain trust. Leadership is a concept reserved for the top-tier roles within the organization and is categorized by Reingold, Schneider, Capell, and Enbar (1999) as one of the most critical topics for executive development.

Changing Demographics and Diversity

Not only is diversity impacting demographic trends, it is also posing challenges and creating opportunities for the business world (Noe, 2002). Diversity in organizations is presenting underexplored issues as organizational positions are increasing in differences of gender, sex, ethnicity, race, generation, culture, value, and nationality (Fenwick, 2004). Organizations must position themselves to address a broader recognition of complex identities and diverse interests (Fenwick, 2004). Through intentional efforts to communicate opportunities to and for varying interest groups, organizations will demonstrate readiness for diversity (Merriam & Caffarella, 1999).

Although there are a number of arguments supporting the importance of diversity efforts, Noe (2002) described managing workforce diversity to be dedicated to increasing performance and gaining competitive advantage. The process of managing workforce diversity involves fostering an environment in which all members feel they can contribute to the vision, mission, and goals of the organization. As Noe (2002) also indicated, diversity as a developmental area in a large percentage of business organizations is merely "seen as a way to reduce costs related to discrimination lawsuits rather than to improve company performance" (p. 19). Business organizations do not appear to focus on valuing or appreciating increased diversity in the workplace, but allow accepting and adjusting to what diversity bring to the workplace.

Case Study

Jenny and Kevin are sitting in a break room discussing the difference between their college environment and work environment. Because they are members of the Millennial generation, they share common characteristics such as special, sheltered, confident, and pressured.

Jenny reminisced about the support she received from her faculty and mentors while in college, which made her more confident in her abilities to perform successfully. Now that she is in the workforce, she realizes that it is a different environment from college. In addition to no longer being actively mentored by her supervisors, she feels overwhelmed and less confident about her abilities. In essence, one of the aspects that differs from college to work is that her supervisor does not continuously provide her with feedback or affirmation concerning her job performance. Although Jenny is confident in her abilities, her poor job performance does not reflect her high expectations of her abilities. Because of her concerns, she e-mailed one of her college mentors to seek advice. Her mentor advised her to speak to her boss, and when she did her boss revealed that they only provide yearly performance evaluations. As a result, Jenny feels lost at her job without the constant affirmations that made her feel special and confident, despite the many pressures she experienced in college.

Similarly, Kevin shared some of his concerns with Jenny about his work and how his college environment differed. He talked about how he felt pressured while in college because of his student involvement; however, the pressure he feels in the workforce is different somehow. In college, he was active in student government, a member of a fraternity, and played intramural sports. Whereas in college he was used to being involved in various activities to break the monotony of the day, which allowed for flexibility in his schedule, he is now pinned into a 40-hour-a-week job with little diversion in his typical workday. In many instances in college, Kevin confided in his mother for help, often regarding issues he encountered in his fraternity. He often found that his issues would be resolved with the help of his mother and without having to be held accountable for any of the concerns. However, he is realizing that the lack of shelter within his work environment is problematic because he is encountering several issues that cannot be resolved with the help of his mother.

How would a student affairs practitioner better equip students to avoid these scenarios in the workplace? What student development theories would be more applicable to address the transitional issues that Millennial students of color encounter as they move into the workplace? What assumptions can be made about the educational experiences and career development of Millennial students of color?

Implications for Student Affairs Practitioners

Based on the case study, five implications have been identified in relation to Millennials in the workplace.

Silence does not mean disapproval (Gleeson, 2003). Since Millennial students often receive immediate feedback in college, they are accustomed to knowing how they are performing. However, in the workplace many employees do not receive immediate feedback via performance reviews. Hence, it is important for Millennial students to know that the lack of feedback in the workplace does not mean that they are performing poorly in their jobs.

Work that is meaningful to them (Gleeson, 2003). In order to reach the full potential of Millennials, organizations have to structure assignments that these employees feel have some meaning to them. In essence, if Millennial employees have a connection to the work, they will give their best efforts and therefore will increase productivity, as well as work efficiently.

Encourage students to create their own solutions but with caution (Gleeson, 2003). In order to allow these students the ability to use all of their capabilities, they should be allowed to think creatively. Nonetheless, this creative thinking, which could be considered thinking outside of the box, should be geared toward problem solving and providing new and creative solutions for the organization, specifically within the constraints of organizational policies.

Mentoring program (Beard, Schwieger, & Surendran, 2008). In order to prepare Millennial students for the workforce, organizations should provide mentorships. The mentors would provide guidance to help students successfully transition from a college environment to a work environment. Additionally, this mentor would also help prepare the students for future leadership within the organizations.

Rewards system (Beard et al., 2008). Along with creative thinking, organizations should establish a rewards system for innovative solutions. Because one of the characteristics of Millennials is that they are competitive, these students should be given the opportunity to continuously think. It is this continuous thinking that will foster Millennial employees to come up with solutions to problems and allow them to work toward a common goal.

Conclusion

In conclusion, this chapter captures the nuances of the Millennial generation as they transition into the workforce. This group of new employees brings to their jobs all of their unique characteristics as well as new and innovative approaches to the organization. As discussed earlier, there is a gap between the new employees' education attainment and whether they are prepared to meet the demands of the workforce. In an attempt to strike a balance, organizations are meeting Millennials where they are currently in their development by providing internships for students (Lindquist, 2008). In order to better understand this populace, managers should be able to address their expectations along with meeting the organization's mission and purpose.

References

Beard, D., Schwieger, D., & Surendran, K. (2008). *Preparing the millennial generations for the work place: How can academia help?* SIGMIS-CPR Conference (pp. 102–105). Charlotteville, VA: SIGMIS-CPR.

Becker, G. S. (1964). *Human capital.* New York: Columbia University Press.

Bing, J. W., Kehrhahn, M., & Short, D. C. (2003). Challenges to the field of human resources development. *Advances in Developing Human Resources, 5*(3), 342–351.

Bosco, S. M., & Bianco, C. A. (2005). Influence of maternal work patterns and socioeconomic status on Gen Y lifestyle choice. *Journal of Career Development, 32*(2), 165–182.

Broido, E. (2004). Understanding diversity in millennial students. *New Directions for Student Services, 106,* 73–85.

Cennamo, L., & Gardner, D. (2008). Generational differences in work values, outcomes and person-organization values fit. *Journal of Managerial Psychology, 23*(8), 891–906.

Chermack, T. J., & Lynham, S. A. (2001). Considering old theories from the theoretical foundations of HRD and performance improvement. In O. Aliago (Ed.), *Proceedings of the Academy of Human Resource Development* (pp. 372–379). Baton Rouge, LA: AHRD.

Cunningham, P. M. (2004). Critical pedagogy and implications for human resource development. *Advances in Developing Human Resources, 6*(2), 226–240.

Egan, T. M., Upton, M. G., & Lynham, S. A. (2006). Career development: Load-bearing wall or window dressing? Exploring definitions, theories, and prospects for HRD-related theory building. *Human Resource Development Review, 5*(4), 442–477.

Elam, C., Stratton, T., & Gibson, D. (2007). Welcoming a new generation to college: The millennial students. *Journal of College Admission, 195,* 20–25.

Fenwick, T. J. (2004). Toward a critical HRD in theory and practice. *Adult Education Quarterly, 54*(3), 193–209.

Fry, L. W. (2003). Toward a theory of spiritual leadership. *Leadership Quarterly, 14,* 693–727.

Garavan, T. N., O'Donnell, D. O., McGuire, D., & Watson, S. (2007). Exploring perspectives on human resource development: An introduction. *Advances in Developing Human Resources, 9*(1), 3–10.

Gilbert, T. F. (1978). *Human competence: Engineering worthy performance.* New York: McGraw Hill.

Gleeson, P. B.; Texas Woman's University, Houston TX; Matrix Rehabilitation, Katy TX. (2003). *Managing and motivating the generations: Implications for the student and the employee.* Combined Sections Meeting 2003 (pp. 1–11). Tampa, FL: Cardiovascular and Pulmonary Section, APTA. Retrieved from http://www. uwsp.edu/education/facets/links_resources/4413.pdf

Gohn, L. A., & Albin, G. R. (2006). Predicting the future based on demographics. In L. A. Gohn, & G. R. Albin (Eds.), *Understanding college student subpopulations: A guide for student affairs professionals* (pp. 37–52). Waldorf, MD: National Association of Student Personnel Administrators.

Holton, E. F. (2002). Theoretical assumptions underlying the performance paradigm of human resource development. *Human Resource Development International, 5*(2), 199–215.

Howe, N., & Strauss, W. (2000). *Millennials rising: The next great generation.* New York: Vintage Books.

Howe, N., & Strauss, W. (2002). Through prism of tragedy generations are defined. *Christian Science Monitor, 94*(210), 9.

Hussar, W. J., & Bailey, T. M. (2009). *Projections of education statistics to 2018.* Washington, DC: National Center for Education Statistics.

Landcaster, L. C., & Stillman, D. (2002). *When generations collide: Who they are, why they clash, how to solve the generation puzzle at work.* New York: Harper Business.

Levine, M. (2005). College graduates aren't ready for the real world. *Chronicle of Higher Education, 51*(24), B11.

Lindquist, T. (2008). Recruiting the millennium generation: The new CPA. *CPA Journal, 78*(8), 56–59.

Macky, K., Gardner, D., & Forsyth, S. (2008). Generational differences at work: Introduction and overview. *Journal of Managerial Psychology, 23*(8), 857–861.

McGlynn, A. (2005). Teaching Millennials our newest cohort. *Education Digest, 71*(4), 12–17.

Merriam, S. B., & Caffarella, R. S. (1999). *Learning in adulthood* (2nd ed.). San Francisco: Jossey-Bass.

Newman, F., Couturier, L., & Scurry, J. (2004). Higher education isn't meeting public's needs. *Chronicle of Higher Education, 51*(8), B6.

Ng, E. S., Schweitzer, L., & Lyons, S. T. (2010). New generation, great expectations: A field study of the millennial generation. *Journal of Business Psychology, 25,* 281–292.

Noe, R. A. (2002). *Employee training & development* (2nd ed.). New York: McGraw-Hill.

Oblinger, D., & Raines, C. (2003). Boomers and Gen-Exers Millennials: Understanding the new students. *Education Review, 38,* 6–7.

Rawlins, C., Indvik, J., & Johnson, P. R. (2008). Understanding the new generation: What the Millennial cohort absolutely positively must have at work. *Journal of Organizational Culture, Communications and Conflict, 12*(2), 1–9.

Reingold, J,. Schneider, M., Capell, K., & Enbar, N. (1999, October). Learning to lead: Executive education results. *Business Week, 18,* 64–71.

Rothwell, W. J., Sullivan, R., & McLean, G. N. (1995). *Practicing organization development: A guide for consultants.* San Diego, CA: Pfeiffer.

Sambrook, S. (2004). A critical time for HRD? *Journal of European Industrial Training, 28*(8–9), 611–624.

Schultz, T. W. (1971). *Investment in human capital: The role of education and research.* New York: Free Press.

Smith, W. S. (2005/2006, December–January). Employers and the new generation of employees. *Community College Journal,* 8–13.

Smola, K. W., & Sutton, C. D. (2002). Generational differences: Revisiting generational work values for the new millennium. *Journal of Organizational Behavior, 23,* 363–382.

Sujansky, J. G. (2009). Spoiled, impatient, and entitled: Why you need strong Millennials in your workplace. *Supervision, 70*(10), 8–10.

Swanson, R. A. (*1999*). HRD theory, real or imagined? *Human Resource Development International, 2*(1), 2–5.

Swanson, R. A., & Holton III, E. F. (2001). *Foundations of human resource development.* San Francisco: Berrett-Koehler.

Swanson, A. D., & King, R. A. (1991). *School finance: Its economics and politics.* New York: Longman.

Sweetland, S. R. (1996). Human capital theory: Foundations of a field of inquiry. *Review of Educational Research, 66*(3), 341–359.

Torraco, R. J. (1997). Theory building research methods. In R. A. Swanson & E. F. Holton (Eds.), *Human resource development research handbook: Linking research and practice* (pp. 114–137). San Francisco: Berrett-Koehler.

Twenge, J. M. (2006). *Generation me: Why today's young Americans are more confident, assertive, entitled and more miserable than ever before.* New York: Free Press.

Twenge, J. M., & Campbell, S. M. (2008). Generational differences in psychological traits and their impact on the workplace. *Journal of Managerial Psychology, 23*(8), 862–877.

U.S. Census Bureau. (2002, February 25). *Race and Hispanic or Latino origin by age and sex for the United States: 2000.* Retrieved http://www.census.gov/population/www/cen2000/briefs/phc-t8/tables/tab03.pdf

U.S. Department of Education. Institute of Education Sciences, National Center for Education Statistics. (2011, February). Enrollment in postsecondary institutions, fall 2009; Graduation rates, 2003 & 2006 cohorts; and financial statistics, fiscal year 2009. Retrieved from http://nces.ed.gov/pubs2011/2011230.pdf

U.S. Department of Labor Bureau of Labor Statistics. (2009a, September). *The employment situation.* Retrieved from http://www.bls.gov/news.release/pdf/empsit.pdf

U.S. Department of Labor Bureau of Labor Statistics. (2009b, November). *A new look at a long-term labor projections to 2050.* Retrieved from http://www.bls.gov/opub/mlr/2007/11/art3full.pdf

Weinberger, L. A. (1998). Commonly held theories of human resource development. *Human Resource Development International, 1*(1), 75–93.

Woodhall, M. (1987). Economics of education: A review. In G. Psacharopoulos (Ed.), *Economics of education: Research and studies* (pp. 1–8). New York: Pergamon.

Wong, M., Gardiner, E., Lang, W., & Coulon, L. (2008). Generational differences in personality and motivation. Do they exist and what are the implications for the workplace? *Journal of Managerial Psychology, 23*(8), 878–890.

15

CURRICULUM DESIGN FOR MILLENNIAL STUDENTS OF COLOR

Rosa Maria Banda, Alonzo M. Flowers, III, Petra Robinson,
Genyne Royal, Rose Anna Santos, and Nicholas Zuniga

Teachers of Millennial students need to consider the diversity of their students as well as individual learning preferences in order to meet their students' needs as effective educators. Millennial students are more open to issues of diversity and social justice and have the potential to change the way they and the larger world view such issues (Broido, 2004). Howe and Strauss (2003) reported that Millennial students are one of the most diverse generations in U.S. history. The authors stated that in 2002, 37% of adults below the age of 20 were non-Whites and Latino/as, and of the entire Millennial population 1 in 5 has an immigrant parent and 1 in 10 has a noncitizen parent. Howe and Strauss have provided foundational work about teaching and learning relative to Millennial students in general. This chapter adds information to the existing literature about teaching and learning specifically related to Millennial students of color.

According to Pendergast (2007), generations that dominate the teacher workforce include Baby Boomers and Generation Xers. Teachers in these generations are considered digital immigrants, and Millennial students are considered digital natives. The diverse makeup of the Millennial student population and their technological savvy influence their learning preferences. They prefer learner-centered instruction, a team-oriented environment, experiential activities, and an educational structure that uses technology (Jonas-Dwyer & Pospisil, 2004). After considering how Millennial students learn best, teachers must be knowledgeable in many areas of technology and learner-centered strategies to best meet the learning needs of Millennial students.

This chapter describes Kolb's experiential learning theory as our guiding framework. We present the following elements of teaching and learning: adult learning theory, learning-centered instruction, cooperative learning, technology, and the integration of curriculum. We also provide recommendations for teaching Millennial students of color, followed by a case study to demonstrate instructional implications.

Theoretical Framework

Kolb's (1984) experiential learning theory (ELT) is one of the most influential theoretical frameworks to assist educators in their construction of their instructional design and platform. This four-stage model illustrates a cyclical process of learning. Kolb's work is paramount to the world of education as it solidifies the need to acknowledge the various experiences that shape and affect the way students learn. Moreover, the theory has implications for instructors as well.

Instructors who are cognizant of the premise of Kolb's (1984) theory recognize the need to create instructional strategies that seek to meet the diverse learning styles students individually possess. According to Kolb, Boyatzis, and Mainemalis (2000), ELT "provides a holistic model of the learning process and a multilinear model of adult development, both of which are consistent with what we know about how people learn, grow, and develop" (p. 2). Although Kolb's (1984) theory outlines the processes of learning for the general population of students, it fails to recognize the variations of learning as it pertains to students of color.

With the implication of any theory, it is vital to recognize that theories cannot be transposed from one population to another. Kolb's (1984) model is no exception, as we suggest that variations within the stages of this model occur when applied to students of color. The ELT model contends that students first have concrete experiences and then learn from these concrete experiences through reflective observation. Once concrete experiences have occurred, students then experience knowledge through abstract conceptualizations in which they learn from active experimentation. However, for students of color, this process of learning through experiential knowledge differs from the learning experiences of their White counterparts. For many students, an individual approach, through experiential knowledge, might contribute to their way of learning. Yet for students of color, a community approach to learning (i.e., interaction with peers and instructors) might yield a different type of experiential learning rather than simply learning, as the model suggests, from their experiences in isolation of others.

Though Kolb (1984) does not mention the cultural experience of students of color and how it relates to his model, Lessor (1976) illustrated different patterns of thinking styles across ethnic groups. Witkin's (1967) similar findings also suggest that differences exist globally in the manner in which abstract conceptualization occurs. Such findings, though dated, reinforce the need to account for the variations in the experiential knowledge that students of color bring to college classrooms. Additionally, the cyclical process of learning for college students of color does not necessarily follow the four-stage process outlined by Kolb's model. Because of their lived experiences, some students of color might have abstract conceptualizations about a particularly topic because they have repeatedly had prior concrete experiences with the topic at hand. Thus, the stage in which students of color learn, because of complex social, cultural, and generational issues, does not necessarily coincide with the model premised in Kolb's work.

Although the baseline approach to Kolb's (1984) ELT model provides a framework for student learning, instructors must remain cognizant that students of color, and their respective forms of experiential knowledge, are framed in a manner that is often not reflective of their White counterparts. Similarly, in the need to extend Strauss and Howe's (2007) Millennial framework, there is also a need to expand our understanding of Kolb's model as it pertains to students of color. A further examination of Kolb's ELT model is only possible when the variation found within Millennial students of color is considered by instructors. Then, and only then, can instructors begin to recognize that one's process of learning is better understood when the generalized attributes of Millennial students are dispelled.

The Millennial generation has been categorized in seven distinct categories, described as their "core traits" (Strauss & Howe, 2007), which may serve as an applicable tool to employ when examining the population in general. However, there are distinct and significant differences in populations of color that would prohibit this framework from being entirely pertinent. With that in mind, a careful analysis of each descriptor and its applicability or relevance to Millennial students of color is essential.

The seven descriptors define Millennials as a cohort of people raised to feel *special* and that have been *sheltered*, primarily by their Baby Boomer–generation parents (Strauss & Howe, 2007). These young people are also classified as *confident* individuals with an affinity for teams and *team orientation*. Millennials have also been classified as *conventional* in their positive outlook on policies and rules that govern their lives, and this generation, unlike many others, has been categorized as experiencing an exceptionally high level of *pressure*. A significant amount of the pressure they endure is associated with their heightened propensity to *achieve*, as many in this cohort have been exposed to various curricular and cocurricular experiences that have amplified their belief in their own abilities. When considering the magnitude of this cohort, generalizations serve as a viable means of gaining an ambiguous snapshot of Millennial students; however, when it is understood that learning is a task that is particular to experiential knowledge and based as much on their learning styles as their life experiences, it is imperative that the nuances of the population are considered.

Although a family's methods of making a child feel special may be limited by the time and resources available to them in particular or through their communities, it is presumable that most families maintain a significant concern about the safety of their children. Millennials are described as sheltered as they have evolved from the previous generation of latch-key kids to those students who witnessed events such as the shootings at Columbine High School and Virginia Tech. However, for youth living in some urban areas, issues of safety are much more varied than occasional, although horrific, acts of violence that have significantly impacted society (Rasmussen, Aber, & Bhana, 2004).

Millennials are also characterized as confident and team-oriented, and some research indicates that they believe they possess the potential to address many of the worlds issues, which those of their generation will resolve. It is critical to understand that all Millennials have not had the opportunities that fostered such confidence and orientation as their cohort peers. In the literature on this population, there is a significant amount of information about Millennials being awarded for their mere participation in activities and not for their individual talents or abilities. As a result, their exposure to team activities has fostered an appreciation for the shared experience of Millennials. Although many schools have phased out cocurricular activities, many students have lost the ability to engage the very organizations that fostered both a sense of self-assurance as well as the collaborative spirit of the generation. While privatized opportunities do exist in many communities, the cost, although relatively inexpensive, is likely prohibitive for some Millennials of color who would have not been able to engage in such opportunities.

Contrary to their predecessors in Generation X, Millennials are also described as conventional as it relates to rules and the traditional values of their parents. Yet, for people of color, personal values are typically very closely related to their cultural and community values. For instance, many first-generation Hispanic American families continue to become acquainted with dominant customs and ideologies as their children go to school and engage a population very different from their own. An example of such a cultural conflict would be reflected in literature in reference to the experience of Latino/as in higher education. Culturally, Hispanic families believe that one's family obligations would surpass that of any possible financial or educational aspirations, and for those who have grown up with such a conviction, to behave in a manner contrary to what is divergent of their own culture (Rodriguez, Guido-DiBrito, Torres, & Talbot, 2000). As this generation is known to be the most diverse, little consideration has been given to the cultural influences of particular Millennial populations that would display a distancing from traditional family values as opposed to the simple acceptance of it as proposed by Strauss and Howe (2007).

As expressed in the literature, this generation will experience much more pressure, yet it is also expected to achieve much more than both of its preceding generations. Millennials are expected to seek admission to college in greater numbers because of their affinity for institutions and their understanding that advanced education will aid them in their ability to succeed. However, a significant divide remains in those families that will be able to access higher education because of their socioeconomic status and academic performance, which is still inequitable in many low-income areas as compared to more affluent communities (Burdman, 2005). According to the 2008 U.S. Census, White students are earning college degrees 3 times more than Black and Hispanic students combined, and the increasing cost of college tuition has continued to impede many students of color who qualify for admission making it difficult to consider higher education a viable option for them (Tierney & Venegas, 2009). Although the majority of Millennials will experience the pressure to succeed or achieve, many Black and Hispanic Millennials will be working to keep pace with the growing economic obligations and striving to maintain a lifestyle that is financially secure (U.S. Census Bureau, 2005).

Elements of Teaching and Learning

By 2012, 75% of all college undergraduate students will be Millennial students (McGlynn, 2005). As a result, the most racially and ethnically diverse generation of college students is embarking on today's college campuses (Howe & Strauss, 2003). Not only do they have the most demographically distinct characteristics, the so-called Millennial generation brings with them new ways of thinking and learning, which seek to transform the teaching and learning methods found within college classrooms. Equally important, institutions of higher education must examine student demographics, in addition to the generational differences in this student population, as such a diverse demographic will have implications for the learning and teaching components within institutions of higher education (Scarborough & Vorah, 2006).

This section provides an overview of learning and teaching pedagogy that will illicit discussion and insight into the necessary considerations and revisions that must be made by educators in order to meet the instructional needs of Millennial students of color. Although Howe and Strauss's (2003) research on Millennial students is a crucial component to understand this generation, it is our intent to create a variation, within this framework, that pertains to the learning and teaching of students of color within the Millennial generation. In addition to a brief overview of adult learning theory, topics for discussion include learning-centered approaches, cooperative learning, technological innovations as a learning component, and integrative curriculum as a means of culturally based instructional methods. A number of recommendations are also offered to provide practical solutions for educators who are concerned about creating optimal learning and teaching classrooms for Millennial students of color.

Adult Learning Theory

The processes of adult learning are multifaceted and require educators to examine experiential learning from various sociocultural frameworks. Experiential learning is the process in which adults learn through formation and reformation of experiences. Thus, for adult learners, "understanding is not a fixed or unchangeable element of thought" (Fry, Ketteridge, & Marshall, 2009, p. 15). This continual process suggests that, as individuals, we learn from our experiences by reflecting, learning, and processing. It is important to note that this process is cyclical in nature and requires adult learners to have concrete experiences, reflective observations, abstract conceptualization, and active experimentation that work to continuously create and re-create knowledge (Fry et al., 2009).

According to Knowles et al. (1984), *andragogy* refers to adult learning as the "art and science of helping adults learn" (as cited in Fry et al., 2009, p. 14). Adult learning theory is premised on the work of Kohlberg (1984) and further expanded by Knowles et al. (1984), which contends that there are five principles associated with andragogy. These principles include (as cited in Fry et al., 2009, p. 14):

1. As a person matures he or she becomes more self-directed.
2. Adults have accumulated experiences that can be a rich resource for learning.
3. Adults become ready to learn when they experience a need to know something.
4. Adults tend to be less subject-centered than children; they are increasingly problem-centered.
5. For adults the most potent motivators are internal.

Because of their unique learning experiences, students of color may construct knowledge and process learning through a variety of lenses. It is essential that instructional strategies emphasize multiple styles of learning so that students of color can be invested in their adult learning processes.

The principles of andragogy suggest that the adult learning process is one of constant change and re-creation of knowledge, which works to facilitate an autonomous cognitive process in adult learners. This creation of knowledge, according to Brown (2000), is found in two dimensions: explicit and tacit. While explicit knowledge focuses on the "know-whats" of concepts, the tacit knowledge focuses on the "know-how" through practices and skills. Explicit and tacit dimensions of knowledge, as they pertains to adult learning theory and students of color, are crucial aspects that educators must take into consideration as they attempt to integrate various instructional methodologies into their classroom curriculum. Thus, we contend there must be an integration of adult learning and the instructional needs of Millennial students of color. Although we recognize that adult learning theory outlines a particular mode of curriculum development for students, it must be done in conjunction with the various instructional needs of students of color in order to optimize the processes of learning by altering traditional forms of teaching within the college classroom through learning-centered approaches.

Learner-Centered Approaches

Even though extant research (Astin, 1993; Chickering & Reiser, 1993; Fink, 2003; O'Banion, 1999; Pascarella & Terensini, 1991) has shown that learner-centered model approaches to student learning are more effective, college instruction continues mainly to consist of teacher-centered approaches to learning. Traditional forms of college instruction tend to focus on teacher-centered approaches that often limit students of color the opportunity to be active participants in the learning process.

Sheull contends, "It is important to remember that what the student does is actually more important in determining what is learned than what the teacher does" (as cited in Biggs, 1993, p. 73). For instance, in curriculum design, it is essential that the instructor remains cognizant of the integration of the various students' instructional needs in relation to their respective teaching philosophy (Biggs, 1993). In essence, a paradigm shift in how students of color are taught within college classrooms is necessary.

This paradigm shift from traditional instructional methods to learner-centered approaches seeks to involve students of color in the various aspects of the teaching process, from syllabus design to reflective cognitive processes that prelude classroom discussion in an active manner. Gosling (2002) surmised:

> Part of being learning centered is recognizing that although there is a subject context which all students must learn in order to pass, each student approaches the subject from their own perspective, their own unique past experiences and their own understanding of themselves and their aspirations. (p. 114)

Learning-centered instruction creates a learning environment where students of color can potentially develop ownership of their cognitive processes in relation to information that is facilitated by the instructors. According to Gosling (2002), in order to learn, students must "recognize their own working needs and find strategies to meet them" (p. 115). However, students' abilities to recognize and find strategies for their respective learning processes can only happen if the instructor serves as a facilitator by modeling appropriate learning strategies that seeks to further expand on the experiential knowledge that students of color already possess.

Cooperative Learning

Based on the description of Millennial students, the most ethnically diverse generation, as being team oriented (Howe & Strauss, 2003), active learning in the form of cooperative and collaborative learning (McGlynn, 2005; Wilson, 2004) is a critical method in which Millennial students of color learn. Wilson (2004) contends that "To promote learning, students need to be engaged and involved" (p. 61). Further, McKeachie (2002) and Guskin (1994) suggested that passive forms of lecture discussion do not promote student learning.

Instructors must include collaborative work through group projects so that students can be actively engaged with the course material. In essence, "active learners tend to be more tolerant of new ideas, are able to develop multiple ways of solving problems, work collaboratively with other students, and are self-motivated" (Cress & Sax, 1998, p. 76). It is vital for instructors to create active learning opportunities for students of color that continue to promote a reciprocal process of learning between instructors and students. Hence, cooperative and collaborative learning approaches within the college classroom will allow students of color to utilize their experiential learning as they build on their cognitive processes.

Technology

To promote the most optimal learning environment, it is critical that instructors utilize various outlets of technology within the classroom. These include visual aids, multimedia devices, and social networking sites. This generation of students has grown up with various technological devices so much that they have been referred to as "digital immigrants" and "digital natives" (Prensky, 2001). Taylor (2006) stated:

> Much of students' engagement to each other and to their learning is through technology. . . . The relationship of today's young people to technology is fundamentally different than the relationship any other generational cohort has with technology and is hard for most instructors and administrators to understand. Many of their interpersonal relationships exist primarily online, and the lines between the online and the live (what we might consider the virtual and the real) are blurred or nonexistent. (p. 49)

As a result, instructors must be cognizant of this generation's desire to receive immediate feedback on grades and responses to e-mail. Despite the immediate gratification needs of this generation, instructors must utilize technology by infusing multiple forms of it within the classroom context (Taylor, 2006). Although this generation is considered to be "technology savvy" (Howe &

Strauss, 2003), we caution against blanket generalizations about the true accessibility of technological devices to Millennial students of color. This distinction, due to socioeconomic factors, is a vital component of existing models and theories that serves as a reminder that variations within students of color exist in any given context, particularly in the realm of higher education.

Integration of Curriculum

Before discussing the integration of curriculum, it is vital to acknowledge instructor perception on students of color. More important, educators must address issues on how they can operate outside the context of color-blind approaches when teaching Millennial students of color. Lewis (2001) termed this a "color blind" approach where these teachers avoid the racial realities and are willing only to address the superficial meaning of race. Additional studies such as Schofield (1989) and Wells and Crane (1997) noted that teachers in suburban (desegregated schools) districts use color-blind pedagogical practices where teachers taught children of color the same as the other children. Therefore, this color-blind perspective resulted in teachers' limited understanding of using culturally relevant pedagogical practices. Thus, teachers often tend to operate their instructional practices with a "color-blindness" lens for students of color found in their classrooms.

Therefore, the instructional methods educators utilize in college classrooms must come from a non–color-blind, culturally relevant perspective so that teaching approaches can be reflective of the diverse learning styles that Millennial students of color possess in order to maximize the learning that takes place. This means assisting students to develop their abilities to think for themselves, develop their knowledge, understanding and self awareness, and become critical thinkers. In so doing, all learning processes (including curriculum design, teaching strategies, support services and other resources) should be designed to help students in their development (LearnHigher, 2008). In order to create optimal learning development of students, the instructor must develop a curriculum framework that best integrates the various learning styles and multiple abilities that students of color bring with them into college classrooms.

Hence, we suggest instructors follow a curriculum outline similar to that proposed by Cowan and Harding (1986). Their logical model of curriculum development focuses on developing curriculum from the viewpoint of all students. This model contends that instructors must first focus on the background of the institution (i.e., students, faculty, and departmental needs).

Second, the instructors must focus on the *intended learning outcomes*. These measures must be specific and measurable throughout the duration of the course. Essentially at this stage, instructors should focus on what knowledge they want students to have ascertained at the end of the course. Next, once instructors develop learning outcomes, they must focus on the various forms of *assessment* they will use to gauge student progression of learning outcomes. After decisions about assessments are made, instructors must consider the core *content* of the course. Subsequently, *course structure* serves as the desired directionality of the content throughout the semester. After taking into account the course structure, the *class structure* must be taken into consideration. At this point, instructors must ensure that instructional methods of employing course content are diverse in its structure (i.e., dialogue, peer-to-peer grouping, active learning activities). Lastly, instructors must provide *evaluations* of course content that allow flexibility in the learning outcomes of students. In essence, this provides instructors with ongoing feedback of their own curriculum design.

Although there are multiple curriculum frameworks that guide course design, we contend that Cowan and Harding's (1986) logical model of curriculum development best meets the needs of the Millennial students of color found on college campuses today. In essence, Cowan and Harding's curriculum development model is not prescriptive in nature. Rather, it recognizes that college classrooms, and the students sitting in them, continue to be situational and contextual. According to Howe and Strauss (2003), the distinct characteristics of the Millennial generation have implications for the methods of teaching and learning that currently take place in college classrooms. However, the caveat here is that it is vital to remember that students of color, within the Millennial generation, and the method in which they learn is a central component that should guide the manner in which instructors develop their curriculum. Thus, recommendations of how to integrate curriculum, particularly for Millennial students of color, utilize the work of Howe and Strauss as a basis that will further extend to the population of students of color.

Recommendations

According to Howe and Strauss (2003), the Millennial generation display the following seven characteristics: special, sheltered, confident, team oriented, conventional, pressured, and achieving. These characteristics serve as a framework for our extension on how these generational characteristics can help guide the integration of curriculum for Millennial students of color. Although this framework is prevalent to the cohort within this generation, students of color must been seen as individuals who are members of this generation. Often theoretical frameworks encapsulate, like with Millennial students, an entire population of students without extrapolating the differences that exists within the cohort. For example, it is vital to understand how the characteristic of "team oriented" is situational and contextual in nature when applying it to various demographics within the generation. Thus, the instructional needs, particularly of Millennial students of color, should not be created on the characteristics that are used to describe an entire generation.

Our recommendations demonstrate the importance of learning and teaching practices pertaining to Millennial students of color. Generational characteristics provided by Howe and Strauss (2003) serve as a baseline for Millennials; however, it is vital to recognize that these characteristics are socially constructed notions. Even though the characteristics are presented as independent characteristics, many of these characteristics, we surmise, particularly for students of color, work interdependently in various situational contexts. For instance, what constitutes being team oriented is contingent upon the availability of resources and technology available to each student prior to his or her arrival on a college campus. Students of color, due to sociocultural factors, often do not have the same availability of resources in high school as their White counterparts who are also members of their generation. Further, the reasons why students of color feel pressured to achieve in the context of education vary from the experiences of students from other racial groups. These examples, though limited and general in scope, serve as a cautionary note to remind instructors that theoretical frameworks, such as the work done by Howe and Strauss (2003), provide a premise based on generalizations. Yet it is crucial to recognize that simply attributing these general characteristics to *every* Millennial would fail to recognize the differences that exist within any framework, particularly regarding students of color. Thus, acknowledging that these differences exists, instructors should utilize differentiation styles of teaching that will support multiple and diverse ways of learning.

Case Study

Here Comes the Millennials: Understanding Millennials' Way of Learning

As a teaching assistant at Woods State University, I recently spent an afternoon in an all-graduate professional development workshop that focused on the learning experiences of Millennial students in higher education. The workshop was built on the framework of Howe and Strauss's (2003) seven characteristics of Millennial students. With these characteristics in mind, I decided to refocus the scope of my next classroom project in order to maximize the student learning outputs based on the information I had learned in the workshop.

The newfound information of the technological savvy of this generation influenced my decision to reevaluate the culminating project for the semester. Thus in designing my final classroom project, I created a learning experience designed around podcasting; a simple yet new technology in which students produce a short audio clip and then post it on the Internet for all to hear. Knowing that Millennial students are technologically savvy, I had my students work in self-selected groups. They were to create a 2-minute podcast that focused on the connection between various presidential speeches in the 20th century. Students were to present their projects in class 2 weeks later. To my surprise, the level of technological sufficiency was not what I had expected based on the concept that I learned about Millennial students from my professional development training. During my evaluation process, I realized that the groups that consisted primarily of students of color had podcasts that lacked the same level of in-depth application of technology when compared to other groups that consisted of students who were predominately White. My first instinct was to attribute the lack of in-depth analysis due to the academic effort displayed by the students of color. But after further examination, I surmised that the levels of technological efficiency between student groups were unbalanced. As an instructor who takes into account the experiential learning of students, I decided to reevaluate the real issue underlying the discrepancies between the various projects.

After referring back to my workshop notes from Howe and Strauss (2003), I had made a blanket generalization about the true accessibility of technological devices to Millennial students of color. I had forgotten that socioeconomic factors are vital components that may have put my students of color at a disadvantage in this particular assignment. Here, I assumed that my entire class of Millennial students was technologically savvy, when in fact I had some technology immigrants.

Although the Millennial generation has been characterized as being technologically savvy, it is vital that instructors do not superimpose Howe and Strauss's (2003) seven distinctive characteristics of Millennial students on the entire student population. Such assumptions about student performance in the classroom adversely affect students of color because variations in their access to resources often affects the level of sophistication in which they can implement technology into school projects. Therefore, before one places the blame on effort, instructors must be willing to acknowledge that variations exist within the seven characteristics generated for the Millennial generation. A framework, though it provides guidance, in no way accounts for the wealth of diversity that inherently exists in students of color. We suggest that instructors pose the following questions to themselves in order to create an instructional curriculum that takes into account the experiential knowledge of Millennial students of color found within their college classrooms.

1. When developing curriculum, who is the target population you are creating it for?
2. What processes have you set forth to continuously check your personal biases regarding student learning?
3. What mechanisms have you created to safeguard and reevaluate the generational influences among the class?
4. How will you deconstruct the learning needs of students of color who are part of the Millennial generation?
5. How does your developed curriculum affect learning outcomes for students of color in your class?

Implications and Conclusion

Teachers of Millennial students of color must consider characteristics of the Millennial population in general along with the learning preferences and influential factors relative to students of color. Kolb's (1984) ELT outlines learning as a holistic process by which students learn through their own experiences. With regard to teachers incorporating ELT into the classroom, it is imperative that teachers understand how Millennial students of color have forms of experiential knowledge that are influenced by issues of safety, cultural, and community values, which may differ when compared to predominately White students.

Experiential learning and andragogy were examined through various sociocultural frameworks to consider the fact that Millennial students of color have diverse experiences largely influenced by their social and cultural values. Teachers should undergo a paradigm shift from traditional instructional methods of learning to reflective processes to ensure learner-centered instruction. Cooperative and collaborative learning approaches will allow students of color to engage in effective experiential learning.

To best meet students' needs, we recommend that teachers utilize multiple outlets of technology in the classroom, provide individual feedback and e-mail responses immediately, and be mindful of the socioeconomic factors that may inhibit the technological needs of students of color. By adhering to the logical model of curriculum development, the integrated curricular framework will consider the various learning styles and multiple abilities of students of color. Teachers' acknowledgment of the differences between the general Millennial student population and students of color will aid in utilizing differentiation instruction that will support the diverse learning methods of students.

References

Astin, A.W. (1993). *What matters in college? Four critical years revisited.* San Francisco: Jossey-Bass.

Biggs, J. (1993). From theory to practice: A cognitive systems approach. *Higher Education Research and Development, 12*(1), 73–85.

Broido, E. M. (2004). Understanding diversity in Millennial students. *New Directions for Student Services, 106,* 73–84.

Brown, J. (2000). Growing up digital: How the web changes work, education, and the ways people learn. *Change, 32*(2), 11–20.

Burdman, P. (2005). *The student debt dilemma: Debt aversion as a barrier to college access.* Berkeley, CA: Center for Studies in Higher Education.

Chickering, A. W., & Reiser, L. (1993). *Education and identity.* San Francisco: Jossey-Bass.

Cowan, J., & Harding, A. (1986). A logical model of curriculum development. *British Journal of Educational Technology, 17*(2), 103–109.

Cress, C. M., & Sax, L. J. (1998).Campus climate issues to consider for the next decade. In K. W. Bauer (Ed.), *Campus climate: Understanding the critical components of today's colleges and universities.* New Directions for Institutional Research, No. 98 (pp. 65–80). San Francisco: Jossey-Bass.

Fink, L. D. (2003). *Creating significant learning experiences.* San Francisco: Jossey-Bass.

Fry H., Ketteridge, S., & Marshall, S. (Eds.). (2009). *A handbook for teaching and learning in higher education: Enhancing academic practice* (3rd ed.). New York: Routledge.

Gosling, D. (2002, Nov.). Personal development planning. SEDA Paper 115. Presented at the Staff and Educational Development Association, Birmingham, England.

Guskin, A. E. (1994). Restructuring the role of faculty. *Change, 26*(5), 16–25.

Howe, N., & Strauss, W. (2003). *Millennials go to college: Strategies for a new generation on campus.* Washington DC: American Association of Collegiate Registrars and Admissions Officers.

Jonas-Dwyer, D., & Pospisil, R. (2004). The millennial effect: Implications for academic development. *Proceedings of the 2004 annual International Conference of the Higher Education Research and Development Society of Australasia (HERDSA),* Sarawak, Malaysia. Retrieved from http://www.herdsa.org.au/newsite/wp/wp-content/uploads/conference /2004/PDF/P050-jt.pdf

Kolb, D. A. (1984). *Experiential learning: Experience as the source of learning and development.* Upper Saddle River, NJ: Prentice-Hall.

Kolb, D. A., Boyatzis, R. E., & Mainemelis, C. (2000). Experiential learning theory: Previous research and new directions. In R. J. Sternberg & L. F. Zhang (Eds.), *Perspectives on cognitive, learning, and thinking styles* (pp. 227–248). Mahwah, NJ: Erlbaum.

Knowles, M., et al. (1984). *Andragogy in action.* Houston, TX: Gulf Publishing.

Kohlberg, D. A. (1984). *Experiential learning.* Englewood Cliffs, NJ: Prentice-Hall.

LearnHigher (2008). LearnHigher—Excellence in learning development. Retrieved from http://www.learnhigher.ac.uk/LearningDevelopment/index.html

Lessor, J. (1976). Cultural differences in learning and thinking. In S. Messick (Ed.), *Individuality in learning: Implications of cognitive styles and creativity for human development* (38-89). San Francisco: Jossey-Bass.

Lewis, A. (2001). There is no "race" in the schoolyard: Color-blind ideology in an (almost) all-white school. *American Educational Research Journal, 38*(4), 781–811.

McGlynn, A. (2005). Teaching Millennials, our newest cultural cohort. *Education Digest, 71*(4), 12–16.

McKeachie, W. J. (2002). *Teaching tips: Strategies, research and theory for college and university teachers* (11th ed.). Boston: Houghton Mifflin.

O'Banion, T. (1999). *Launching a learning-centered college.* Mission Viejo, CA: League for Innovation in the Community College.

Pascarella, E. T., & Terensini, P. T. (1991). *How college affects students: Findings and insights for twenty years of research.* San Francisco: Jossey-Bass.

Pendergast, D. (2007). Teaching Y generation. *Journal of the HEIA, 14*(3), 15–21.

Prensky, M. (2001, October). *Digital natives, digital immigrants. On the horizon.* Lincoln: NCB University Press.

Rasmussen, A., Aber, M. S., & Bhana, A. (2004). Adolescents coping and neighborhood violence:Perceptions, exposure and urban youths' efforts to deal with danger. *American Journal of Community Psychology, 33*(1–2), 61–75.

Rodriguez, A. L., Guido-DiBrito, F., Torres, V., & Talbot, D. (2000). Latina college students: Issues and challenges for the 21st century. *NASPA Journal, 37*(3), 511–527.

Scarborough, J. D., & Vorah, P. (2006). *The scholarship of teaching: CEET initiative and learning.* Retrieved from http://www.eric.ed.gov/ERICWebPortal/search/

detailmini.jsp?_nfpb = true&_&ERICExtSearch_SearchValue_0 = ED498370&
ERICExtSearch_SearchType_0 = no&accno = ED498370

Schofield, J. (1989). *Black and White in school.* New York: Teachers College Press.

Strauss, W., & Howe, N. (2007). *Millennials go to college: Strategies for a new generation on campus.* Great Falls, MT: Life Course Associates.

Taylor, M. L. (2006). Generation next comes to college: 2006 updates and emerging issues. *A Collection of Papers on Self-Study and Institutional Improvement, 2,* 48–55.

Tierney, W. G., & Venegas, K. M. (2009). Finding money on the table: Information, financial aid, and access to college. *Journal of Higher Education, 80*(4), 363–388.

U.S. Census Bureau. (2005). *People and families in poverty by selected characteristics: 2004 and 2005.* Retrieved from http://www.census.gov/hhes/www/poverty/data/incpovhlth/2005/table4.pdf

Wells, A. S., & Crane, R. L. (1997). *Stepping over the color line: African American students in White suburban schools.* New Haven, CT: Yale University Press.

Wilson, M. E. (2004, Summer). Teaching, learning, and millennial students. *New Directions for Student Services, 106,* 59–71.

Witkin, H. (1967). A cognitive style approach to cross-cultural research. *International Journal of Psychology, 2,* 233–250.

FROM ONE GENERATION TO ANOTHER GENERATION

New Realities, New Possibilities, and a Reason for Hope

Aretha F. Marbley

As African Americans from the two preceding generations (Baby Boomers and Generation X), we approached the writing of *Diverse Millennial Students in College: Implications for Faculty and Student Affairs* with a posture of eternal optimism for this generation. As lifelong multicultural social justice scholars, we embarked on this journey knowing that some things would be markedly different from our experiences as college students of the two preceding generations, and sadly, some things from our generations' experiences of segregation, discrimination, and disenfranchisement as college students would have remained virtually unchanged for this youngest generation of college students, deemed and labeled *Millennial*. We are products, like most of the authors of these chapters, of generations laced with racism, homophobia, classism, sexism, and hatred that filters down through generations, yet we profoundly believe that every new generation brings with it new realities, new possibilities, and a reason for hope.

Our quest was to find answers to questions such as: Does the term *Millennial* college student apply to underrepresented college students such as people of color (African American, Asian American, Native American, and Hispanic and Latino); people who identify as bi- or multiheritage and racial; and LGBTQIA populations (lesbian, gay, bisexual, transgender, transsexual, queer, questioning, intersex, ally, and asexual)? What role does technology, pop culture (e.g., hip-hop), and race politics play in the identity development for these populations? Are our current minority development theories applicable to these groups? And ultimately, are higher education institutions prepared to meet both the cultural and developmental needs of minority groups, that is, Millennial college students from marginalized backgrounds?

We also knew upfront that one of the challenges we faced in writing a book on diverse Millennial college students, specifically those marginalized and from underrepresented groups, would be finding research on those populations. True to form, before embarking on this book, what we found was only an infinitesimal amount of research that disaggregated the diversity found within this generational cohort. For us, the challenge of a lack of easily accessible research on underrepresented college Millennials then became the necessary and key justification for writing this book. Strayhorn (in chapter 2) wrote that "additional research was needed to understand whether and how the central tendencies often associated with today's college students related to students of color" and other marginalized groups. This book assembled together a group of renowned higher education scholars of multiculturalism and social justice, who together, tackled the tough questions and were able to excavate data in a way that has helped profile and create recognizable portraits of the diverse Millennial college student.

Diverse Millennial Students in College has attempted to address the questions and provide some answers, leaving plenty of opportunity for additional discourse, and at the same time evoke more questions for future scholars and future generations to answer. In essence, in a profound and unique way, through the chapters in this book, Millennials from underrepresented groups have entered their voices into the scholarly discourse on Millennial college students. Further, implications for faculty and staff in student affairs contexts, practice, policy, and future research are delineated in each of the chapters.

The authors focused on the Millennials from their cultural backgrounds or their professional experiences within these groups. All too often they were faced with the arduous task of using large databases, census reports, tangential studies, and narratives and counternarratives in order to flesh out or unravel extant information. For example, Museus (in chapter 5) discovered, that for the Asian community, the phenomenon of a high level of connectiveness is not just a characteristic of the Millennial generation. Americans of Asian ancestry have always been connected to Asian American and Asian communities around the world, such as the early Chinese immigrants to America who sent money back or returned to their homeland in the 1800s.

At the end of this journey, though we know that there is still much work left to be done, progress has been made—we were not disappointed. In the end, the Millennials from traditionally underrepresented groups, though different in some aspects than their White counterparts, will nonetheless, as projected, achieve much *greatness*. They will, as our generation did and all the previous generations have done, take their rightful places as leaders.

It is our hope that this book engages the broader higher education community in critical diversity and social justice conversations about the unique challenges diverse Millennials students face on college and university campuses. To the question, Does the term *Millennial* apply to these underrepresented students? Through the powerful chapters in this book, these scholars have all answered in unison with a resounding *Yes!*

ABOUT THE CONTRIBUTORS

Rosa Maria Banda is a doctoral candidate in the Department of Educational Administration and Human Resource Development at Texas A&M University. Rosa received both her BA in Communications with a concentration in public relations and her MA in higher education with an emphasis on bicultural/bilingual studies from the University of Texas at San Antonio. While Rosa's primary research interests include the persistence of Mexican American females in science, technology, engineering, and mathematics (STEM) disciplines, her secondary research interests include millennials, gifted poor, and high achieving students of color.

Fred A. Bonner, II is a professor of higher education administration in the Educational Administration and Human Resource Development Department at Texas A&M University–College Station. Bonner has been the recipient of the American Association for Higher Education Black Caucus Dissertation Award and the Educational Leadership and Counseling Foundation's Dissertation of the Year Award from the University of Arkansas College of Education. Bonner has completed a book (*Academically Gifted African American Males in College,* 2010) that highlights the experiences of postsecondary gifted African American male undergraduates in predominantly White and historically Black college contexts. He is anticipating the publication of *Diverse Millennials in College: Implications for Faculty and Student Affairs* with Stylus Publishing in fall 2011. He spent the 2005–2006 academic year as an American Council on Education (ACE) Fellow in the Office of the President at Old Dominion University in Norfolk, Virginia. Additionally, he has been awarded a $1 million National Science Foundation (NSF) grant that focuses on factors influencing the success of high achieving African American students in STEM disciplines in historically Black colleges and universities (HBCUs).

Lonnie Booker, Jr. has a PhD in higher education administration from Texas A&M University. He holds an MSin interdisciplinary studies with an emphasis in criminal justice from Texas A&M University–Texarkana and a

BS in sociology from Jarvis Christian College. He also was a police officer and detective, and has amassed more than 13 years of experience in this field. Additionally, he served as an adult probation officer. Dr. Booker's research and scholarly interests include campus safety and institution crisis management planning, student affairs, and generational students of color.

Bryan McKinley Jones Brayboy is an enrolled member of the Lumbee Tribe of North Carolina. He is Borderlands Associate Professor of Culture, Society, and Education at Arizona State University and President's Professor of Indigenous Education at the University of Alaska Fairbanks. Most recently, his research has been focused on exploring the role of Indigenous Knowledge Systems in the academic experiences of Indigenous students, staff, and faculty. His research has appeared in journals such as *Anthropology and Education Quarterly, Harvard Education Review, Journal of Black Studies, Review of Educational Research, Review of Research in Education,* and *The Urban Review.*

Angelina E. Castagno is an assistant professor of educational leadership and foundations at Northern Arizona University. Her teaching and research centers on issues of equity and diversity in U.S. schools, and she is especially interested in issues of race, whiteness, and Indigenous education. Her publications include articles in *Anthropology and Education Quarterly, Race and Ethnicity in Education,* and the *Review of Educational Research.*

Mitchell James Chang is professor of higher education and organizational change at the University of California, Los Angeles and also holds a joint appointment in the Asian American Studies Department. His research focuses on the educational efficacy of diversity-related initiatives on college campuses and how to apply those best practices toward advancing student learning and democratizing institutions.

Stephanie Chang is a third year doctoral student in the College Student Personnel Program at the University of Maryland, College Park. She studies issues of diversity, social justice, and qualitative research methods. Her concentration is on critical theories and pedagogy, and she also teaches courses on human diversity, advocacy, and leadership.

Gwendolyn Jordan Dungy is executive director of NASPA–Student Affairs Administrators in Higher Education, the leading association for the advancement, health, and sustainability of the student affairs profession. In her capacity as a national advocate for students and the primary spokesperson for student affairs administrators and practitioners, she draws on more than 30 years of experience in higher education. While at NASPA, Dr. Dungy has pursued a number of initiatives designed to enhance the association's role in public policy, research, professional development, and student learning and assessment, with a particular interest in student populations that are newly emerging and/or traditionally underrepresented.

Alonzo M. Flowers, III is a full-time instructor at Blinn College in the humanities division. His PhD is in higher education administration from Texas A&M University. Dr. Flowers specializes in educational issues including academic giftedness, teaching and learning, and student development theory. He holds an MA in adult and higher education administration from the University of Texas at San Antonio and a BA in political science with a minor in multicultural studies from Texas State University. Dr. Flowers's dissertation research topic focuses on academically gifted poor African American males in engineering disciplines. He is also on the editorial board for the landmark *Journal of African American Males in Education* (*JAAME*). Noteworthy too is his recent article in *TEMPO*, a leading peer-reviewed journal for the Texas Association for the Gifted and Talented (TAGT) entitled "Becoming Advocates for the Gifted Poor."

Manuel Gonzalez is a doctoral student in the Higher Education Administration program at the University of Texas at Austin. He is also the president of the UT Graduate Student Assembly, and he recently completed an internship in the White House through the Archer Fellows Program.

Corey Guyton is assistant director for student leadership, training, and development at North Carolina Central University. He received his bachelor's degree from Clayton State University and his master's degree from the University of Louisville, and is currently a doctoral candidate at Indiana State University.

Mary F. Howard-Hamilton is a professor in the Department of Educational Leadership, Administration, and Foundations, Higher Education Program at Indiana State University. She received her BA and MA degrees from The University of Iowa and a Doctorate of Education (EdD) from North Carolina State University. Dr. Howard-Hamilton has served as a higher education student affairs administrator for 15 years and a full time faculty member for 20. She has published over 80 articles and book chapters. The most recent co-authored books are, *Multiculturalism on Campus: Theories, Models, and Practices for Understanding Diversity and Creating Inclusion, Unleashing Suppressed Voices on College Campuses: Diversity Issues in Higher Education,* and *Standing on the Outside Looking In: Underrepresented Students' Experiences in Advanced Degree Programs.*

Sylvia Hurtado, PhD, is a professor in the Higher Education & Organizational Change program at the University of California, Los Angeles. She is also the Executive Director of the Higher Education Research Institute (HERI) at UCLA.

Gabriel Javier is assistant dean of students and director of the LGBT Campus Center (LGBT CC) at the University of Wisconsin–Madison. Prior to joining the LGBT CC at Madison, he was senior assistant director of the Spectrum Center at the University of Michigan, where he completed his master's degree in higher education administration. Gabe is also a former chair of the Consortium of Higher Education Resource Professionals.

Carrie Kortegast is an assistant professor of the practice of higher education at the Peabody College, Vanderbilt University. She received her BA from Mount Holyoke College, MEd from the University of Massachusetts Amherst, and her PhD from Iowa State University. Prior to her faculty appointment, she served as an assistant dean of students and director of housing and residential. Her professional experience and research interest also include LGBT issues in higher education.

Aretha F. Marbley is professor and director of Community Counseling in Counselor Education at Texas Tech University. She received a PhD from the University of Arkansas and is a licensed professional counselor, board-approved supervisor, and national certified counselor. She is a critical social justice womanist activist teacher, servant, and scholar, with a research focus on global multicultural-social justice. This includes the stories and counter-narratives of silenced voices—specifically, those of women, people of color, and communities of color in oppressive social structures. Her multicultural-social justice and human rights work has spanned over three decades. She has published extensively, served in a leadership capacity on over 150 committees, provided professional development, and presented numerous papers in the area of human, social, and cultural rights. She is the recipient of numerous awards for her work, including a national human rights award and a national research award.

Samuel D. Museus is assistant professor of Educational Administration at the University of Hawaii at Mānoa. His scholarship is focused on college success among underserved student populations. Specifically, his current research is aimed at understanding the role of institutional environments in minority college student adjustment, engagement, and persistence. His books include *Using Qualitative Methods in Institutional Assessment* (2007), *Conducting Research on Asian Americans in Higher Education* (2009), *Racial and Ethnic Minority Students' Success in STEM Education* (2011), *Using Mixed Methods to Study Intersectionality in Higher Education* (2011), and *Creating Campus Cultures: Fostering Success among Racially Diverse Student Populations* (2011).

Anna M. Ortiz is professor of educational leadership at California State University, Long Beach. She studies ethnic identity development in college students, multicultural education, and career trajectories in higher education professionals. She received her MA from The Ohio State University and her doctorate from UCLA.

Nana Osei-Kofi is an assistant professor of social justice studies and a women's studies affiliate faculty member at Iowa State University. She earned her MA in Applied Women's Studies and PhD in education at Claremont Graduate University. Her scholarship focuses on critical education, transnational feminist thought, cultural studies in education, and arts-based inquiry.

Lori D. Patton is associate professor and coordinator of the higher education program at the University of Denver. She is best known for her research on Critical Race Theory applied to higher education, African Americans in postsecondary contexts, student development theory and campus environments, and culture centers on college and university campuses. Her most recent research examines issues of intersectionality in the experiences of African American lesbian, gay and bisexual students attending HBCUs. Professor Patton's research has been published in *The Journal of Higher Education*, *Journal of College Student Development*, *International Journal of Qualitative Studies in Education*, and several other well-respected journals, edited books and monographs, and professional magazines.

Dorali Pichardo-Diaz is a counseling faculty member at Rio Hondo College. She earned her bachelor's degree in sociology, Spanish and translation/interpretation studies, and her master of science degree in counseling from California State University, Long Beach. She teaches courses on career and life planning and enjoys advocating for students regarding transfer issues, and is also passionate about working with first-generation and underrepresented student populations.

Tammie Preston-Cunningham is the Coordinator of Leadership and Community Involvement in the Department of Greek Life at Texas A&M University. She received her master's degree in Higher Education from Texas A&M University and is currently pursuing a PhD in Agricultural Leadership Education and Communication. Her research interests include college student development, leadership development, and underrepresented students.

Kristen A. Renn is associate professor of higher, adult, & lifelong education at Michigan State University. She was a student affairs professional for 12 years before joining the faculty. Her research focuses on issues of identity in higher education, including studies of mixed race identities, LGBT students, and leaders of identity-based student organizations. She is associate editor for international research and scholarship of the *Journal of College Student Development* and chair of the Editorial Advisory Board of the *Journal of Higher Education*. With support from the Spencer Foundation, she is currently conducting an international study of women's higher education institutions.

Petra Robinson is a research associate in the Graduate School of Education at Rutgers, The State University of New Jersey. She received her PhD in educational administration and human resource development from Texas A&M University. Her research and teaching interests include social justice in education, adult education, postcolonialism and culture, and faculty professional development.

Genyne Royal is a doctoral student in the higher education administration program at Texas A&M University. She has several years' experience both as a student and as a student affairs professional at a number of HBCUs as she earned degrees from Shaw University and North Carolina Agricultural and Technical State University. She also has several years of experience working in student affairs, with her most recent appointment being executive director of campus life at Lincoln University in Pennsylvania. Her primary research interest is in student development and academic resilience in students of color.

Victor B. Saenz, PhD, is an assistant professor in the higher education administration program at the University of Texas at Austin. He is also a faculty associate with the Center for Mexican American Studies and a faculty fellow with the Division of Diversity and Community Engagement at UT Austin.

Rose Anna Santos is a doctoral student in the Department of Education Administration and Human Resource Development at Texas A&M University. She received her bachelor's degree from Baylor University and master's degree from Texas A&M University–Corpus Christi. She has taught in Corpus Christi Independent School District and currently teaches in Bryan Independent School District. Her research agenda focuses on the experiences and educational persistence of Latina doctoral students, home literacy practices in adult learner families, and literacy learning in Latino single parent households.

Mattyna L. Stephens is a doctoral student in adult education and human resource development at Texas A&M University. Her research interests include urban poverty, economic development among low-income adults, and adult literacy. She currently works as a researcher at the Texas Center for the Advancement of Literacy and Learning (TCALL). As a Barbara Bush Family Literacy fellow during 2011–2012, she will be conducting research examining African American grandmothers who are the primary caregivers of their grandchildren and how they promote literacy for themselves and those in their care.

Terrell L. Strayhorn is associate professor of higher education at The Ohio State University, where he also serves as senior research associate at the Kirwan Institute for the Study of Race & Ethnicity, faculty affiliate in the Department of Africana Studies, and director of the Center for the Study of Higher Education Research & Policy. His research focuses on the experiences of historically underrepresented students in American education, as well as issues of equity, diversity, and social justice. He earned his bachelor's degree from the University of Virginia (UVA), master's degree in educational policy from UVA, and PhD in higher education from Virginia Tech. Strayhorn is co-editor of *Spectrum: A Journal About Black Men.*

Theresa Survillion is a doctoral student in Higher Education Administration at Texas A&M University. She is proud to be the Diversity Education Specialist and Program Advisor for the Department of Multicultural Services at Texas A&M University. Her research interests focus on issues related to women in higher education, student development theory, college teaching, and social justice education. Theresa continues to teach various courses both at the undergraduate and graduate levels on culture and leadership, and serves on various professional committees promoting research on diversity education and academic integration.

Tonya Turner-Driver is a doctoral student in educational human resource development at Texas A&M University, College Station. She serves as the associate director of multicultural services at Texas A&M University, where she has spent over 10 years in the field. She received her bachelor's degree in marketing and master's degree in leadership education from Texas A&M University. She has studied and developed numerous student development programs focusing on retention, engagement, cultural programming, and pre-college initiatives in efforts to understand and foster the growth of student leadership and behavior.

Stephanie J. Waterman, Onondaga, Turtle Clan, is an assistant professor at the Warner Graduate School of Education and Human Development at the University of Rochester in the Educational Leadership, Higher Education Department. She researches Native American college experiences and the interaction between university staff and students.

Nicholas Zuniga is the assistant director of Greek Life at Texas A&M University. He received degrees in journalism and public relations from Ball State University and is currently obtaining his PhD in higher education administration at Texas A&M. Nicholas actively facilitates to campuses and organizations on hazing and member development in fraternity and sorority life, and is an international volunteer for his fraternity, Lambda Chi Alpha.

INDEX

transgender, 177. *See also* GLBT Millennial
  students
Transitional Generation, 6
tribal colleges and universities (TCUs),
  159–160
Tribally Controlled College or University
  Assistance Act, 159
TRIO programs, 143
Tulgan, Bruce, 11
Twenge, Jean M., 10

urban *vs.* suburban, 119

validation, 123, 129
values and attitudes
  African American Millennial students, 32
  all Millennials, as a group, 32

Asian American and Pacific Islander
  (AAPI) Millennial students, 60
human performance improvement theory
  and, 250
Latina/o Millennial students, 109–112, 122,
  123
video games, 17. *See also* technology
volunteerism. *See* service

Williams, Erica, 71
workplace issues
  all Millennials, as a group, 10–12, 251–255
  human performance theory, 247–250
  implications for student affairs prac-
    titioners, 255–256
  Latino/a Millennials, 101, 103–104
  preparation for entering workforce, 246
  work-life balance, 251

Also available from Stylus

Multiculturalism on Campus
Theory, Models, and Practices for Understanding Diversity and Creating Inclusion
Edited by Michael J. Cuyjet, Mary F. Howard-Hamilton, and Diane L. Cooper

"Not just another book on multiculturalism, this book is a much-needed practical resource on how to prepare a campus to identify the diverse identities of all its students, their commonalities and differences. These seasoned authors have prepared a comprehensive guide for all in higher education, from professionals to students. Examining the student experience with the knowledge provided here could make a positive difference in the retention of all students."—*Gwendolyn Jordan Dungy*, *Executive Director, NASPA—Student Affairs Administrators in Higher Education*

"In two words: impressively comprehensive. New professionals and seasoned administrators alike will find much that is useful in this book. The editors have assembled a dynamic constellation of scholars who offer rich insights into the texture and substance of multiculturalism on contemporary college campuses. Anyone who aspires to become a more culturally competent and responsive educator should read this text."—*Shaun R. Harper*, *Graduate School of Education, Africana Studies and Gender Studies, University of Pennsylvania*

This book presents a comprehensive set of resources to guide students of education, faculty, higher education administrators, and student affairs leaders in creating an inclusive environment for under-represented groups on campus. It is intended as a guide to gaining a deeper understanding of the various multicultural groups on college campuses for faculty in the classroom and professional staff who desire to understand the complexity of the students they serve, as well as reflect on their own values and motivations.

The contributors introduce the reader to the relevant theory, models, practices, and assessment methods to prepare for, and implement, a genuinely multicultural environment. Recognizing that cultural identity is more than a matter of ethnicity and race, they equally address factors such as gender, age, religion, and sexual orientation. In the process, they ask the reader to assess his or her own levels of multicultural sensitivity, awareness, and competence.

The Evolving Challenges of Black College Students
New Insights for Policy, Practice, and Research
Edited by Terrell L. Strayhorn and Melvin Cleveland Terrell
Foreword by Lemuel Watson

Presenting new empirical evidence and employing fresh theoretical perspectives, this book sheds new light on the challenges that Black students face from the time they apply to college through their lives on campus.

The contributors make the case that the new generation of Black students differ in attitudes and backgrounds from earlier generations, and demonstrate the importance of understanding the diversity of Black identity.

The book offers new insights and concrete recommendations for policies and practices to provide the social and academic support for African American students to persist and fully benefit from their collegiate experience. It will be of value to student affairs personnel and faculty; constitutes a textbook for courses on student populations and their development; and provides a springboard for future research.

Culture Centers in Higher Education
Perspectives on Identity, Theory, and Practice
Edited by Lori D. Patton
Foreword by Gloria Ladson-Billings

"Lori Patton's book is stunning! It has closed the decades-long absence of a definitive compilation to inform Culture Center communities as they function in American Higher Education. As many colleges and universities struggle with issues of recruitment and retention of underrepresented students, this work provides a splendid blueprint for the development of Culture Centers for years to come."—*Willena Kimpson Price*, *Director African American Cultural Center, University of Connecticut, Storrs*

This book fills a significant void in the research on ethnic minority cultural centers, offers the historic background to their establishment and development, considers the circumstances that led to their creation, examines the roles they play on campus, explores their impact on retention and campus climate, and provides guidelines for their management in the light of current issues and future directions.

For administrators and student affairs educators who are unfamiliar with these facilities, and want to support an increasingly diverse student body, this book situates such centers within the overall strategy of improving campus climate, and makes the case for sustaining them. Where none as yet exist, this book offers a rationale and blueprint for creating such centers. For leaders of culture centers this book constitutes a valuable tool for assessing their viability, improving their performance, and ensuring their future relevance—all considerations of increased importance when budgets and resources are strained. This book also provides a foundation for researchers interested in further investigating the role of these centers in higher education.

22883 Quicksilver Drive
Sterling, VA 20166-2102

Subscribe to our e-mail alerts: www.Styluspub.com